CHARL

The Logic of

Perfection

OPEN COURT PUBLISHING COMPANY · LASALLE, ILLINOIS

Library of Congress Catalog Card Number: 61-11286

THE LOGIC OF PERFECTION

©1962 by the Open Court Publishing Company

Printed in the United States of America

Third Printing, 1973

To Dorothy

WHOSE SKILLFUL AND PAINSTAKING EDITING OF MY WRITINGS
HAS BEEN INCIDENTAL TO A LIFE IN WHICH CREATIVITY,
AND JOY IN THE CREATIVITY OF OTHERS, HAVE BEEN
CONSTANTLY APPARENT, AND WHOSE IMMENSE
HUMOROUS LOYALTY HAS SO GREATLY AIDED THE
PURSUIT OF THAT REASONABLE WISDOM
WHICH THE PHILOSOPHER NEVER QUITE ATTAINS.

Prologue: Some Fragments of Neoclassical Philosophy

... the moving unbalanced balance of things. . . . JOHN DEWEY, in *Experience and Nature*, p. 420.

. . . . the concept of increase or growth, a *That* whose *What* consists of *being ever more than itself* . . . . seems to me best suited for a first principle or absolute *Prius*. WILLIAM PEPPERELL MONTAGUE, in *Ways of Things*, p. 534.

The infinity of the Ultimate Ego consists in the infinite inner possibilities of His creative activity . . . .
The future certainly preexists in . . . . God's creative life, but it preexists as an open possibility, not as a fixed order of events with definite outlines. MOHAMMAD IQBAL, in *The Reconstruction of Religious Thought in Islam*, p. 61.

The eternity of God is His being without commencement or termination; He is eternal inasmuch as He exists and cannot not exist. FAUSTO SOCINUS and JOHANNES CRELL, as expounded by OTTO FOCK, in *Der Socinianismus*, p. 427.

Should we say that because the later God develops beyond the earlier there was a defect in the earlier? But it was no other defect than that which progress to the higher itself measures, and each earlier time stands in this relation to a later time, and each later time stands in this relation to the one following; in *this* respect the world never advances, because this is the ground of the whole progress, to will something transcending the present. . . .

In the earliest time, as in the latest, God with equally flawless wisdom fulfills the task of properly leading the world, in the condition in which it is, out beyond this condition; and the perfection of God generally is not in reaching a limited maximum but in seeking an unlimited progress. In such a progress, however, that the whole God in each time is the maximum not only of all the present, but also of all the past; He alone can surpass Himself, and does it continually, in the progress of time.

Therefore, if we desired to call the earlier condition of God inferior, then our inferior concept of inferiority would be unsuitable. We call that inferior which is small in relation to something higher, or which is not equal to a difficult task. But in every time everything is small compared to God, and in every time God satisfies the most difficult task. Only the later God looks down upon Himself — perceiving, however, in that same earlier God the one who has elevated Him to His present height.

G. T. FECHNER in *Zend Avesta*, p. 241.

Preface

I feel chiefly indebted, in connection with this study, to my Harvard teachers of many years ago, to some discussions with Rudolf Carnap (who shares very few of my opinions), and to the advice on some logical points given me by Richard M. Martin and Lucio Chiaraviglio. If I knew all that any of the three men mentioned knows about logic, this book would be at least somewhat different. It might be simply a more rigorous statement of essentially the same thoughts. Or . . . I wish I knew!

I also feel deeply grateful to the members of my "Summer Seminar" of 1958 in Kyoto, for their patient and friendly interest, as we met five days a week for four weeks to discuss metaphysics, particularly the dominant theme of the present work. It was during these discussions that some of the key ideas first occurred to me. It is a temptation to mention every professor and advanced student of this group, but I must refer to my very understanding and dear friend, Professor Matao Noda of Kyoto University.

Mention should be made of the kindness of Brand Blanshard, of Yale, in bringing the essay which, slightly revised, forms Chapter Two to the attention of Dr. Eugene Freeman of The Open Court Publishing Company, whose idea it was that the argument of the essay ought to be embedded in a larger context. From this idea, and Dr. Freeman's understanding and encouragement, grew this book. It is a singular good fortune and pleasure to have as publishing editor a man who is also a trained and thoughtful philosopher, experienced in this capacity both as teacher and as author.

The second chapter deals, in a manner not hitherto represented in the literature, with the ontological argument for belief in God. It is my conviction, and as will be shown not only mine, that this subject has been scandalously mishandled. In my own view, this is true of nearly all schools of philosophy which have attempted to deal with it. If I am mistaken in this, I hope to be corrected.

The subject-matter of the rest of the book is less restricted, but the theme of the ontological argument is central to much of it. Various topics in metaphysics, cosmology, and philosophy of religion are dealt with.

The first half of the book, through Chapter Three, is entirely new; the remaining chapters are based on articles previously published — often, however, in media not widely accessible to students of philosophy or theology. These articles have also been more or less drastically rewritten, and in some cases greatly expanded (Chapters 4, 7, 13).

The general philosophical standpoint may be described as that of philosophical rationalism, the "search for the coherence of the presuppositions of civilized living" (Whitehead), but a rationalism which has earnestly striven to learn what it could from modern empiricism and modern logic. I feel closest to Peirce, Bergson, and Whitehead; but I believe the present work is sufficiently different from anything hitherto published to constitute a challenge to my philosophical colleagues.

About the age of seventeen, after reading Emerson's *Essays*, I made up my mind (doubtless with a somewhat hazy notion of what I was doing) to trust reason to the end. In pursuit of this ideal, I have tried to make my thinking about metaphysical and religious questions good thinking, good by the proper criteria of thinking, rather than of persuading, edifying, or expressing emotion. This is an ideal easier to proclaim than to adhere to. One obstacle in adhering to it has been the dearth of careful criticisms of my writings. Such criticism is indeed welcome. For Popper is right, the rational way is the way of criticism. Objectivity is not in the individual thinker but in the process of mutual correction and inspiration.

Another obstacle is the widespread conviction that the deepest questions simply elude or transcend the rational or critical process. On the contrary, a basic technical conviction of all my writings is expressed in the word "logic" as it appears in the title of this book. The conviction is that the ultimate concepts have a rational structure, lucid, intellectually beautiful. When I meet an opponent of metaphysics or theology who shows an awareness of this logic, then indeed I shall wonder why we disagree. And when I meet a theologian who shows it I shall be pleased. But theologians seem often to agree with skeptics that theism is unintelligible. This matter will receive some attention in Chapters One, Two, and Four.

Another conviction which has haunted me for many years is that a great deal of the discussion of metaphysics and philosophy of religion in our time has been rendered idle by the assumption that if "metaphysics" (meaning, an a priori theory of reality) were possible it would have to be the sort of thing which Hume and Kant knew and criticized, or perhaps Kant's own queer and truncated sort of metaphysics, or else the Absolute Idealism of the last century. On the contrary, what I take to be the basic metaphysical issues were not clearly seen by Kant or Hume, nor yet by Green or Bradley. What these authors dealt with were forms of what may be called "classical metaphysics," metaphysics of being or substance. There is another form — in some respects admirably worked out in Buddhism, but in some respects left unfinished in that tradition — the metaphysics of becoming or creativity. I call this the "neoclassical" tradition. Beginning

THE LOGIC OF PERFECTION

in the West with Socinus in theology, with some anticipations in Origen and Tertullian, there has been an inconspicuous, but, to the careful student of its representatives, impressive, development of a metaphysics of creativity. This development is not comprehensively criticized, but is largely ignored, in the current debates. Yet when one examines these debates one sees that little if anything is established in them which is capable of deciding the questions posed by neoclassical metaphysics. It is as though one were to suppose that the estimation of physics can be made to turn upon "classical physics," its limitations being taken as insuperable. There was a Greek-Newtonian attitude, both in physics and in metaphysics. Has it not had its day?

We may, for better or for worse, be entering upon a new period in the metaphysics of religion. Peirce, Bergson, James, Dewey, Whitehead, and many others before and after them cannot (if culture endures) have written simply in vain; contemporary eddies cannot stop the slow change of four centuries from the mode of philosophizing which ignored or belittled the responsibilities and opportunities of creative becoming—from which in a sense even deity may not be exempt—to the mode which, after three millenia of evasion, accepts these responsibilities, not skeptically or because nothing better can be reached, but with faith and enthusiasm, and because the very notion of "better" presupposes the "creative advance" which is reality itself.

Another way in which the challenge of neoclassical metaphysics may be missed is through the supposition that frankly antirationalistic rhapsodies, such as those of Heidegger or Berdyaev, or the intuitionism of Bergson alone are capable of expressing the standpoint of becoming or process in metaphysics. This is not so; Peirce and Whitehead are among the distinguished rationalists of modern times, and it is my clear conviction that an uninhibited rationalism is possible only if what Berdyaev in his rhapsodic way called the "slavery to being" is overcome in philosophy.

There are many who suppose that a metaphysics of becoming, if logical, will be non-theistic. In a later book I hope to deal with six or seven theistic arguments in a systematic manner. None will be simply the old well-known arguments, all will express neoclassical principles, both in assumptions and in conclusions. But at the same time all will have affinities with standard arguments, and the idea of God which they support will be relevant to religion, that is, to "worship," or devotion of the whole man.

A distinguished ornithologist begins a book with a preface in which he ironically offers assistance to his future critics by telling them what is wrong with his work, even giving page references for some of the defects. I shall indulge in a bit of the same kind of irony and follow his example.

Taking this book as a whole, and apart from Chapter Two, the reader may complain that it is: (1) loosely organized and repetitious (note how the explanation of evil recurs over and over); (2) excessively polemical (see almost any chapter); (3) too much like a lawyer's brief, with many pros and few cons (note how the tremendous difficulty of reconciling a general "creative advance" with the denial by relativity physics of a cosmic simultaneity is dismissed in a brief footnote in Chapter Seven); (4) without a definite subject-matter, since half the problems of human life seem to come in eventually.

My defense or excuse in each case is as follows. (1) Since some of the central ideas are very widely ignored or casually repudiated almost or quite without examination, they evidently need the emphasis of repetition; also, since metaphysical ideas are global not linear in their interrelationships, repetition is scarcely avoidable, and a satisfactory order of exposition is extremely difficult. (2) Since the theories I reject are often deeply entrenched majority opinions, it seems unlikely that moderately expressed objections, unspiced with occasional argumenta ad hominem, will even be noticed. (3) For similar reasons counterarguments to my views are sure to be urged by others. (4) The subject of the book is The Logic of Perfection, but since abstract ideas permeate life and culture mainly through their applications to more concrete matters, a number of these applications have been included as illustrations (above all in Chapter Thirteen). Also, besides applications to special topics, the ultimate or metaphysical abstractions (wholly summed up, I contend, in the concept of Perfection) have implications for one another (the global nature of metaphysics above referred to): accordingly, many of these are considered, especially in Chapters 3, 5, 6, 7, 8, and 12. Chapters 4, 9, 10, and 11 try to relate the philosophical and religious aspects of the position.

In spite of the apparent impossibility of a non-arbitrary linear order, I shall hope in a subsequent work (referred to above) to achieve a more systematic analysis, besides profiting by the critical responses which I hope for from the present volume. In the later essay, I shall also pay more attention to certain epistemological and methodological questions. Perhaps some readers will find the standpoint naively realistic, and yet not realistic enough; for I seem to take it for granted that, just as men and elephants exist, so do atoms, or even particles, forgetting that these are but scientific constructs, based on everyday modes of perception of sticks and stones and chemicals. I suspect, but hope later to be able to see more clearly and show, that this matter is not crucial for my argument, since science has at least shown that sticks and stones and chemicals, as merely that, are entities which are but slightly understood; moreover, the extension of our understanding through science exhibits as illusory, not indeed any positive aspects of physical reality as experienced, but certain negative ones, such as mere inertness, lack of organization or of spontaneity. It is from these negations, and nothing positive, that materialism, determinism, and dualism derive their plausibility.

Undoubtedly some critics will think that I take language too much for granted, or pay too little attention to the normal meanings of words. Perhaps so; I am open to conviction on this point.

Besides supplying some criticisms gratis, the ornithologist above referred to suggested that any critic ask himself this question, "Do I know as much about the subject as the author?" Whereas, however, not many would imagine themselves to be experts in a class with Meinertzhagen on "the birds of Arabia," a great many apparently claim expertness as to the right way to think about metaphysical questions. All I say here is, if there be those who have thought about them, even in some small aspect, more carefully or precisely, or with more intellectual freedom, or more adequate acquaintance with the various standpoints and writings, than four and one-half decades of effort have enabled me to do, it will be an honor to be instructed by them. It is they from whom we need to hear.

Since, as will be pointed out in Chapter Four, conceptions of God and of the creatures are correlative, mistakes in one tending to produce or be produced by mistakes in the other, a thorough consideration of the case for and against theism is possible only within a general speculative philosophy or metaphysics. A sane philosophy of religion cannot be fully articulated save as a sane comprehensive philosophy. What I take to be such a philosophy is indicated in Chapters Three to Thirteen but not systematically developed. This development I hope to accomplish in the subsequent volume. It will then, I think, appear still more clearly that a Neoclassical Theism belongs in a Neoclassical Metaphysics, and that many of the recent discussions of the possibility, impossibility, or nature of metaphysics have little relevance to this theism or metaphysics, but are at best applicable either to the classical form or to non-classical, eccentric metaphysics (Heidegger, Russell). Classical metaphysics is a metaphysics of being, substance, absoluteness, and necessity as primary conceptions; neoclassical metaphysics treats these as secondary abstractions, the primary ones being those of creative becoming, event, relativity, and possibility.

Since Chapter Two is more technically philosophical than considerable portions of the remaining chapters, readers untrained in philosophy may find it better to begin with the latter; however, they would probably do well to read first sections I–III, especially II–III, of Chapter Two, since in these the neoclassical idea of divine perfection is explained. Note, the idea is explained, not the actual God. To "explain God" would mean explaining absolutely everything. Our knowledge of God is infinitesimal. Nevertheless it is, I am persuaded, the only adequate organizing principle of our life and thought.

C. H.

Contents

The Logic of Perfection

CHAPTER ONE

Preliminary Survey

"I said to myself, . . . would not the existence of time prove that there is indetermination in things? Would not time be that indetermination itself? . . . Reality is . . . growth, progressive invention. . . .

. . . Philosophy has never frankly admitted this continuous invention of unforeseeable novelty. . . .

We shall feel we are participating, creators of ourselves, in the great work of creation which is the origin of all things and which goes on before our eyes. By getting hold of itself, our faculty for acting will become intensified. Humbled heretofore, in an attitude of obedience, slaves of certain vaguely felt natural necessities, we shall once more stand erect, masters associated with a greater master. In this speculation . . . let us guard against seeing a simple game. It can be a preparation for the art of living."

HENRI BERGSON, in *The Creative Mind*, pp. 109–110, 112, 123, 124–25.

PHILOSOPHY CAN scarcely refuse to deal with the idea of God. For (in spite of some psychoanalysts) no other idea more obviously transcends the scope of the empirical sciences. Yet "God" properly stands for the object of worship. Can a worshipful deity

3

be the object of rational analysis or demonstration? Must not what we analyze be an *it*, rather than a *thou*? We encounter God, it is said, as we do friends and enemies; we do not define or prove Him or them. I believe that this objection rather inconsistently presupposes a rationalistic theory of the nature of deity, a theory which I wish to challenge. This is the theory that God is a single something, an entity so essentially "simple" that there can be no distinction between His reality as a whole and any definable positive characteristic by which we could conceptually identify Him, in contrast to other beings. My own rationalistic theory implies that while no essence, to be captured in a human concept, could possibly be the entire actual God whom we confront in worship, yet such an essence could very well qualify God and no one else. It would be an *it*, though God is not. But the *Thou* could include the it, and indeed the personal includes the impersonal, not vice versa. My friend is not an it, but friendship is, and my friend embodies this it. The God who loves us now is no essence; yet love, and even in a fashion divine love, is an essence. God is infinitely more than divine love, as a definable concept, an abstraction. He is the unimaginable actual love of the unimaginable vastness of actual things; what we call His essence, or His attribute of "perfection," is the common denominator of God loving this world, *or* that world, *or* a third world, and so on, out of the absolute infinity of possible kinds of world and of possible ways in which each kind of world could be divinely loved. The view that such distinctions cannot be made with respect to deity is itself, I hold, a theory derived from Greek philosophy, rather than from any religious testimony faithfully interpreted. Thus, whether one can distinguish between rationally defining or demonstrating "God" as abstract concept and defining or demonstrating God as unfathomably mysterious reality is itself a question of how one has defined "God." The rationalistic question is begged by the antirationalistic argument.

One may admit the impenetrable divine mystery but believe also in the unrivalled lucidity of the divine essence as an abstract aspect of the mystery. God may be at once the most baffling and the most intelligible of all realities, depending upon whether we have in mind the concrete or the abstract in His reality. To reject this distinction between abstract and concrete on the ground that it is only human minds who need abstractions, whereas God who knows intuitively is without them, is again a piece of metaphysical theorizing, not a religious insight. God has not "told us" that He in no sense thinks universals, as well as perceives particulars, or that for Him the Hegelian "concrete universal" (as some interpret it), in which all distinctions of abstract and concrete are transcended, is sound doctrine. Nor has He told us that He distinguishes between abstract and concrete only with respect to the world, not with respect to Himself.

That "God" stands for the supreme concrete reality does not prevent the word from standing also for the supreme abstract principle. If the supreme abstract principle were not uniquely divine, then God would either come under no concept and be inconceivable (and the word "God" without meaning) or He would be but another instance of the principle, which would thus in a sense be super-divine. This seems blasphemous.

Men judge a philosophy or a religion partly by its practical applications, its "fruits." Whatever our religion or philosophy of life, its fruits can hardly be judged adequate unless it can be used to illuminate two momentous practical questions of our time. These are: how can we have liberty with peace, or at least with the avoidance of totally destructive warfare; and how can we bring the human birth rate into reasonable relation to the unprecedentedly low death rate achieved by scientific hygiene? The tendency of human groups to quarrel to the death, the tendency of technological man to destroy the approximate balance found almost everywhere in nature between births and deaths, these are the over-riding dangers. No attitude toward life which fails to help at these points can serve our minimal needs.

The dangers of group quarrelsomeness are generally conceded; the dangers of excess births relative to deaths are widely conceded by thoughtful people. However, there are many who fail to put the proper emphasis upon one or the other set of dangers. And there are some who virtually deny the second set. They speak about increasing production or populating other planets as sufficient solutions. If those who talk in this way would themselves colonize another planet, the prospects on this planet might indeed be improved. It has been calculated that in 11,000 years, at the present rate of increase, the human race would weigh as much as all the known universe.[1] In other words, the increase at the present rate will not go on indefinitely. The relevant questions are: how far, if at all, will the rate be reduced by increase in the death rate, and how far by reduction in the birth rate, and what role, if any, will conscious choice play in the affair? Shall we try to reduce births, or try to increase deaths, or simply drift? Of course, we shall increase production, and also do some space-exploring; but, since it is mathematically proved that these alone will not suffice, we must either make plans to reduce the birth-death ratio, or expect that the reduction will be forced upon us, perhaps in some brutal and ugly fashion.

It is similarly evident that group quarrelsomeness, including modes of treating racial traits or religious differences which are bound to generate quarrels, must be reduced — if in no other way, then by the destruction of a species which cannot moderate its internal animosities. But how far shall peace come through destruction and coercion, and how far through reconciliation?

The religious-philosophical question is, How can we so interpret life that we shall be motivated to deal wisely and nobly with these dilemmas? Inherited attitudes in all religions seem insufficient to enlighten us. At least their representatives fail to make the sufficiency manifest. Nor is this surprising, since both problems are somewhat novel. The novelty is due to science and technology. Is it not reasonable to suppose that a closer relation-

[1] See Fred Hoyle, *Man and Materialism* (London: George Allen and Unwin, 1957), pp. 135–136.

ship between science and religion, or reason and faith, is what is required? There are many ways to look at the contrast between modern intellectual methods — as exhibited, say, in empirical science and mathematical logic — and the ancient faiths. No one man can hope to give us *the* truth here. At best he may furnish helpful suggestions. But clearly we should all search for means to transcend individual and group selfishness and bias. The great religions have professed this aim, but how far have they achieved it? I believe they can achieve it, relative to the needs of our time, only by learning from each other and from science.

In this context, Philosophy is included under science, in the sense of employing the critical method. A philosophy should be open to criticism from every point of view, that of the natural and social sciences, that of the various religions, that of symbolic logic, that of rival philosophies. Existentialism and "linguistic analysis" seem to me lacking here; they have adroit ways of making criticism seem irrelevant, or of failing to assert anything sufficiently definite to make criticism seem worth while, for instance by saying that philosophy is not a doctrine but an activity, or a personal way of realizing the human situation. All these contentions have their point, but they do not exhaust the responsibilities which philosophers, or somebody, must assume if our cultural needs are to be met. Someone must seek for the principle or principles which will enable us to clarify the "meaning of life," in relation to the new sciences and the old religions. Mere unbelief is scarcely a possible attitude; and mere belief in humanity is either an idolatrous exaltation of man which, in my opinion, unlike belief in the superhuman, is without rational basis, or if it is realistic about man and his cosmic prospects, it fails to furnish even the minimum of religious inspiration and integration of life and thought.[2] "When the gods go, the half-

[2] This case is temperately but forcefully argued by A. C. Garnett, in his *Religion and the Moral Life* (New York: The Ronald Press Co., 1955), Chs. 2–4.

THE LOGIC OF PERFECTION

gods arrive" is still a true picture of human affairs. However, there are half-gods which many revere in all good faith as God. Theologians have tried hard to distinguish between worship and idolatry. I believe they cannot succeed without the help of philosophy. For, historically, theologians have always been steeped in some philosophy, and they seem always to have read elements of this philosophy into their "revelation" before reading them out again as revealed truths.

For instance, the text translated "I am that I am" is made to support the primacy of being and thus classical metaphysics, although, as scholars tell us, the verb in the Hebrew original may be translated in quite other ways, as meaning "I live (or breathe) as I live, I act as I act, I become what I become, etc." My good friend Professor Tetsutaro Ariga of Kyoto University has wittily suggested that instead of ontology, what theologians need to cultivate is *hayathology* or *hayathontology*, utilizing the Hebrew verb in question.[3] Who can doubt that Greek philosophy of being presided over the early interpretations of the text? Again, the Biblical passages affirming the changelessness of Jahweh are shown by their contexts to refer to ethical steadfastness, constancy of purpose; and so far from entailing complete metaphysical immutability, they may more naturally be taken as implying a succession of acts or decisions implementing for diverse occasions a single basic intention. Finally, in its context the injunction to be perfect "as the heavenly father" obviously has nothing to do with immutability but enjoins impartiality as between conflicting claims of ourselves and our neighbors. Yet to this day, when "God" is spoken of, theologians and philosophers, believers or otherwise, are likely to suppose without question that the term means a wholly immutable reality. Is this revelation — or is it prejudice and ignorance? How can we ever

[3] See *Proceedings of the IX Intern. Cong. for the Hist. of Religions* (Tokyo: Maruzen, 1960), pp. 223–228. Also "An Inquiry Into the Basic Structure of Christian Thought," *Religious Studies in Japan* (Tokyo: Maruzen, 1959), pp. 418–419.

deal rationally with the religious question if we proceed in such hit or miss fashion? After two thousand years of ontology, why not experiment a bit with hayathology? Even the "Ontological" argument, when freed of fallacious aspects, turns — as we shall see — into a hayathological one.

Among philosophers of this century who have contributed the most to the central philosophical task indicated above I should include James, Bergson, Peirce, Whitehead, Berdyaev. C. Ehrenfels (in his *Cosmogony*), S. Alexander, and B. Varisco also deserve mention. Among living thinkers, at least in this country, those with the greatest comprehensiveness and courage are perhaps the two Pauls, Weiss and Tillich. Their example is a stimulus and inspiration. In both, however, there seems to be a certain eclecticism, a hesitation to choose between what I call classical and neoclassical doctrines, with consequent ambiguity or vagueness in the basic concepts. Both rely somewhat heavily upon rhetorical devices where I prefer to strive for (though I may not often attain) the impersonal lucidity of the formal logicians.

Tillich's doctrines that religious thought must be largely nonliteral and that *God is Being Itself* furnishes the sole literal description of God (recently he has appeared almost to exclude even this core of literalness)[4] are capable of various interpretations. (This problem is dealt with in Chapter Four.)

Weiss's complex system puts together four conceptions, Ideality, Actuality, Existence, and God, without telling us, so far as I have made out, which is concrete relative to the others. Apparently all are concrete or all are abstract in the same sense.

---

[4] *Systematic Theology* (Chicago: The University of Chicago Press, 1957), II 9–10. We are here told that statements like, "God is infinite, or is being itself," are both symbolic and nonsymbolic, since they mark the boundary between the symbolic and literal. I have dealt, perhaps with insufficient subtlety, with Tillich's view in "Tillich's Doctrine of God," in *The Theology of Paul Tillich*, edited by C. W. Kegley and R. W. Bretall (New York: The Macmillan Company, 1952) pp. 164–197.

I have trouble with the logic of such a contention. Ideals I view as abstract elements in more concrete entities. Even existing individuals are for my neoclassical or neoBuddhistic view abstractions concretized only in actual events or states — the truly concrete units of reality — and God is the universal Individual, who, through His states, with unique effectiveness and adequacy, includes all actuality, hence all entities whatsoever. I admit that there are aspects of this picture which are not wholly clear to me; but it does have a certain definiteness which I cannot find (perhaps it is mostly my fault) in the thought of these two justly admired contemporaries. However, they are wise, humane, and brilliant writers, and moreover if they had not been there I (and doubtless others) should at times have suffered far more than I have from the sense of being almost alone in the cause of speculative philosophy. One hates to think of what might have happened to this cause without Weiss's influence, or how little communication there might have been in our time between theology and philosophy without Tillich.

The two men mentioned are not the only encouraging or challenging figures in the almost chaotic variety which is, in a way, the glory of the philosophical scene in this country. Thus the following have conceived the metaphysical task in an imaginative or stimulating way: the late DeWitt H. Parker and W. P. Montague; among the living, F. S. C. Northrop, A. C. Garnett, Milič Čapek, Stephen C. Pepper, and Richard McKeon. There are a number of others. None of these seems to me to have seen clearly and in its full sweep the issue between classical and neoclassical metaphysics (Parker and Montague came closer to this than most of the younger men, which is discouraging); at least one, Pepper, has had a bias against theism which I feel has blinded him to the essential metaphysical issue (see Chapter Three); and none of them in my judgment does justice to the relevance of modern exact logic to the metaphysical issues. Or, putting it in another way, there is not enough Leibniz in them.

I agree with Leibniz that metaphysics is essentially a question of the logical structure of concepts, and that the mathematical method is the technical key — one which I may have used far too little, but nevertheless, thanks to Sheffer, Peirce, Whitehead, Scholz, Carnap, Martin, Chiaraviglio, and other friends among the logicians, have always respected. In short, the present writer is more of a rationalist than his contemporaries in speculative philosophy, although even farther than they are from traditional rationalism with respect to the relative roles of being and becoming, or necessity and creative contingency. If this be thought a paradox, since metaphysics seeks necessary truth, the answer is simple: it may be necessary, and I think is necessary, that almost everything (and everything concrete) should be contingent. Contingency itself is a necessary category, and in a sense more fundamental than the category necessity. In a similar way, becoming as a category eternally is; but no category has any reality except in the actual becoming which, taken concretely, is everlasting but not eternal or necessary.

The reader may still be wondering what connection the two practical problems which were mentioned early in this introduction (and to which we shall return in Chapter Thirteen) can have with the fortunes of metaphysics. There are two ways of doing without an explicit and sound metaphysics: to content oneself with a merely implicit metaphysics, or to adopt an explicit metaphysical system which is unsound (meaning, as we shall see, unclear or inconsistent). In the absence of metaphysics, in some fairly explicit form, men are likely to feel confused as to their basic aims and aspirations. They do not know how to combine the sense of the importance of their actions with the essential facts of life, such as the inevitability of death, the conflict of aims among men, and the partial or complete failure of many of these aims, if not perhaps all of them, when looked at from the widest perspective in space-time. Accordingly, there is a tendency toward dull despair or cynical indifference.

To escape these evils, many turn to one or another of the old religions, or to a new religion or quasi-religion, such as Humanism, or Communism. But there are many religions, new and old, and it less and less suffices merely to have been brought up in some one of them. But the deeper difficulty is that the religions, in their obvious popular forms at least, are infected with ambiguity in their metaphysical implications. For instance, what does the conception of providence, taken seriously, really mean ? Does it mean that nothing can go wrong in the world, that all tragedy and missed opportunity are but apparent ? In that case, let us give no thought to the dangers and threatened ills confronting us, for they cannot be real. The conclusion has no clear, consistent meaning, and neither have the premises from which it is "deduced." But such confusion is not, I believe, altogether harmless, especially today. All life involves choice and avoidance of danger; the advice just derived from one way of trying to construe "providence" cannot, strictly speaking, be followed. What advice then are we to derive from religious faith, advice useful for today's needs ?

We confront, for example, the possibility that all increase in food production and other results of human ingenuity will be absorbed, and perhaps more than absorbed, by increase in population. Some highly trained men have dealt carefully with this matter, and, so far as I have read them, they are nearly unanimous in finding little hope of any very happy solution during the next fifty or one hundred years.[5] We seem to face grim tragedy in this regard, even if atomic war be avoided. (Such war might well reduce production as much as population, and so it also provides no solution.) Then there is the difficulty of even imagining a plausible escape from the dilemma: how to preserve liberty without incurring intolerably great danger of destruction of the

[5] See, for example, C. G. Darwin, *The Problems of World Population* (Cambridge: Cambridge University Press, 1958), and *The Next Million Years* (New York: Doubleday, 1952–1953); also, Harrison Brown, *et al.*, *The Next Hundred Years* (New York: Viking Press, 1957).

populations seeking to be free, along with those seeking to re-strict their freedom.

It seems, then, that there must be something deeply tragic in the world. The highest species on the planet apparently not only fails to solve its own gravest problems, but in failing to solve them it threatens to wipe out the other forms of terrestrial life also. Indeed, even without atomic warfare, it is hard to see how very much of the non-human life on the planet can survive if the present rate of man's self-multiplication goes on very long. For this rate would in 1100 years leave but a yard of standing room per person! And what would then (or long before then) be left for the 9000 species of birds, for example, with their necessary forests, swamps, and savannahs gone into human utilization?

Man is a destructive creature indeed, compared with whom all other animals are gentle and harmless. What in the nature of things made this human destructiveness possible? Is it original sin, bad luck, divine punishment, divine weakness? Or the non-existence of any divine power? Man is too conscious an animal to be able to deal well with difficulties unless he has some under-standing of them.

One form of metaphysics encourages a refusal to take life's evils and dangers seriously. They are held to belong to mere appearance, or perhaps to a merely provisional existence im-portant only because exit from it will be into heaven or hell, or into the direct grasp of Reality. Or, again they are temporary evils which will somehow disappear under the workings of providence. These attitudes are soothing, but are they sufficient? Are they intellectually clear and responsible? On the other hand, the rejection of all metaphysics may leave us without the courage to face the disturbing situation in which we find ourselves. For how, in a universe as a whole "meaningless" or "valueless" (sup-posing this itself means anything), can courage have meaning or value, any more than anything else?

Marxian metaphysics seems excessively vague: for (in spite of some helpful suggestions) it leaves the cosmic question of meaning almost as confused as it finds it. The dialectical process of nature produces man, but will presumably also destroy him eventually; and no clear reason is given for supposing that reality as a whole will have gained any increment of value from the episode.

What we need seems to be a combination of two factors: an explanation of the root of tragedy in the world, an explanation which the mere idea of providence seems not to furnish, even with the traditional doctrine of the Fall (for instance, the sufferings of animals are left unexplained); and a ground for hope, love, and faith in the basic goodness of life, in spite of the truth that tragedy is no passing episode but somehow deeply interwoven in the structure of existence. More tersely expressed, we need a clarified cosmic optimism which understands the element of validity in pessimism. It is my belief that neoclassical metaphysics, in which freedom and chance are inseparable from law and design, can best effect this combination. The root of tragedy, as Berdyaev has so well insisted, is in free creativity, and if freedom or creativity is reality itself, tragedy is necessarily pervasive. But if Supreme Creativity inspires all lesser creative action, and takes it up into its own imperishable actuality, then the opportunities of existence outweigh its risks, and life is essentially good. In such a doctrine, escapism and despair can alike be overcome. All free creatures are inevitably more or less dangerous to other creatures, and the most free creatures are the most dangerous. Optimistic notions of inevitable, and almost effortless, progress are oblivious to this truth. They have tended to unfit us for our responsibilities. Man needs to know that he is born to freedom, hence to tragedy, but also to opportunity. He could be harmless enough, were he less free. Freedom is our opportunity and our tragic destiny. To face this tragedy courageously we need an adequate vision of the opportunity, as well as of the danger.

Merely positivistic or empirical philosophies try to achieve courage without paying its full price, which is recognition of the ultimate metaphysical principle whereby existence has a beauty somehow triumphant over death and destruction. Man cannot properly live on the merely human plane, for the reason, which Bergson so well pointed out (in his *Two Sources of Religion and Morality*), that man faces negative aspects of existence which are cosmic and infinite. For example, he knows (as the other animals can scarcely be imagined to do) that when he is dead, he is, as the vulgar saying has it, "all the time dead" — for infinite time, that is. We live in the finite, but we know that for good or ill we tend toward the infinite. This infinite toward which we tend is either good, bad, or indifferent. Whatever it be, it is that which at last essentially qualifies our lives. The whole cannot be for the sake of the part merely, but the part can very well be for the sake of the whole. The concrete whole we are unable to know, but metaphysics can give us its most abstract principle, and with that, together with fragments of the whole which we get from science and personal experiences, we can be content. Not with less! That metaphysicians sometimes claim, and even more often are accused of claiming, without benefit of the special sciences, to give us concrete or particular features of the whole merely shows how prone men are to err.

There is another way (also pointed out by Bergson) in which we can see the need for metaphysics. Man's power of reflection, which is the essence of his excess of freedom over that of the other animals, easily leads him into anti-social behavior. For whereas instinct can ensure that an animal will give heed to the needs of its young, or to the dangers confronting other members of the group, the clever human individual may all too easily ask himself, "Why should I make sacrifices or run risks for others"? Our entire Western tradition is shot through with crude or subtle self-interest doctrines, derived from philosophies of being, and our whole future is now endangered by the practical consequences springing partly from these doctrines.

It is notable how little communist propaganda addresses itself to individual self-interest. It appeals to groups, not to individuals as such. Indeed Marx sharply rejected self-interest as the basis of action (for example, in his posthumously published and as yet untranslated critique of Stirner's egocentric theory; see part two of the *Deutsche Ideologie*).[6] His objection was that the mere self is an unreal abstraction from the social reality, the group, which is the sole concrete bearer of interests and values. In this communist avoidance of the self-interest motif, there is a deep source of strength; for men "in their hearts" know that they are "members one of another," and do not live for themselves alone, or even essentially. But is the Marxian remedy for the insufficiency of self-interest adequate? Does not the group become merely an extended quasi-self, or greater individual, one lacking in the unity of awareness which, after all, the human individual, at least in any given moment, does have? And this greater individual, as such not aware of itself, is by no means all inclusive; it too is but a fragment, not the whole. One group, as against another, can still fall into the fallacy of trying to absolutize the merely relative validity of its aims. The root of this difficulty goes deep, and the whole Western tradition is weak or unclear at this point.

How can I love my neighbor "as myself" if, whereas I am simply identical with myself as one and the same personal "substance" or "being" from birth or death and perhaps beyond, I am simply non-identical with my neighbor, a second being? The confusion is subtly connected with the classical metaphysics of being at the expense of becoming. The world is many beings, I am one, you are another; this is the basic assumption. And God, in this language, is the Supreme Being, or "Being Itself." But then does He too love Himself by sheer identity and everything else by sheer non-identity? Or is there really but one Being, and are we "unreal"? There is no adequate classical solution. But

[6] I owe this reference to a student, H. L. Ruf.

there is a neoclassical one. According to it, the relation between "me" and "myself" as at another time is in principle, though not generally in degree, the same as that which connects me with my neighbor, or even — subject to suitable qualifications, which also express a principle — with God. In this way we can mitigate the excessive individualism which has tended to weaken our ethics.

From this weakness Buddhism has been largely free. But this advantage has been paid for by a certain negativism, a certain inadequacy, or at least ambiguity, in the Buddhist view of the values of existence. This defect does not derive from the fact that Buddhism is a philosophy of becoming and events, rather than of being and substances. It is connected instead with a certain radical pluralism in the Buddhist conception of event. Some Buddhists tried to defend a doctrine of the present reality of the past, but they failed to carry full conviction, and the reason may have been that they spoke in the same breath of the reality of past and also of future events.[7] This symmetrical way of arguing the case always blurs the issues between classical and neoclassical doctrines. For if all events are real together, then the totality of events simply is, and being not becoming is the inclusive conception. The Buddhists meant to be philosophers of becoming; but they could see no way to do so except by a symmetrical denial of past and future events, leaving only the present event as real. But then all life is vain, for all actual experience is doomed to destruction. So the ethical defect which most Westerners feel in Buddhism is tied in with a metaphysical one, just as the ethical defect which Asiatics often feel in Christianity is tied in with its individualistic philosophy of substance.

Western neoclassical philosophy has produced a synthetic-

[7] See Th. Shcherbatskoi (Stcherbatsky), *The Central Conception of Buddhism*. See also T. R. Murti, *The Central Philosophy of Buddhism* (London: George Allen and Unwin, 1955), pp. 138–139. Note repeated reference to "relativity or *mutual* dependence" (pp. 138 f., my italics), indicating the symmetrical interpretation.

conservative theory of events in which the "immortality of the past" is provided for, without any relapse from the standpoint of becoming. (I have so far failed to find a clear anticipation of this in Asiatic sources.) Events endure — but in later events, not in any mere being. Fechner, Bergson, and Peirce adumbrate this doctrine; Whitehead is perhaps the first clear expositor of it. It separates entirely the Buddhist insight expressed in the "no-soul, no-substance" standpoint from the negativism of much Buddhism. The resulting philosophy seems essentially Christian and Judaic, at least to the extent of congruence with the two Great Commandments (which Jesus repeated rather than invented). By de-absolutizing self-identity, one opens the way to an ethically valuable de-absolutizing of non-identity of self with others. The only strict concrete identity is seen as belonging to the momentary self, the true unit of personal existence, as Hume and James rediscovered long after the Indians, Chinese, and Japanese. (Alas, the rediscovery included considerable repetition of the radical pluralism which plagued the Buddhists.) Each momentary self is a new actuality, however intimately related to its predecessors. It is self-enjoyed rather than self-interested. All aim beyond the present is interest taken by one momentary self in others. A kind of "altruism" is thus the universal principle, self-interest being but the special case in which the other momentary selves in question form with the present self a certain chain or sequence. But this chain has no absolute claim upon its own members. Only the cosmic Life has absolute claims.

These matters are to be clarified on the metaphysical level, the level not of facts but of principles so general that they are presupposed or expressed even by the bare notion of "fact" itself, any fact no matter what.

We say today that we are defending freedom. But we have inherited a metaphysics of being which cannot coherently construe freedom. As will be argued in Chapter Six, freedom includes creativity, and it is through its aspect of creativity that "becoming" is distinguished from mere "being." Almost every month, in our philosophical journals there is a new "reconciliation of determinism and freedom." What is not seen is that determinism is merely one of the corollaries of the denial of the reality of becoming. Things change, oh yes, but there is, in the present or past causal conditions and the laws of change, a complete and unchanging blueprint of all changes. Thus, the entire factuality of the world, its definiteness of character, simply is, in any state no matter how far back or forward in time. This is the Parmenidean paradox, in one of its several forms: being simply is, it does not become. The Stoics worked out such a view long ago. They also, following Aristotle, worked out a version of the currently popular apologetic which attempts to attenuate the idea of freedom, divesting it of the implication of creativity, so that men will think they have nothing to lose by accepting determinism.

According to such apologists, we are free if we are not coerced or constrained, if we do what we want to do. But suppose we want to add to the definiteness of the world, to decide the previously undecided, to settle the unsettled, to close some previously quite open alternative? Ah, then, the determinist tells us, we want too much. We must be content if the concrete acts we perform are those we wish to perform. This is like telling us that we are not in chains in so far as we do not mind or notice the chains. We have all heard of the tyrant who says to his subjects, "Not only will you do what I want you to do, but you will like it." The subtle tyranny is not coercion. Are the Russian rulers aiming to make us feel coerced into being their puppets? Surely they are cleverer than that: they aim to inspire enthusiasm for puppetry, and we dangerously underestimate them if we do not see how far they succeed.

Augustine's theory of freedom was that the divine blueprint defines our decisions for us, and the divine power makes us accept our role as though it were our own. (Adam before the Fall was a bit different, but even this distinction is of doubtful consistency in Augustine's system.) We are free because we do indeed *will* what the blueprint provides. So we are responsible and may be punished. Leibniz repeats the argument. Such freedom of course has nothing to do with creativity. That is reserved for God alone. He has perfect, absolute creative power; we have not even imperfect, limited creative power, power to add to the definiteness of reality. The theory passes from the supreme case of this power to zero, with nothing between. This scarcely coherent doctrine is a common form of our inherited metaphysics of being. Is it good enough for our present responsibilities?

The connection of determinism with the philosophy of being comes out also in attempts to elucidate freedom as action proceeding from the self. I do what my character determines me to do, so my actions are "self-determined." But by what self, what character? The actual self alive in the moment of decision and its character? This self came into being with the decision, and was not among its antecedent causal conditions; hence, its self-determination cannot support determinism in the sense of causal predictability. Is the action determined, rather, by the previous self? But this is the paradox that the decision was already made beforehand and only seemed to be awaiting determination. In any case the previous self is not simply identical with the self now acting, taken as given its full concreteness by that act itself; and this concrete self of the moment either does or does not have at least some slight power of decision de novo, some genuine options despite all prior determinations and commitments.

To think of "oneself" as simply a "being," identical from birth to death, is to accept an abstract common denominator of many concrete subjects — as far apart as an almost mindless infant, a man in deep sleep, coma, or pitiful senility, and a highly conscious adult — in exchange for the living self now acting, a self which in its concrete fullness never existed until this moment. It is not enough for freedom that other persons or circumstances refrain from predetermining my decision; my past selves also may not deny to my present self its power of self-creation, conditioned but not fully determined by all the past. To argue that acts must express character is to forget that character is but the balance of past acts; it presupposes decisions and cannot in principle explain them.

Would we not be in a better position to defend freedom if we were clearer as to what it is? It is curious to see critics of all metaphysical thinking, one after another, appealing to Spinoza as sponsor of the view that freedom sets no limits to causal determinism. Spinoza was one of the most penetrating and honest of the metaphysicians of being. The entire definiteness of the world, he held, is an eternal truth (to see truly is to see "from the standpoint of eternity," that is, the standpoint of mere being). Philipp Frank, who admirably understands many things I am ashamed not to grasp, solemnly propounds Spinoza's absurd paradox that if a stone knew it was falling it would claim to do so freely. This assumes what was to be shown, that it makes sense to speak of a conscious action so utterly devoid of moment to moment decision as falling is held to be.[8] Consciousness is inseparable from decision, and it must lapse the instant action becomes merely inevitable. So Spinoza was here talking nonsense. In all conscious (if not in all sentient) action there must be details, however trivial, which are decided de novo. This is the view taken by the philosophy of creativity.

The customary examples of predictable, or causally inevitable, yet "free" acts merely show that in a voluntary act there are some uncreative and hence foreseeable aspects (and this no careful thinker has denied); they do not show that such action has no creative aspects.

[8] See Frank's instructive book, *Philosophy of Science: the Link Between Science and Philosophy* (Englewood Cliffs, N.J.: Prentice-Hall, 1957), p. 257. In this book there is much about metaphysics, and it is worth reading on that subject too, but there is not a suspicion of what a metaphysics which has learned to think critically about the traditional bias against creativity would be like, and this in spite of quotations from and appreciative remarks about Whitehead.

Russell suggests that indeterminists claim exemption from prediction for themselves though we all are confident that we can foresee some of the actions of others. The indeterminists I have studied are not guilty as charged. Nor in my whole life have I ever been able to foresee accurately and certainly a single slice, however short or simple, of the action of a single person or animal, and the only sense in which it seems to me harder to do something like this for oneself is that the process of prediction or the memory of it might be a disturbing factor.[9]

In my own most difficult decisions I recall sometimes seeing, long before I had ceased to debate with myself, the probability (and more we cannot have with other persons) of a certain outcome. But the reason for the continuance of the deliberation was not merely that probability is less than certainty, but also that the "outcome" in question was but an abstract aspect common to all reasonably likely outcomes, and what had to be decided were the exact concrete steps through which this abstract feature would be actualized. Always and in every moment something is not yet settled, or awareness must cease altogether. Until determinists show us how their examples refute this contention, they are not offering any very pertinent evidence. That creativity is always conditioned, causally influenced, and hence partially predictable, no sane person has ever denied (unless with respect to God, and not necessarily wisely even then). But the predictable aspects are precisely the uncreative aspects. One can predict that the poet will be poetic, and in a certain general style, for this has become his "character" and needs no further creation, but one cannot predict the poem. Think of a prosaic psychological predicter setting out to compose a poem beforehand from his knowledge of the poet's past and the causal laws of poetic composition, thus rendering poetic ability superfluous!

[9] For an original and ingenious treatment of this topic see D. M. Mac-Kay, "On the Logical Indeterminacy of a Free Choice," *Mind*, LXIX (1960), 31–40. I cannot accept his solution, but it is worth studying.

The usual reference to the complexity of the conditions in such cases does not, I think, dispose of the absurdity in the very idea of predicting what, according to the neoclassical view, has to be creatively determined before it can be definite at all. The complexity merely shows that the claim "in principle to predict all" is idle even apart from any truth in the idea of creativity. The determinists' claim thus amounts to positing an absolute where only something relative has practical utility, and in addition, if we must raise ultimate theoretical issues, it is the wrong absolute. For it may be argued (See Chapter Six) that being, in the form of fixed law, cannot be absolute, since this would make becoming an illusion; however, being too would then be illusory, because all terms involve contrast, and if there is only being, "being" is meaningless. On the other hand, becoming can be absolute in a certain sense, without making being an illusion. How this may be is one of the semi-open secrets of the new metaphysics.

The basic issue about determinism is this: the world is full of arbitrary matters of fact, arbitrary definiteness; *either* this definiteness was already given, once and for all, even in the remotest past, *or* new definiteness is added from time to time (more reasonably, in every instant). In the latter view, we human adults may, in higher degree than most creatures, contribute to the definiteness of the world. It is no mere question of liking our causally-appointed roles — finding our chains agreeable or imperceptible — but of making these roles in some degree. Either we have a hand in the authorship of the play, or we are mere actors, and even less than actors, for these in concrete fact always in some measure, and unpredictably, create the play as enacted. This is the real metaphysical question of freedom.

It is true that we can and should defend political freedom, whatever our metaphysics, and co-operate to this end with others, whatever their philosophies. But if we are philosophers, or interested in philosophy, we may well feel some obligation to try to understand the metaphysics which takes freedom as first principle of reality. For doing so might help us to have a more intelligent and a stronger faith in our cause, and a firmer grasp even of its practical meaning.

Close to the center of the metaphysical problem is the status to be assigned to theistic proofs, arguments favoring belief in God.

It was maintained by Kant, and has been widely accepted, that the theoretical reasons which have been given for believing in God all depend upon the Ontological Argument (invented by Anselm and used by Descartes, Spinoza, Leibniz, and Hegel) and that this argument is a mere sophism. Recently, however, there have been signs that the prolonged "dogmatic slumber" on this topic may be nearly over. In a very able article, J. N. Findlay some years ago contended that Anselm's procedure did prove something, even though not what he hoped to prove — indeed, rather the contrary, since the famous inference, properly evaluated, turns out to furnish a disproof of theism.[10] For, contended Findlay, the only way in which the idea of God could be valid would indeed be in the form of the necessarily existent; in so far, Anselm was right. But we know from modern logic that "necessarily existent" is logically impossible; ergo, the idea of God is not only not shown by the proof to be valid, it is shown to be invalid. No such being as God could exist.

If this position is correct, then Kant's criticisms and those of Russell and others who, armed with modern logic, have embellished Kant are antiquated. The Argument is no mere sophism — it is a discovery; apparently that of the impossibility of God, surely one of the most momentous discoveries of all. Yet not a single opponent of theism has taken up Findlay's cue! Everyone continues to reiterate Kant's contention that the proof leaves the issue where it was before. Rather, it forces us to choose between

[10] "Can God's Existence Be Disproved?" *Mind*, LVII (1948), 176. Reprinted in Anthony Flew and A. Macintyre (eds.), *New Essays in Philosophical Theology* (London: SCM Press, 1955), pp. 47–56.

the view that theism is logically invalid or impossible and the rejection of the doctrine of "modern logic" that necessary existence is an absurdity.

A second sign that Kant failed to dispose of the question is the recent appearance of a notable article by Norman Malcolm which demonstrates (I had already pointed it out repeatedly) that Anselm had two forms of ontological argument, not one, and that the standard criticisms are clearly relevant only to the first of them.[11] The second argument Malcolm vigorously and adroitly defends, and his reasoning here is in line with Findlay's, except that he rejects the contention that necessary existence has been shown to be illogical.

Where these two authors agree with each other and with Anselm (also with Descartes, as Malcolm notes), they are disagreeing with the standard treatment of the Ontological Argument in no fewer than hundreds of books. And they are in partial agreement with what I have been writing on this topic for years.[12] How long, one wonders, will this challenge be ignored? Here are three of us who, with otherwise very different philosophical standpoints, declare (in effect) that this matter has up to now been gravely mishandled.

It is true that we disagree in the end as to the conclusion to be drawn. Findlay thinks it should be anti-theistic, Malcolm, theistic, and I think it should be both, depending upon which form of theism is in question. The sense in which logic can show necessary existence to be impossible is relevant (and in my judgment fatal) to one such form, but not to every form. As so often, the disagreement turns at least in part upon an ambiguous concept, in this case the concept of "perfection" which is employed in the argument. There are really two essentially different

[11] "Anselm's Ontological Arguments," *Philos. Review*, LXIX (1960), 41–62.

[12] See especially *Philosophers Speak of God*, written and edited by C. Hartshorne and W. L. Reese (Chicago: The University of Chicago Press, 1953), pp. 96–98; 103–106; 134; 135; 136–137.

ideas of perfection, and of its existence; and there is no reason why Findlay should not be right as to the one, and Anselm and Malcolm as to the other. Since neither party seems aware of the ambiguity, this might explain their reaching opposite conclusions, the one more or less unconsciously resolving the ambiguity in one direction, the other in the other. My own position is simply that, with this understanding, both are right. What is needed is to clarify the choice between the two conceptions of divine perfection, which I term the classical and the neoclassical.

The points of agreement among Findlay, Malcolm, Hartshorne, Anselm, and Descartes are these: for an individual to exist contingently is a defect, hence either "perfect individual" exists non-contingently, or it fails to exist; but since where contingent existence is impossible, failure to exist cannot be contingent failure, either perfection exists necessarily or its non-existence is necessary ("perfect individual" is impossible). Findlay then argues on logical grounds against necessary existence and infers impossibility; Malcolm argues against impossibility and infers necessary existence. I take both positions, the one with regard to the classical and the other with regard to the neoclassical concepts of perfection and its manner of existing. My contention is further that the classical view not only makes trouble in connection with the ontological argument, but has many other disadvantages, philosophical and religious. It is one of our legacies from Greece (not from Palestine), and like most such legacies, as it stands it is inadequate to our intellectual and spiritual requirements.

Malcolm's essay was published after Chapter Two, in nearly its present form, was completed. If the reader will consult the section on Anselm in *Philosophers Speak of God*, he will see that to Malcolm's two Anselmian or Cartesian Ontological "Arguments," correspond the "two forms" which I there recognize (pp. 96–97, 99, and 135), and that we agree rather well as to the value of the two, except that Malcolm misses the element of validity in

Findlay's contention that it cannot be possible to infer the concrete from the abstract, from which it follows that unless God is a mere abstraction He must be more than the necessary being demonstrated by the Argument, and must have contingent properties as well as necessary ones. In addition to this implication deriving from the Ontological Argument, we have excellent reasons, both religious and philosophical, for conceiving divine perfection neoclassically as requiring contingent states in God. The future of the argument, and that of metaphysics itself, depends upon the fortunes of the new philosophy of creativity.

CHAPTER TWO

Ten Ontological or Modal Proofs For God's Existence

"It is possible to conceive of a being which cannot be conceived not to exist; and this is greater than one which can be conceived not to exist. Hence, if that, than which nothing greater can be conceived, can be conceived not to exist, it is not that, than which nothing greater can be conceived. But this is an irreconcilable contradiction. There is, then, so truly a being than which nothing greater can be conceived to exist, that it cannot even be conceived not to exist; and this being thou art, O Lord, our God." ANSELM, *Proslogium* (*trans.* S. N. Deane).

"In the idea or concept of a thing existence is contained, because we are unable to conceive anything except under the form of an existent; that is, possible or contingent existence is contained in the concept of a limited thing, but necessary and perfect existence in the concept of a supremely perfect being . . .

"To say that something is contained in the nature or in the concept of anything is the same as to say that this is true of that thing . . . But necessary existence is contained in the nature or in the concept of God.

"Hence it is true to say of God that necessary existence is in Him, or that God exists." DESCARTES, *Second Replies to Objections* (*trans.* Marjorie Grene).

28

I. The Nature of the Problem.

For forty years I have been thinking with some care about the Ontological Argument of Anselm and Descartes, and its rebuttals in Hume, Kant, and various other writers. It has been strange to observe the procedures of those who apparently have paid but casual attention to the matter. (It is even, in a somewhat different way, strange to recall how I myself looked at it a few years ago.) Since this sense of strangeness is likely to be a two-way affair, and accordingly the reader may be startled, amused — or worse still, bored — by some of the things I shall say, I ask him to exercise patience until he has familiarized himself with what, I predict, will be more or less new conceptions. I also remind him that — as I have heard a scientist (Alfred E. Wilhelmi) declare, with a certain quiet intensity — the growing point of knowledge is where a solitary individual decides to risk his time, energy, and perhaps reputation, in testing, and if the tests turn out well, in challenging, a proposition which all his fellow investigators regard as established.

It is in some such position that I find myself. To be sure, instead of saying that I am forced to disagree, I might about as well say that I am forced to agree, with almost everyone; for it proves possible to reconcile, in surprising degree, though not completely, the contentions of Anselm and Kant, or of Descartes and Russell. This often happens with new perspectives and is one sign of their probable superiority. But however it is described, the position is not an altogether comfortable one to be in. Intellectual history shows only too clearly how, in well-trained, even gifted and creative, minds, incredulity is not only a common initial response to novelty, but often a prolonged response. If the reader of what follows comes to judge that I am a fool, either he will be right — or (for I confess I can scarcely see a third possibility) he will be one more of the innumerable members of the class of those by whom new discoveries have been greeted with scorn. At any rate, he has now been warned.

One conviction which prolonged concentration upon "the Proof" or "the Argument" (as I shall call it) has produced is that the subject is much more complex and subtle than has been realized. Anselm and Descartes were rather simple-minded in their claim to have found a clear and obvious logical connection, scarcely open to intelligent dispute, between their "idea" of divine perfection and the existence of something perfect. But have opponents of the Argument been less simple-minded in proclaiming a clear, obvious, and non-controversial lack of connection? I expect to show that any such simplicity, favorable or unfavorable, to the Argument, is a fairy tale. These are deep waters — or sheer mirage: the idea of divinity, if it has any cognitive meaning, cannot have an altogether obvious one; and we have only to look with a little care into the ramifications of its conceivable relations to existence to see that many, in a sense all, of the questions of metaphysics, in the classical sense of ontology, are at stake in this one. Above all, the status of metaphysics itself is at stake. That those who dismiss the Argument as a mere sophistry also, and especially in recent times, dismiss the possibility of metaphysical inquiry (unless in some trivialized form having little to do with historical models) seems to me only what should be expected. Nor is it surprising that as a result philosophy threatens to become the elegant trifling we have often witnessed of late.

The remedy, I am persuaded, cannot be found until the Argument has been examined with more care than has yet been bestowed upon it. For this is the crucial case: here if anywhere a sharp focus upon ontological matters must be achieved. I shall contend, moreover, that the theory of the modality of existential judgments (their uniform contingency) upon which rejection of the argument chiefly rests has little to commend it, being supported solely by an exceedingly loose form of analogy, assimilating to ordinary contingent judgments (those which nearly all philosophers agree are such) two forms which are radically distinct from them and from each other, and whose contingency is by no means non-controversial. The theory can be replaced (see Secs. XI, XII) by one which accepts all the clear evidences of contingency, but avoids heaping together in one modal basket propositions differing both from the ordinary type and from each other in the most radical ways conceivable, the differences having definite logical connections with the modal status of the propositions.

The question to be discussed is not the crude alternative, "Did Anselm (or Descartes) prove God, or did he not?" Of course he did not, if "prove" means, achieve absolute cogency and clarity by means of a single brief course of reasoning. But the significant question is rather, "Did Anselm discover something, or give us indications following which we may discover something, concerning the relation of 'divine perfection exists' to ordinary existential judgments?" Is this simply one more instance of such judgments? "Why not?" some will ask. The answer is, "Because divinity is not simply one more existing, or not-existing, property." According to nearly all theologians and metaphysicians who have accepted the idea of God, deity is not simply one being among others, but *the* Being, identical in some sense with "Being itself." How then do we know that judgments in which this allegedly incomparable term occurs are not of a distinct logical type? Even if "identical with Being itself" is nonsensical, it will still follow that judgments which imply it are not of the same logical type as ordinary existential judgments capable of being contingently true or false!

We shall see that perfection cannot be of one type with ordinary predicates, and this for at least ten reasons, almost any one of which seems decisive, and the totality of which forms one of the strongest of philosophical arguments. Not that this, of itself, proves theism: "divinity exists" may still be open to rational rejection, even though not for the same sort of reason as can lead us to reject an unjustified existential judgment of the ordinary type. The opponents of the Argument, with rare exceptions, assume a simple logical analogy here; Anselm did not assume, he argued rationally for, the absence of such analogy, and of his several reasons only one, and that the weakest, is even mentioned in most of the critical literature. This seems remarkable. Here is a man everyone thinks worth refuting, but almost no one thinks worth studying. And here is a problem few refuse to deal with, but almost everyone refuses or fails to deal with in a free and intellectual manner.

As Karl Popper says, one of the rules of rational method is, choose for criticism the strongest, not the weakest, form of the theories you reject. Applied to philosophy, especially, it is a hard saying — but a sound one.

An empiricist critic has advised me not to run counter to the overwhelming sentiment against the Ontological Argument. "People's minds are closed, on this subject," he said; "you should not openly defend the old Proof. Label it differently, appear to be talking about something new." I have decided not to be so coy; but still, I do propose an alternative label, the Modal Proof; and I do somewhat revise, not only the proof, but its conclusion. And — I appeal to Popper's rule, and seek to act according to it myself (see especially Sec. IV).

An opponent may argue: If there is no analogy between the theistic assertion and other existential judgments, then "exists" in the case of God is a mere equivocation and has no specifiable meaning. The defender of the Argument replies: existence is of two kinds, the division between which is intelligible and indeed logically necessary. "But" — persists the critic — "there should be some common generic, or at least analogous, meaning, and the burden of proof is upon the user of the Argument to show that and how the division into two such radically different kinds leaves the unitary meaning intact." Now here is where the plot really begins to thicken. For, we shall see (Sec. VIII), Anselm was in no position to meet this challenge. As Findlay, almost alone among the critics of the Argument, has seen and brilliantly argued, Anselm had made a definite logical discovery, but not quite the discovery he thought he had made.[1] Perfection (in the theological sense) belongs indeed to a different logical type from ordinary predicates; and its existence cannot be a purely contingent question, but must involve either a positive necessity or a negative one (i.e., an impossibility); yet the question remains, How do we decide between the two? *If* "necessary existence" is logically inadmissible, as many hold, then Findlay is right in taking the Argument as a "disproof" of theism: the divine existence must be impossible. If, on the contrary, "necessary existence" is logically possible and if, further, "perfection" in its other implications is likewise possible, then the Argument furnishes a valid proof of theism. It is thus careless to suppose, as has so generally been done, that the Argument merely displays Anselm's ignorance of certain logical principles, leaving the theistic question where it was before. Rather, it is an objective and important contribution, though not by itself a demonstration of theism.

I shall show my hand at once. If perfection or divinity must be defined and conceived as Anselm, Descartes, and many another philosopher or theologian, conceived it, then I hold that the Proof amounts to a cogent argument against theism. For, as will be explained, it would commit us to necessary existence in a form which really does violate logical principles.

However, another definition — "the neoclassical," I shall term it — can be given (Secs. II, III) which has the following properties:

a) It not only preserves, but actually strengthens, the cogency of the inference from the logical possibility to the non-contingency of the divine existence;

b) It gives necessary existence a meaning which seems logically defensible;

[1] J. N. Findlay, "Can God's Existence Be Disproved?" *Mind*, LVII (1948). Reprinted in Anthony Flew and A. Macintyre (eds.), *New Essays in Philosophical Theology* (London: SCM Press, 1955), pp. 47–56.

c) It is free from other well-known antinomies which mar the "classical idea" of perfection, and it thereby removes the chief ground for doubting the logical possibility of perfection;

d) It recognizes a sense in which the assertion of theism makes no empirical difference and also a sense in which the divine reality does make empirical differences; hence, even the "empirical criterion of meaning" does not establish an absence of significance for "perfect."

e) The revised idea can be derived from ancient and widely-acknowledged religious sources, and therefore it would not be correct to say that the redefinition is a mere "changing of the subject" from the "existence of God" to something else; rather it is arguable that the classical definition had already changed the subject, being an idolatrous substitute for the religious idea, whereas the redefinition is in effect a resumption of the original subject. For even Anselm intended to deal with the God of religion! That he, along with most classical theologians, including Kant, failed in this, is not merely my opinion.[2]

Not the Gospels and the Old Testament, but Greek philosophy was the decisive source for the classical idea of divine perfection. Yet precisely for philosophical purposes, this idea has been a failure. Anselm's defeat, which led finally to the discrediting of all the theistic arguments, in their classical forms, is one indication of this. The fate of theism depends, I believe, upon the possibility of an alternative idea of divinity.

II. The Neoclassical Idea of Perfection as Modal Coincidence.

What both ideas of divine perfection have in common is that they connote an excellence definable a priori, or in comparison to any other individual, possible or actual. Anselm's version of

[2] Out of many theologians and philosophers who hold this view I choose three: Nicolas Berdyaev, *The Destiny of Man* (New York: Charles Scribner's Sons, 1937), esp. pp. 33, 37; Reinhold Niebuhr, *Human Destiny* (New York: Charles Scribner's Sons, 1943), II, p. 71; Edgar Sheffield Brightman, *The Problem of God* (New York: The Abingdon Press, 1930), Chs. III, IV.

this was "such that none greater is conceivable." This is wholly a priori, referring to nothing empirical, but only to what, in purely abstract terms, is conceivable. An a priori proof obviously must start with such a non-empirical definition. But Anselm's formula, in addition to being perhaps impossibly vague (what is "greatness"?), is ambiguous. It may mean (a) no individual greater than God is conceivable, or (b) not even God Himself in any conceivable state could be greater than He actually is. Those who, as Anselm himself did, take the meaning as in (b) say that the very idea of alternative possible states of an individual is inapplicable to deity; but those who take the meaning as in (a) accept the distinction between divine individual and divine states. The neoclassical idea results if we affirm the legitimacy of divine states, and take the formula to mean: God cannot conceivably be surpassed or equalled by any other individual, but He can surpass himself, and thus His actual state is not the greatest possible state. This implies that there is potentiality as well as actuality in the divine reality.

The classical doctrine, of course, regarded deity as exclusively actual (*actus purus*). Whereas an ordinary or imperfect individual (we normally assume) always fails to actualize some of its potentialities, this was denied of the perfect. All that God has power to be, that, it was held, He is. What the classical theologians failed to note, apparently, is that by choosing (a) we can define perfection in a fashion which (1) is no less a priori; (2) excludes merely contingent existence, though not all contingent properties; (3) is free from the logical difficulties that are otherwise inevitable.

Ordinary or imperfect individuals, it is true, fail to actualize all their potentialities; but is this, in itself, a defect? A person selecting a career cuts off from realization opportunities such as could not be thought of in relation to an ape; and an ape, at every moment, confronts choices far richer than an amoeba can have. Thus the power of selection among partly incompatible possibilities of self-realization seems a measure of excellence rather than of deficiency. Nor is it obvious that this would not apply to deity. God makes this sort of creation, or that instead, but not both: hence He possesses this actual world or that, but not both. (A world which actualized all worldly possibilities would be sheer confusion, not a world.) The classical view was, in effect, that it is all one to the deity whether His world be this or that; the unactualized possibilities for worlds were not conceived as unactualized divine potentialities. God could, it was thought, be conceived to have acted differently, or at least with different results, but not to have been different.

This divorce between being and doing is a strange notion which nothing in our experience illustrates, even by analogy, except where the analogy implies the reverse of what the theist intends. Thus we may conceive that Plato could, after his death, have had a different influence upon subsequent generations, without having in his lifetime been other than he was; for we may conceive later thinkers as having responded differently to the *Dialogues*, just as they were. But this action or influence of Plato is, in either case, conceived as unconscious and involuntary: Plato, he lived in Athens, could not know his posthumous effects. God, on the contrary, is supposed to know and will what He elicits in the world, and indeed to love His creatures. That so many could think they believed this, and at the same time could hold that, no matter what world there is, God remains in exactly the same state, is to my mind one of the great oddities in human development. The degree of lovingness, its perfection, would of course not vary with varying worlds; but by definition, to "love" is to care about differences, and to respond to them differentially. Otherwise love would indeed be "blind" in the most absolute sense. Even Nygren can scarcely mean that to God a normal man and an idiot, or a man and an insect (his comparison is of saint with sinner, but why not take the radical case?) are simply equivalent.[3] If this were so, what would it

[3] Anders Nygren, *Eros and Agape*. Trans. by P. S. Watson (Philadelphia: The Westminster Press, 1953), pp. 68–73, 77.

mean to say that God knows what these creatures are, since certainly they are different?

On the classical view, any other world or none would have actualized the very same state of divine love and knowledge. Yet consider: *one* divine possibility is plainly unactualized if world W^1 is created and world W^2 is not; this is the possible knowledge that W^2 exists and W^1 does not. Since W^2 is non-existent, so is divine or any other knowing that it exists; since W^1 exists, knowledge of its non-existence does not. So if it be denied that there are unactualized potentialities in God, it is contradictory to say that He could have produced other worlds, and that He is sure in any case to know the truth. To cover the nakedness of this inconsistency with talk of the merely "symbolic" or analogical meaning of theological terms is only to announce one's intention of not standing by any affirmations or denials which one makes in these matters. Even analogical affirmations should commit one to something.

Let us then try the other tack, and say that unactualized possibilities increase, rather than decrease, with the rank of a being, and that, accordingly, perfection does not mean a zero, but a maximum, of potentiality, of unactualized power to be, as well as to produce beings in others. To define this maximum in purely a priori terms, we have only to say that the divine power-to-be is absolutely infinite, or is all power to be.

Perhaps the reader objects: What, God can be anything, for instance a murderer, or a worm! If this means, can be identical with a murderer or a worm, then of course not. But if it means, can include the reality of the wicked man or the worm in His own divine reality, then there is no absurdity. We have only to think of the divine knowing to see this. If a worm exists, then so does divine knowledge-of-the-worm-as-existent. And how can this fail to include the worm? And so with anything else which exists or is conceivable. If its existence can be thought of, so can God's knowledge that it exists. But not even God can be conceived to know as actual what is merely potential. And since there are mutually incompatible possibilities (all logic and mathematics stand or fall with this idea) it is contradictory to say, God knows as actualized all conceivable things.

The absolute infinity of the divine potentiality might also be called its *coincidence with possibility as such.* (Perhaps "co-extensiveness" with possibility would be more accurate.) To be possible is to be a possible object of divine knowing. But it immediately follows that one thing is not possible — the non-existence of the divine knower. For no subject can have knowledge of the fact of its own non-existence, certainly not perfect, infallible knowledge. Thus either the non-existence of the perfect knower is impossible, or there is one possibility whose actualization the perfect knower could not know. But the second case contradicts the definition of perfection through the coincidence of "possible" and "possible for God." Does this constitute a proof that perfection exists? Scarcely, in itself. But it does suggest that the relation of perfection to existence is at least peculiar. For in ordinary cases there is no reason why a property must be conceived as coincident with possibility in general. Indeed this would ordinarily be nonsensical.

So much for the relation of "perfection" to potentiality. What of its relation to actuality? Here too, if our Argument is to be possible, we need a principle definable a priori. The same notion of coincidence can be used: the divine actuality is all-actuality. This too is implied by the ordinary notion of infallible knowledge. God is thought of as actually knowing the existence of whatever does actually exist. His actuality, like His potentiality, is all inclusive. Item for item, everything actual is accounted for in His actual knowing, as everything possible is in His potential knowing. Thus we may define perfection as *modal coincidence,* and we may interpret this under the analogy of infallible knowledge.

If then someone says, "Perhaps there is no being modally coincident with actuality and possibility in general," he seems to be saying, "If such a being were to exist, this would be because a certain possibility (that it might have failed to exist) had not been actualized, and another possibility, that it might exist, had been actualized." But it follows, contradictorily, that the modally coincident would exist as not modally coincident, since one possibility would be outside its own potential possession, the alleged possibility of its own non-existence. Do we not here face an absurdity?

One may put the matter a little differently. If God is conceived as Creator, this means, "Whatever world actually exists, God is thought of as having created it; and whatever world might exist, God is thought of as capable of creating it." Thus the actual is what God is or is the maker of; and the possible is what God could be, or be the maker of. Again we have modal coincidence. Now suppose it "possible" that God should not exist: then, if it were the fact that He did exist, this fact would, on the assumption, be the actualization of a possibility not resting upon God's own creative action. But this makes no sense, in terms of the Creator-Creature dichotomy with which we are operating. Not merely does it falsify it factually, it even destroys its meaning. Ordinarily a contingent hypothesis concedes the conceivability of facts contradicting it. Indeed this conceivability is required for the hypothesis. But the theistic "hypothesis" claims to cover not only all facts but all conceivable hypotheses about facts; for it views them all as descriptions of what God might be conceived to be or do! A very strange "hypothesis"!

It is to be noted here that according to "Becker's Postulate," which has some standing in modal logic, modal status can be affirmed or denied in the mode of necessity only.[4] Thus, to say,

[4] See *e.g.*, R. Carnap, *Meaning and Necessity* (Chicago: The University of Chicago Press, 1947), pp. 185–186; A. Church, "A Formulation of the Logic of Sense and Denotation," in *Structure, Method and Meaning: Essays in Honor of Henry M. Sheffer*, edited by P. Henle (New York: The Liberal Arts Press, 1951), p. 22; Henry S. Leonard, "Two-Valued Truth Tables for Modal Functions," *op. cit.*, pp. 60–63; G. H. von Wright,

"p is possible," is the same as to say, "necessarily p is possible." And to say, "it is possible that p is necessary" is to say, "necessarily p is necessary." (See Sec. VI.) If this is correct, a concept of perfection as modal coincidence is not a factual hypothesis that might be true or false. If it could be true, it must be. I am sure that the reader is still far from convinced. But I hope he will have patience.

III. The Religious Idea of Perfection

Let us now look at a more obviously religious way of conceiving deity. (For we do not want our Argument to be impugned on the ground that its conclusion is irrelevant to the religious question.)

"God is perfect," in the religious sense, means, He can be worshipped without incongruity by every individual no matter how exalted. But what is worship? It has been very accurately defined. To worship X is to "love" X "with all one's heart and all one's mind and all one's soul and all one's strength." Perfection is the character which X must have to make sense out of this. The genius of Tillich first perceived that this formula is potentially the clearest definition in religious literature of the term "God." Yet (as has been shown elsewhere) even Tillich, through undue reliance upon the classical idea of perfection, and classical metaphysics generally, fell into ambiguity in interpreting his great suggestion. The fault is not in the Judeo-Christian text quoted. Its lucidity is virtually mathematical; One hundred per cent of our interest (mind), devotion (heart), energy (strength), and whatever else is in us (soul) is to have God as its object. It follows that if there be anything additional to God, it must receive zero attention! Yet we are to love ourselves and our fellows. A contradiction? Yes, save upon one assumption, that there cannot be anything "additional to God." Rather, all actu-

An Essay on Modal Logic (Amsterdam: North-Holland Publishing Co., 1951), pp. 66–77. Von Wright expresses some misgivings about the postulate, but they seem irrelevant to the present inquiry.

ality must be included in His actuality, and all possibility in His potential actuality. (For we must be interested in possibilities, if we are to love and help our neighbor, or ourselves.)

It immediately ensues as logical consequence that the notion of a "possible non-existence of God" must be contradictory. For suppose it is not contradictory. Then even were God to exist, His never having existed would still be or have been a logical possibility. Yet an interest in this possibility would contradict the religious commandment, and thus, since all thought expresses interest in its objects, a "contingently-existing God," or "a being whose non-existence is not contradictory and which is yet worthy of worship," involves a contradiction.

It is plain that Anselm and Descartes did not identify possibility with divine potentiality. Rather, like myriads of classical metaphysicians, they thought that God must be devoid of potentiality, incapable of acquiring any actuality He does not eternally and necessarily possess. But then our inevitable interest in creating value is not an interest in God, since He is thought to be incapable of receiving any created value. Created value or reality becomes thus bare nothing, or something external, and genuinely additional, to God. This is contrary to the meaning of religious perfection, as defined through worship.

If perfection has (even though necessarily) contingent instances or states, what becomes of the uniqueness of God? Does He become a member of a class of possible perfect individuals? The answer is no. For any two states which coexisted must coincide in their actuality with each other as inclusive of all that coexisted with either of them. The sole way in which more than one state can be actual and yet distinguishable is by forming a sequence, first the one state existing without the other, then the second state coming to be, as wholly embracing its predecessor in complete "memory." This is intelligible only if there is "genetic identity," or "personal order" (Whitehead), including continuity of character and purpose, through the sequence.

Once we grant that divinity has potential as well as actual

states, there is no longer any reason for denying successiveness to the divine life, and the old paradoxes of a non-successive divine "consciousness" need no longer trouble us. Nor need the perfection of the divine knowledge mean that later states must be fully anticipated in earlier; for until a state is actualized, it does not exist to be known. It would be error, not knowledge, to know as determinate what is as yet only a somewhat indeterminate potentiality. The Socinians stated this very plainly centuries ago; but the world was too busy to trouble itself with the opinions of a tiny and ephemeral group of heretics. It has not yet had time to catch up.[5] The theory that the truth about actual occurrences is timeless is all of a piece with the classical idea of God and ought not to survive its abandonment.

If the acceptance of the classical idea of perfection was the one fatal flaw in Anselm's use of his Argument, then Kant was not the man to correct him; for Kant never dreamt of conceiving God except in the classical manner.

In favor of this classical manner, certain arguments are also more or less classical. It is said that the assertion of coincidence between God and reality is "pantheistic," and hence irreligious. But, as Tillich sagely remarks, "pantheism" needs to be defined before being used polemically. When defined, it will either not agree with the neoclassical idea, or it will be religious. For the religious meaning which agrees with the neoclassical idea, I prefer the term Panentheism.[6]

It is said that the perfect could change only for the worse, since it must be already complete. This neatly begs a metaphysical question: is "completeness" in the sense here employed a consistent cognitive idea? It seems not, since there are incompatible possibilities, and therefore no reality, inclusive of God

---

[5] See Otto Fock, *Der Socinianismus* (Kiel, 1847), pp. 438–442. Trans. in Hartshorne and Reese (eds.), *Philosophers Speak of God*, p. 226.

[6] See Hartshorne and Reese, *op. cit.*, Ch. VII. Also my article, "Panentheism" in V. Ferm's *Encyclopedia of Religion* (New York: Philosophical Library, 1945).

or not, can contain all possible actuality or value, all actualized. To deny unrealized potentialities to God merely makes the total reality, as including such potentialities, "God and something additional." This is irreligious. It is also illogical; for, after all, the content of omniscience can only be all reality, and if there could be still further realities, there could be further real objects for omniscience to know. Hence there must be cognitive potentialities in God.

It is said that certain arguments for the existence of God, such as that for an unmoved mover, imply the absence of potentiality in God. However, the weakness of the said arguments is notorious — even though exaggerated in some accounts; moreover (this essay furnishes part of the evidence for the statement I am about to make), to strengthen the arguments, nothing is more truly essential than dropping the classical idea of perfection!

How is the divine inclusion of all values, actual and potential, to be conceived? Thus: God must Himself value all things; for nothing possesses actual value but an actually-enjoying subject, while the potential possession of value can only be the potential enjoyment of a subject.

The old objection was, "A subject must be relative to an object, contingent so far as that is, and so forth, whereas God must be wholly absolute and non-contingent." [7] But this indicates that the "whereas . . ." is an idolatrous distortion of the meaning of perfection. Hume came perhaps the closest of any nontheist (if he was that) to understanding all this. [8]

An apparent objection to the neoclassical idea is this: if per-

---

[7] In his *Ueber einem neuerdings erhobenen vornehmen Ton in Philosophie* Kant tells us that God must have no limitations, hence he cannot be conceived to have any positive properties known to us, such as will, which would make His happiness dependent on what happened in the world, or understanding, for it would have to be intuitive yet active, which we (with our sensory or passive intuition) cannot conceive. Neoclassicism admits and affirms a certain dependence and passivity as inherent in perfection, and compatible with omniscience.

[8] See especially the *4th Dialogue Concerning Natural Religion*.

fection is coincidence of reality with an all-valuing process of experience, then of course all evil is experienced by the perfect. However, to experience or perceive moral evil, wickedness, as such, is not necessarily to be wicked; indeed, to perceive it fully in its wickedness makes being wicked impossible. But it is otherwise with suffering. How does one perceive a particular, concrete suffering in its concrete particularity? I see no way but to sympathetically share it. And hence for me the old heresy of a suffering deity is no heresy.[9]

The neoclassical idea of perfection entails a sheer absence of suffering neither in God nor in the world. Its principles imply, as we shall see in later chapters (6–8, 13), an element of indeterminacy and uncertainty in reality as such: it therefore conceives supreme power not as a monopoly of power, unilaterally determining all things, but as an ideal form of give and take.[10] It views providence and chance, not as alternatives, but as complementaries, both applying universally to events, which in details must always be unintended. Thus any support given by the Ontological argument to the neoclassical idea cannot be nullified by a simple inference from the fact of evil.

IV. Twenty Objections to the Proof

Let us now return to the Argument. I should like to try to win something of the reader's confidence in my competence to judge this matter by giving here as complete and cogent an account as I

[9] See my article, "Whitehead and Berdyaev: Is There Tragedy In God?" in *J. of Rel.*, XXXVII (1957), 71–84.

[10] Three recent British discussions of religion proceed on the assumption that metaphysical or absolute determinism makes sense. See *New Essays in Philosophical Theology*, pp. 26, 144–169; also J. L. Mackie, "Evil and Omnipotence," *Mind*, N. S., LXIV (1955), 200–212. Such writers are ignoring a large part of the work that has been done in metaphysics during the last five generations. It is not alone physicists who have been reexamining the "*uses*" of the word cause. But alas, Lequier, Boutroux, Bergson, Varisco, Fechner (in his later writings), Peirce, and many others have written almost in vain.

can, in brief compass, of the case against an argument of the Ontological type. The following considerations seem to constitute such a case.

1) "Any sensible man" must see that we cannot find out what exists merely by analyzing our ideas (Kant: Commonsense Objection).

2) All other forms of existential judgment are contingent, hence presumably this one is so (Inductive Counterargument).

3) If we can deduce existence from a concept we must have presupposed existence, and the Argument is thus a tautology, a result of defining something to exist. But a definition is always open to rejection as inapplicable to anything. Tautologies or analytic judgments are empty, trivial (Kant: Charge of Tautology).

4) Even if existence is necessarily included in a certain kind of thing, there is contradiction, not in rejecting the thing with all that it would include, but only in admitting a thing of the kind and rejecting some of its properties (Kant). The necessary existence of God could thus at most mean that *if* He exists, He exists necessarily (Objection of Hypothetical Necessity Only or Begging the Question).

5) The Argument assumes the real possibility of a God. But logical possibility is not enough to prove real or ontological possibility (Kant). Similarly, logical necessity does not prove real necessity, nor logical nor conceptual existence, real existence (Ambiguity of Necessity, Possibility, Existence).

6) If "perfect" or "greatest conceivable" guarantees existence, why not greatest conceivable, hence necessarily-existing, island, mermaid, or what you will (Gaunilo: *Reductio ad Absurdum* Counterargument).

7) It is not individuals but properties which exist; hence, to say, God or the perfect being necessarily exists is contrary to logical grammar (Ryle's Objection).

8) If we can prove the existence of God from the divine essence, we must be able to know the latter. But God is the great

45

mystery: we may perhaps know that, but scarcely what, He is. A dog may know his master, but surely not his master's nature, the essence of a man. Something like this should be our relation to deity. The Argument thus reverses the natural order of knowledge in this sphere (Gaunilo: Anti-gnostic Objection, Thomist Objection — Thomists also support the 5th Objection).

9) Going a step further, it is held that there is no meaning, other than an emotive, "convictional," or inconsistent one, for the assertion of the divine existence (Positivistic Objection).

10) Existence is not a predicate: for if there is said to be a thing with a certain property, then it must be that very property, without addition or subtraction, which the exemplifying instance embodies (Kant). Hence the existent is no more perfect than the non-existent (Objection that Existence is not a Predicate).

11) Existence is on a different logical level, or of a different logical type, from a predicate, being more concrete, and hence an addition to the mere predicate, not contained in it (Russell, Carnap). A mere universal or definable abstraction such as "perfection" (Anselm defines it) cannot entail an actual individual exemplifying the universal (Logical-type Objection). I am here indebted to a conversation with Carnap. With him I regard this, and Nos. 9 and 17, as the crucial objections.

12) It is scarcely a rebuttal of (11) to hold, as theologians often do, that God does not "have," but "is," His goodness. This, it seems, can only mean that logical principles collapse in relation to God; but in that case, so far from furnishing a valid argument for belief in Him, they constitute an argument against such belief (The Identity Paradox).

13) Logical necessity connects concepts with concepts, or propositions with propositions, not concepts or propositions with things. How can logical necessity transcend the logical sphere of thought, or language? (Paradox of the Self-transcendence of the Logical).

14) If God's reality follows from our idea, then this idea must be (or contain) God himself (Kant: Mystical Paradox).

15) In some forms, the Argument commits the "homological" mistake of taking a predicate as an instance of itself. There is no need that perfection be perfect, only that instances of it, if any, be so (Homological Fallacy).[11]

16) If God exists necessarily, this can only mean, "He is reality itself" (the real can only be the real, the existent does exist), and hence "God" stands either for an empty abstraction, or else for the totality of things which happen to exist, including perhaps the possibility of a vacuous case in which nothing concrete exists (Lack of Distinctive Character for the Necessary Being).

17) Logical analysis shows that the necessary can only mean, "what all contingent possible alternatives have in common," the abstract residuum left when we leave out of account all that distinguishes one state of affairs from any other, actual or possible; hence, as necessary being, God would be an extremely abstract entity (Paradox of the Abstractness of the Necessary: Findlay).

18) "All necessary propositions say the same thing, namely nothing" (Wittgenstein).

19) Anselm was not trying to convince unbelievers, but was trying to understand his faith; his argument can be used neither against unbelievers, nor as a secular philosophical proof (Fideist or Barthian Objection).[12]

20) Anselm was a Platonic Realist, and it is only on this basis that his Argument has any weight (Objection of Assumed Realism of Universals).

V. Bias and Short-circuited Inquiry

It is idle to deny that the foregoing objections, especially 8–11, 17–19, constitute an impressive case. It is therefore not to be

[11] Murray Kiteley, "Existence and the Ontological Argument," *Philosophy and Phenomenological Research*, XVIII (1958), No. 4, 533–535. I shall always be grateful to this author; for his article was somehow the spark that kindled the fire burning in this essay.

[12] Karl Barth's book, *Fides Quaerens Intellectum* (Zolikon: Evangelischer Verlag, 1931), is a scholarly discussion of Anselm's reasoning.

greatly wondered at that modern philosophy has in consequence fallen into an attitude toward this topic which may be described as one of unwary wariness, or credulous incredulity. History has shown that philosophical truth, if there be such a thing, is hard to attain. It may never be safe to lean back and say, "That, at any rate, is proved or disproved once and for all." Even scientists are cautious about adopting such an attitude, although they may have more excuse for it.

That the Argument should be given short shrift is the more natural in that both Anselm and Descartes, in their initial statements, wrote as though existence, even in the ordinary sense, were a predicate, in a simple and obvious manner which could be directly exploited by the Argument without further ado. Only later in their discussions (as in the quotations prefacing this monograph) did they indicate a different and more complex basis for the ontological inference. I used to think that this delay in arriving at the essential point was the chief ground for the premature confidence of the critics, causing them to dispense with prolonged and careful study. However, I now realize that there was a more respectable reason. So long as the classical idea of perfection is taken for granted as premise of the Argument, the more adequate approach (via modality rather than simple existence) can be shown logically to entail the same difficulty as the direct method via mere existence (see below, Sec. VIII.).

Nevertheless, natural as the modern attitude may be, it is not altogether in accord with an exacting ideal of inquiry. Read the refutations, especially those coming after Kant. Is this not the attitude they convey: "We know that existence can never be inferred from a mere concept; so let us get this necessary refutation of a silly though ingenious fantasy over with as quickly and decisively as possible." Or perhaps, "Of course the Argument must be refutable, who does not know that? But the interesting thing is to see what slightly new slant we can give the inevitable refutation." Unfortunately, as Peirce said, those who know too well where their reasoning must lead them are doomed to play the confidence game upon themselves. Theirs is likely to be "sham reasoning." It is not inquiry in the best sense.

To show this failure to maintain an inquiring attitude toward our topic, it seems to me almost sufficient to remark that whereas I, who believe in the possibility of the ontological inference, have been able to set out by far the most complete inventory in print (unless I am much mistaken) of the case against the argument, the opponents have never given any such inventory of the favorable reasons, even those offered by Anselm and Descartes; and as for the ten versions of the Argument which I am going to present, scarcely a single one (so far as I can see) is clearly stated or implied in the classical refutation by Kant. Nor have Kant's successors made good the deficiency. Where can the explanation lie, if not in a general bias and lack of interest?

This bias is not due solely to the prima facie case against the ontological inference. It has at least two further sources. There are many who take religion to be essentially subrational; there are others who take it to be essentially suprarational. In either case, it will seem unlikely that painstaking examination of alleged proofs for theism may be rewarding. The trouble with both views is that until we have made such an examination, we do not know how far religion is either sub- or suprarational. Again we face the confidence game possibility. It happens that I have had neither of the two attitudes just mentioned, but have on the whole regarded religion, in its traditional forms, as more or less prerational, the question of its capacity or incapacity for achieving rational consciousness by this or that development or modification being one for reason itself to adjudicate. Anselm's proposal is a possible instrument for such inquiry; but instead of taking it so, we have either used or rejected it cavalierly. I have myself not been guiltless on this score.[13]

VI. The Irreducibly Modal Structure of the Argument

The reader will have noticed the label "modal" in the title of this

[13] *E.g.*, in *The Philosophical Review*, LIII (1944), 225-245.

chapter. Had the proof been known as the Modal Argument, the chances of genuine inquiry would have been greater. Critics have generally discussed the problem as though it concerned a mere question of fact, of contingent existence versus contingent non-existence. This is not a modal distinction in an unambiguous sense, inasmuch as the mode of contingency is the neutrality of a predicate as between existence and non-existence, and the denial of such neutrality is the disjunction: necessarily existent or necessarily non-existent (i.e., impossible). To squeeze this modal complexity into the mere dichotomy, "existent versus non-existent," is to fail to discuss what Anselm was talking about. He repeatedly expressed the principle that "contingently-existing perfect thing" is contradictory in the same way as "non-existing perfect thing." However, since what is not exemplified in truth is certainly not necessarily exemplified ($\sim p \rightarrow \sim Np$), and since what is not necessary could not be necessary ($\sim Np \rightarrow N \sim Np$), to exclude contingency (this exclusion being the main point of the Argument) is to exclude factual non-existence as well as merely factual existence, leaving, as the only status which the idea of perfection can have (supposing it not meaningless or contradictory), that of necessary exemplification in reality; and it then, by the principle $Np \rightarrow p$, "the necessarily true is true," becomes contradictory to deny that perfection is exemplified. (Here, and throughout, we use the arrow sign for strict, not material, implication.)

Is it this subtle, beautifully logical reasoning that we meet in the numerous refutations? Rather we find a gross simplification which amounts to the straw-man procedure.

The logical structure of the Anselmian argument, in its mature or "Second" form, may be partially formalized as follows:

'q' for '$(\exists x)Px$' There is a perfect being, or perfection exists

'N' for 'it is necessary (logically true) that'

'$\sim$' for 'it is not true that'

'$\vee$' for 'or'

'$p \rightarrow q$' for 'p strictly implies q' or '$N \sim (p \& \sim q)$'

1. $q \rightarrow Nq$ "Anselm's Principle": perfection could not exist contingently
2. $Nq \lor \sim Nq$ Excluded Middle
3. $\sim Nq \rightarrow N \sim Nq$ Form of Becker's Postulate: modal status is always necessary
4. $Nq \lor N \sim Nq$ Inference from (2, 3)
5. $N \sim Nq \rightarrow N \sim q$ Inference from (1): the necessary falsity of the consequent implies that of the antecedent (Modal form of modus tollens)
6. $Nq \lor N \sim q$ Inference from (4, 5)
7. $\sim N \sim q$ Intuitive postulate (or conclusion from other theistic arguments): perfection is not impossible
8. Nq Inference from (6, 7)
9. $Nq \rightarrow q$ Modal axiom
10. q Inference from (8, 9)

Those who challenge the Argument should decide which of these 10 items or inferential steps to question. Of course one may reject one or more of the assumptions (1, 3, 7); but reject is one thing, refute or show to be a mere sophistry is another. To me at least, the assumptions are intuitively convincing, provided perfection is properly construed, a condition Anselm did not fulfill. Moreover, no absurd consequence seems derivable from them by valid reasoning.

Concerning (1). Note that we do not take as initial assumption that $\sim q$ is directly contradictory, or that a nonexistent being must therefore be imperfect. Nonexistent subjects cannot be said to have predicates, even inconsistent ones. Rather we reason that by virtue of (1) and certain principles of modal logic,

$$((\exists x)Px \, \& \sim N \, (\exists x)Px) \rightarrow \sim Px$$

and thus the antecedent is necessarily false, since it both asserts and by implication denies perfection, not of a supposed nonexistent but of a supposed contingently-existent subject. Such a subject can very well have predicates, and indeed all ordinary subjects are precisely of this kind. Thus we make contingency and its negation, not existence or non-existence, the predicates with which the argument is concerned, in connection with the predicate perfection.

The postulate of logical possibility (7) is in my view the hardest to justify. One way of doing this is to employ one or more of the other theistic proofs, some forms of which demonstrate that perfection must be at least conceivable. Here, however, we encounter Kant's contention that the other proofs themselves need support from the ontological. Yet Kant's own analysis showed that what the other proofs need from the ontological is not really its conclusion (8 or 10), but only the exclusion of contingency from perfection (6), and this is a mere logical transformation of Anselm's Principle (1). Thus there need be no vicious circle in employing all the proofs in mutual support. They are all complex, involving a number of assumptions and steps, and where one is weakest another may be strongest. There need be no simple linear order, and indeed there is none, among them. Here too we must do our own thinking, and not expect Kant or Hume to have done it for us.

That modality with respect to existence is a predicate is assumed by the critics of the Argument themselves. For they hold, in effect, that to every predicate there is attached the status of contingency, i.e., its existence and non-existence must alike be conceivable. Obviously, if "contingent" is a predicate, so is "noncontingent"; just as, if "perfect" is a predicate, so is "imperfect." This is then, so far as it goes, an answer to the crucial Logical-type Counterargument: modality is (at least) as high in the type-sequence as property! We shall see presently, however, that only neoclassical theism can consistently avail itself of this rebuttal.

It is to be noted that Anselm's Principle does not say that perfection would be imperfect if it were unexemplified, but that anything exemplifying it merely contingently (so that it could have been unexemplified) would be imperfect, and so would not exemplify it after all. Thus the "homological mistake" is not committed (12th Counter-argument). Moreover (and here too Anselm is subtler than most of his critics), "is necessarily exemplified" follows by Becker's Postulate from "could be necessarily exemplified," since $\sim N \sim N p \rightarrow N p$. This disposes of the 5th Counter-argument, "Hypothetical Necessity Only."

Something should be said about the meaning of "necessity," symbolized by 'N'. As every logician knows, there are many interpretations of this symbol. In general it means analytic or L-true, true by necessity of the meanings of the terms employed. This is the sense intended in the present essay. However, what is analytic in one language may, as Quine and others have sufficiently emphasized, not be so in another.[14] (Here, too, we see how absurd it is to suppose that the Ontological question is a simple one.) I cannot exhaust the modal subject here and now. But I must make clear the difference between merely conditional necessity and absolute necessity. As von Wright has it, this last is the same as "necessity upon tautological conditions": not necessity assuming p, or necessity assuming not-p, but necessity, p or not-p. Since "p or not-p" must be true, it is meaningless to say, "q might be necessary but is not," when "necessary" is taken in the sense of "upon tautological conditions." This is the only sense at issue in connection with the ontological argument. The divine existence is by definition unconditioned, and its necessity can only be absolute, valid no matter what, or "given p or not-p." Thus if God logically could be necessary He must be, since no contingent condition can be relevant.

The technical difficulty with regard to the Argument is that the idea of God is apparently not a conception of formal logic. Hence even if the idea implies the necessity of a corresponding object, so that the denial of such an object is contradictory, still the whole question seems to fall outside the basic rules of any

[14] Quine's conclusion that all truth is synthetic is fairly but powerfully criticized by A. Hofstadter in "The Myth of the Whole, a Consideration of Quine's View of Knowledge." *J. of Phil.*, LI (1954), 397–417.

language. However, the matter is not so simple. There ought to be a formal rule concerning the division between necessary and contingent statements, and as we shall see, by some reasonable criteria for this division, the statement "Divine Perfection exists" falls on the side of necessity. Moreover, there may well be an aspect of the idea of God which is formal in the logical sense. If for instance, "deity" connotes, among other things, "the sole individual definable a priori" (distinguished a priori from all others, actual or possible), is this not a formal characterization? Or suppose it follows from the meaning of "God" that it can only refer to an individual "such that, given any statement about any other individual whatever, this statement can be translated without loss of meaning or truth into a statement about God." (Thus for *S is P* we can always say *God knows that S is P*.) Of no other individual than God, I believe, could the quoted stipulation hold; yet it is a formal or logical stipulation. No special fact is mentioned, but only the ideas of individual, statement, and translatability or equivalence. No doubt some problems arise here, but I shall not attempt to deal with them now.

Carnap has proposed the notion of "meaning postulates," as a device for introducing analytic judgments, other than the merely logical, into a language.[15] The objection has been that apparently any scientific law could be turned into an a priori necessity by suitable meaning postulates, thus trivializing the procedure. However, as Bowman Clarke, in an unpublished thesis, has proposed, the trivialization may be avoided if we limit meaning postulates to ideas of metaphysical generality, ideas of unlimited range in space-time, and applicable to all grades of existence, low or high.[16] I think also that metaphysical univer-

[15] See R. Carnap, *Meaning and Necessity*, Second Ed. (Chicago: The University of Chicago Press, 1956), pp. 222–229; and R. M. Martin, *The Notion of Analytic Truth* (Philadelphia: University of Pennsylvania Press, 1959), pp. 87–90.

[16] See Carnap's somewhat analogous proposal in *Meaning and Necessity*, Sec. 21. Also my paper, "Existential Propositions and the Law of Categories." *Proceedings of the Tenth International Congress of Philos-*

sality is the same thing as the absence of exclusiveness to be discussed in § IX, and that God (in His necessary essence only) is universal or non-exclusive, involved in all possible things. It may be that Carnap's proposal, qualified and developed in some such way, will solve the technical problem of reconciling the logical meaning of "necessary" with the ontological in the unique divine case.

One way to put the argument is this: any language adequate to formulate the meaning of "perfect" in the theistic sense will make "perfection exists" analytic or L-true. Moreover, a language which does this will not thereby become inconsistent. This is more than can be said for a language making "perfect island exists" L-true (using "island" in anything like the dictionary sense). Since modal status is always necessary, mistakes in assigning such status can only lead to contradiction. Suppose, for instance, we should speak of a "necessarily-existent" island. Since the necessarily so is of course so, said island must exist. What is wrong? Simply that the notion of island is that of a contingent thing, resulting from causes whose operation is not infallible and everlasting. If an island could be necessary, anything could be so, and since the possibly necessary must be necessary $(\sim N \sim Np \rightarrow Np)$, there would be no contingency or necessary in a significant sense. Thus a language which required one to admit as a genuine concept "necessarily-existing island" would be self-inconsistent. The "necessarily-existing island" must exist, but also it must not and cannot exist. We can only start over again, by dismissing the alleged definition as ill-formed. If then the notion of "necessarily-existing perfection" were likewise illegitimate, a contradiction would result from its use. If the contradiction can be exhibited, there is an end of the matter. But can it? If not, then the notion may be legitimate. And since religion seems to require the idea, there is some burden of proof on the negative. (In the foregoing I assume that we are not limited to

ophy, Amsterdam, August 11–18, 1948, edited by E. W. Beth, H. J. Pos and J. H. A. Hollak, Fascicule 1, pp. 342–344.

classical theism as explication of "perfect," for if we were, then I would grant the charge of inconsistency without further ado.) To reason, "If the metaphysically perfect could be necessary, anything could be so," would be silly, as we shall see in more detail later. The metaphysically perfect is a radically exceptional case, on any analysis. "Perfect island" never did mean metaphysically perfect island, to any honest and careful thinker; for the phrase is too glaringly absurd. It never meant, *either* (classical theism) the exhaustion, through an island, of all possibility so far as positive or valuable, *or* (neoclassical theism) coincidence of actuality with the island's actuality and of possibility with the island's possibility. And if it did mean either of these things, then it meant nonsense. To be thus is not to be an island, but to be God.

The Cosmological Argument, not to be dealt with here, would perhaps show that any language adequate to formulate the universal categories, or to discuss the most general cosmological questions, would also make "perfection exists" L-true.

The foregoing meaning of 'N' justifies the axioms that all modalities reduce to three: $Np, N \sim p, (\sim Np \& \sim N \sim p)$; and that $\sim N \sim NP \rightarrow Np$, and $\sim Np \rightarrow N \sim Np$ (*what could be* necessary is so, and what is not necessary could not be so). It must be understood that propositions are here identified by their meaning, not in some extrinsic way. As Church remarks, "the proposition occurring first on a certain page" may happen to be, in a certain language, a necessary proposition, but "it" might also have been a contingent proposition.[17] Clearly one is not in such cases dealing with the same proposition, so far as meaning is concerned. Some modal systems, at least, recognize the above axioms (Lewis, Prior, Carnap).

In systems of "strict implication," it has been termed a paradox that a necessary proposition is strictly implied by any proposition whatever. I agree with Lewis in not finding this paradoxical, at

[17] A. Church, in his article in *Structure, Method and Meaning: Essays in Honor of Henry M. Sheffer*, edited by P. Henle (New York: The Liberal Arts Press, 1951), pp. 22–23, footnote.

least if we consider only those cases which are free from empirical concepts. That "blue cheese contains micro-organisms" (if this is part of what we mean by cheese) is only trivially a priori or necessary; for there might have been no such thing as cheese, or even any idea of such a thing. What is strictly a priori and purely necessary here is only some such principle as that the consequences of a defined term must be accepted if the term is accepted. This much more abstract proposition, or something like it, is, I believe, in a genuine sense implied by any proposition and any thought at all. I hold similarly that the validity of the Argument, if it be valid, can only mean that the existence of perfection is non-trivially necessary, an implicit or more or less hidden ingredient of any concept or any belief whatever. It follows that it must be highly abstract, highly general; and this consequence I accept and emphasize. We shall see that while this is no threat to neoclassical, it is to classical, theism.

VII. Is Existence a Predicate?

Logicians, including some who would rather be seen in beggars' rags than in the company of the Ontological Argument, have held that existence is, after all, a sort of predicate, even of ordinary things.[18] But for our purpose this is unimportant, since the Argument does not depend upon the treatment of ordinary existence. The status which Anselm and Descartes (when, as in the quotations with which this essay begins, they are being most careful) deduce from "conceived as perfect" is not "conceived as existent," but rather "conceived as existentially non-contingent," i.e., conceived as that which "cannot be conceived not to exist." It is the existential modality which is taken as part of the meaning of the conceived property perfection. But whereas, in the ordinary or contingent case, neither "existent" nor "non-existent" can be inferred from the modal status, from "non-contingent" one may infer "necessarily existent unless impossible." (To ex-

[18] See H. Reichenbach, *Elements of Symbolic Logic* (New York: The Macmillan Company, 1947), pp. 333–334.

clude impossibility, the Argument as it stands does not suffice, except for one who grants that "the fool's" or non-theist's idea of God is self-consistent. But here the other theistic arguments may help.)

VIII. The Incompatibility of Perfection and Contingency

Anselm's intuition was that God exists in a superior manner, the ordinary way of existing being a defect. "Thou dost exist so truly that Thou canst not be conceived not to exist," and "this is greater than a being which can be conceived not to exist." Show me where the critics (Hume, Kant, e.g.) deal with this idea! They discuss whether or not what exists is greater than what fails to exist, which by any logic I know is not the same proposition at all. That Anselm argues also from this more dubious premise does not justify the critics. Their job (after the progress of centuries) was to be clearer than Anselm, not less clear, as to the problem confronting him.

Will the reader admit that (by Double Negation and Excluded Middle) "existing" is identical with "not (not existing)," rather than with "not conceivable as (not existing)?" By what rules do the critics convert "not conceivable as" into a mere "not," or show that if an argument is invalid with the latter as premise, it must be so with the former? This is a challenge. I shall be inclined to take no answer as admission that my point is correct, that the Argument does not depend upon whether or no (mere) "existing" is a predicate. How much longer will ink — and students' time in a thousand colleges — be worse than wasted upon the supposition that it does?

Of course, if to be *conceivable as not existing* is a defect, then so in a sense is simply *not existing*, inasmuch as what is not existent is also conceivable as not existent. But non-existence is thereby shown to be a defect solely in comparison with what is inconceivable as non-existent. Since dollars or islands (the examples which have fascinated so many) are always conceivable as non-existent, there is no implication that existing dollars are greater than non-existent ones. The defect of contingency goes with being a dollar. This whole line of criticism has nothing to do with the case. I beg indulgence for my severity; I am trying to call the attention of those deafened by thousands of shouts (echoing previous shouts) to a manifest mistake which no one seems to want to notice.[19] This king really is naked. The king is not Anselm's argument, or not that only; it is Kant's chief criticism of it.

There is a sense in which the existent can be said to be more excellent than the merely possible, namely, it is more determinate or concrete. Mere possibilities are abstract or in some way indefinite, and this defect can be overcome only by their actualization. Mere multiplication of stipulations will not do it. I shall not argue this thesis here since it is not essential to the Argument before us. But I do wish to point out that, even if the thesis be granted, one may scarcely reason, "the existent is better, since more determinate, than the merely possible, hence the best conceivable, the perfect, must be conceived as existent." For, in the first place, though a real, i.e., determinate dollar is better than an indeterminate or merely possible one, it remains only a dollar, not a man or a deity, from which it appears that a determinate thing is not a better kind of thing, in comparison with other kinds; it is only a thing, an existent, of some kind or other. It is thus not apparent what the comparison has to do with the superiority of the perfect to other kinds of thing. And a critic could reply to the suggested argument as follows: "By 'best conceivable or perfect thing' one only means one which, if it had determinate actuality, would surpass any other actual or possible thing; we thereby refer not necessarily to something which is best, but perhaps only to what would be best if it existed." (A classical theist would also reject the proposed proof because he

[19] For a recent example, see T. Penelhum, "Divine Necessity," *Mind*, LXIX (1960), 175–186.

regards perfection as sheer infinity, hence as an "indeterminate sea of being," in the Thomist phrase; but this way of speaking confirms the suspicion of the neoclassicist that, in philosophies of being, God is confused with the abstract or possible, and is not genuinely viewed as an actuality at all.)

Non-existence is indeed a defect; if it were not, we should all have whatever we wished, the world of possibility being wide open to our dreams. Nevertheless, it is not the sort of defect which will yield an ontological inference. If the indeterminate or non-existent perfection is *therefore* not perfect, this is no contradiction, since an unexemplified property neither need nor normally can apply to itself. If, or insofar as, Anselm meant this, he did commit the homological fallacy! Moreover, let us for a moment assume the actualization, and thus the determination, of the otherwise indeterminate possibility of perfection. The "defect" of indefiniteness will thus be remedied. We shall then, it seems, have an exemplified property applying to that which exemplifies it. So again, where is the inconsistency? Do not logical criteria fail to decide the issue?

The answer is that the inconsistency is in the supposition that perfection is capable of being actualized in determinate form and also capable of being left unactualized, a mere indefinite possibility; for from this latter supposition it follows that *if* perfection is actualized it is so without necessity. Can perfection be thus actualized? What Anselm and Descartes saw unclearly and intermittently is that there is a deficiency in the ordinary manner of failing to exist which carries over into the ordinary manner of existing; and, therefore, neither makes sense in combination with perfection. If there is to be a valid ontological inference, avoiding the homological fallacy, it is exemplified perfection which, conceived in a certain way, must be contradictory; and this "certain way" must be deducible from the mere supposition that "perfection does not exist" is logically admissible, i.e., capable of being true. What is thus deducible? The contingency of perfection's existence, if it exists at all. By the definition of "contingent," if non-existence is a possibility, then existence can only be contingent. This logical truism is critical for Anselm's reasoning.

The pertinent question is not, is the fact of non-existence, but is the bare possibility of non-existence, a defect, and one which, being admitted, must infect the thing *"even if it exists"*? (Anselm's use of this phrase makes it quite clear that he saw the point, even though he did not hold onto it tightly enough.) To repeat, the pertinent question is not, is non-existence a defect, but is the contingency which is deducible from the mere possibility of non-existence a defect? To exist contingently is to exist precariously, or by chance (for to say, by cause or intention is to prompt the query, is the cause or intention necessary — achieving its result necessarily? — or non-necessary?). But to exist precariously or by chance is an imperfection, appropriate only to imperfect individuals. That "humanity" might not have been at all means that each of us exists, and has any particular excellence, thanks to accidental factors only. This total dependence on the way things happen to be, this radical "iffyness" or precariousness of our existence and nature (how easily it could all have been, or could yet be, indefinitely otherwise!) is a defect in principle from which various limitations follow, for instance, having a temporal beginning of existence. If, then, an individual of a kind which can only exist contingently is necessarily imperfect, no such individual could exemplify perfection. Perfection either could not possibly exist, or it exists necessarily. And the necessarily true is true. The existence of divine perfection is a question not of contingent fact, but of necessity, positive or negative. Logical analysis, not observation of nature, alone can settle it.

Anselm did not worry much about the choice between positive necessity and negative necessity (or impossibility); for he assumed "the fool [who] hath said in his heart there is no God," with the implied admission that "God" stands for a genuine idea, and not an impossibility like round-square. In addition he was writting for men of religion who would scarcely doubt that their faith was at least conceivably true. Still, under Gaunilo's prodding, he did produce an argument or two against the positivistic doubt. Today, however, we must do far better on this point, or the Argument will be of little use to us.

Whether or not perfection is conceivable, certainly multitudes of people have thought that it was. But who, except someone trying to refute the Argument, would even pretend to know what is meant by "perfect island"? Perfect for what purpose, by what criterion? Only the divine is consistently conceivable as transcending such relativities, and it is only this transcendence which justifies Anselm's Principle. An "island than which none greater can be conceived" could have nothing in common with what anyone means by "island." Even more obviously, if possible, is this the case with dollars. Therefore, either the first or the sixth principle of the Argument fails in the case of islands, dollars, or mermaids; and thus the traditional reduction to absurdity does not get under way. Anselm was quite justified in his humorous rejection of these.

There is some question as to the interpretation of the variable in $N(\exists x)Px$. It seems to state merely that perfection must be exemplified in some individual or other. But it is an old insight that perfection characterizes a unique individual, rather than a class of possible perfect beings. There can here be no *principium individuationis*. Thus what is necessary is not merely *a* property of the perfect individual, but its very individuality. And in this interpretation x is not a variable, but a unique individual.

In this connection between perfection and uniqueness we have an additional basis for Anselm's principle; for if perfection could fail of exemplification we should have the anomaly, rightly rejected by many logicians, of a nonexistent individual. Here and here alone we deal with an individual which is specifiable as such purely a priori, or in terms of pure concepts. In all other cases individuals have to be identified partly-by some empirical reference or other. We know that God is a priori because we know who He is a priori.

Yet there is still a fatal difficulty with the argument as traditionally used. This difficulty is that the Logical-type Objection seems inescapable. We have held that modality of existence can be a predicate, though simple existence perhaps cannot. In the case of contingency there is no difficulty: for a predicate may be contingent yet non-existent; this modality does not entail actual, but only conceivable, or as Descartes said, "possible existence." By contrast necessity of existence logically includes existence: $Np \rightarrow p$. So how can the necessity of perfection be of higher or more abstract type than its real existence? On the removal of this difficulty depends the fate of the Argument!

The conditions of a solution are as follows: there must, on the lowest logical level, be a concrete form of divine actuality which remains extrinsic to the property perfection and is (in one of two senses to be distinguished presently) its contingent exemplification or instance; and there must be another form, which is necessary, and thus not outside the property, but which, therefore, like the property, is abstract. The distinction of logical levels will here lie between two aspects or kinds of existence, not between property and existence in general, or as such. Furthermore, we must be able to find a basis, even in ordinary cases, for the distinction between the two forms of existence; otherwise, we should be treating the theological case not only as exceptional, but as a blind and groundless exception, without rational standing in our knowledge.

Fortunately for the Argument, there is a very plain basis in ordinary instances for the distinction in question. That I shall (at least probably) exist tomorrow is one thing; that I shall exist hearing a blue jay call at noon is another. The latter is the more specific or concrete statement, and it is not entailed by the former (unless one accepts the logical structure of Leibniz's theory of the monad). Furthermore, the existence of "human being" (the bare fact that there are such beings) is less concrete than the existence of you or of me. There are thus at least three levels of existence: the occurrence of certain actual states of individuals;

the existence of certain individuals; the existence of certain kinds of individuals or of certain class-properties. True enough, the kinds cannot exist save in individuals, nor the individuals save in states; still, in which individuals or which states they exist remains a further, a contingent determination. It follows from this that to conceive existence as necessary we need not deny all distinction between abstract and concrete, or between property and instance. The necessity need not be for this or that instance, but only for "some instance or other," an idea which is certainly abstract; for it treats different concrete cases as equivalent. Thus, while in ordinary cases we have two forms of contingency: (1) whether there happens to be an instance at all, and (2) whether, if there is, it is fa, fb, fc, or . . . , in the necessary case we have only the second form of contingency. Existence is always arbitrary selection or determination among the possible values of a variable x in $(\exists x)fx$. Ordinarily, however, the possibilities include the vacuous case of no value. In necessary existence, $N(\exists x)fx$, the x is still a variable with a range of possible values; however, the vacuous case of no value, $\sim \exists x)fx$, is here logically excluded. Opponents of the Argument must claim that such logical exclusion of the vacuous case is not possible; but they cannot prove this by the Logical-type Objection. For, with or without the vacuous possibility, a value of the variable x is not on the level of the f. So I submit: the classical refutation stands or falls with the possibility of applying the property-instance distinction to perfection. Can it be thus applied?

It seems not, at least to the divine perfection as classically conceived. For God was said to be no member of any kind of class, and to exist not in actual contingent states, but rather in a reality necessary through and through, or in all its properties. This was the meaning of "pure actuality," "the absolute," "the infinite," the wholly "self-sufficient," etc. Our analysis has just shown that an ontological Argument can meet the Type difficulty if and only if there can (and must) be contingent states in which divinity exists, contingent as to which states, but not as to there being some appropriate states or other. There must be alternative possible values for the variable in "$(\exists x)Px$," even though if x is taken as ranging over individuals (rather than states, events) x becomes ix, the name of a unique individual.

The question then arises: is divine perfection properly conceived as open to embodiments, states, which are contingent — save only in the logical exclusion of no-embodiment? If so, we can meet the essential conditions of the Argument, Anselm's Principle can apply, and the strongest of the classical refutations falls. Moreover, the patient reader will find, upon reflection, that the counter-arguments in general lose their force, once we have made a clear distinction between necessary embodiment of perfection in *some* concrete instance, and the particular instance itself. We saw in Sec. II that a promising way to define perfection a priori is through the conception of modal coincidence. It is clear enough that this implies a distinction of the sort we have just seen to be required, between an individual (a) in its abstract identity and (b) in its concrete actual states. For, in the neoclassical view, God may know all sorts of worlds and be in this sense all sorts of knowers, analogously to any knower who may know p to be true if p is true, or may know p to be false if it is false, and yet may be "Himself" in either case — Himself, however, in alternate cognitive states. Thus the conditions of an Ontological Argument are met.

Some readers may find it paradoxical that admitting potentiality in God should strengthen the case for His necessary existence. They forget that contingency is arbitrary selection among possibilities. It is true that limited potentiality must be entirely contingent in its realization; for the limits could not even be defined save empirically. But to be coextensive, by absolute necessity, with all actuality (in the individual's actual states) and with all possibility (in its potential states) is to have a wholly non-selective, and therefore non-arbitrary, a priori definable, relation to actuality and potentiality. The states themselves do involve arbitrariness and therefore contingency, and this is not only compatible with religious perfection, but, as we have seen, is required by it. Individuals exist in states, each of which can only be contingent; but that there *are* states embodying the individual may or may not be contingent, depending upon whether or not the definition of "state of X" involves any arbitrary selection. In the case of perfection, it does not. Only the completely general and a priori requirement obtains that "whatever else is actual must be included in the divine actuality and whatever is possible, in the divine capacity to be." This will be valid "for all possible substitution instances" or values for the variable "whatever." Thus it agrees in a general way with the requirements of formal logicians for logically true or analytic statements.[20]

Besides retaining and, as we shall see (Sec. XI), strengthening the connection of individual existence with non-contingency, the neoclassical view preserves intact the indispensable distinction between instance and property. What "has" the divine perfection is not the divine individuality, in its fixed, eternally identical character; for that is not an instance, but is the divine perfection itself. It is the de facto states which "have" or instance perfection, rather than "being" it. God-now is something perfect, rather than is perfection; and the numerically distinct God-tomorrow will also be perfect, though He will exhibit perfection in an enriched state of actuality. (This is no contradiction, as we have defined "perfect.") Analogously, the man in his fixed identity does not have, but is, his character or individuality; and only the man-now has or exemplifies it. Events, not things or individuals, are the final subjects of predicates, as Scholz, Whitehead, Carnap, and others have maintained. But only the divine individuality can be expressed in a definition or pure concept. In all other cases, a mere concept, without empirical content, without what Peirce called an indexical sign, a reference to a "this-here-now," to the actual world, is unable to designate a unique individual. But "divinity" or its equivalent is the sole property definable purely

[20] R. Carnap, *Introduction to Symbolic Logic* (New York: Dover Publications, 1958), pp. 48–49.

66

abstractly which but one individual can have. The perfect individual is his perfection. It therefore is all one to say, divine perfection exists, and to say, God exists. Hence the latter phrase is not, in spite of Ryle, bad grammar. To be sure it is analytically true, but you merely beg the question of the Ontological Argument if you make that an objection.

For similar reasons, the charge of a homological fallacy must be handled with care. The question of such a fallacy can arise only where something exemplifies a property rather than coinciding with it. Yet the notion of non-coincident exemplification is logically necessary with all properties, even perfection, since the notion of property stands or falls with it. Indeed all our logical machinery does so. God, however, is the one individual in respect to whom the line between property and instance falls only between individual and state, not also, as it usually does, between individual and some broader class property, such as humanity. Perfection is not a class of similar individuals, but only a class of similar and genetically related states of one individual.

It may seem that a contingent state of divinity could not be "such that none greater can be conceived," hence it could not exemplify perfection. But the states exemplify perfection by being such that the individual possessing them is thereby made such that no other individual could conceivably be greater. They do this by containing all actuality, ideally integrated into one actuality, and by having, as sole alternatives, states which also would have been ideal integrations of their given worlds. As I have been trying to explain for many years, perfection has two aspects, the absolute aspect, A, which cannot be surpassed in any way whatever, and the transcendentally relative aspect, or the aspect of transcendent relativity, R, which is surpassable only by the perfect itself, not by any other individual. Or better, and positively: as A, God surpasses all things save only Himself; as R, he surpasses all things, including Himself. The religious meaning of perfect requires both of these aspects. It is a strange notion that one might cease to worship God because of His self-surpassing.

THE LOGIC OF PERFECTION

Why should you or I be puffed up because God can be in a sort of rivalry with Himself? That does not in any way make *us* rivals of His greatness! This is excluded alike by *A* and by *R*.

Neither *A* nor *R* could merely happen to be exemplified. For then an individual would be conceivable whose states exemplified them necessarily, without risk of failure, and this would be a superior individual.

IX. The Argument from Universal Existential Tolerance

Critics of Anselm and Descartes have paid insufficient attention to the crux of the problem, the meaning and criterion of contingency. Unless this is clear, how can its contrasting term, necessity, be understood? We have said that contingency is a matter of arbitrariness. One may also say that it is a matter of specificity or exclusive definiteness. You may do this, or that, but not both; this may happen, or that, but not both. The contingent is always something "instead of" something else which is incompatible with it. But suppose an assertion compatible with any positive and consistent hypothesis; if such an assertion were contingent, this would be at least a very unusual kind of contingency.

Logic does know propositions which are compatible with any positive and consistent assertion whatever, namely necessary propositions. Granted Np, then p is compatible with any logically possible assertion. This is how the proposition, Perfection exists, behaves. It conflicts with no assertion about the imperfect beings which may also exist.

I hold that the existence of perfection is compatible with any other sort of existence whatever. The perfect shows its superiority precisely in this, that it can maintain itself regardless of what else does, or does not, maintain itself. It can tolerate or endure any state of affairs whatsoever. This alone should convince us that we have to do here with something other than a contingent truth, positive or negative.

It may be objected that while the perfect perhaps could maintain itself, or exist, no matter what else existed, it does not follow that it does maintain itself, or exist. But note that if nothing could conflict with the existence of perfection, then (since compatibility is a mutual or symmetrical relation), perfection, by existing, could prevent nothing else from existing, and therefore its non-existence could have no positive significance whatever. It would be, not only a negative fact, but a purely negative fact, a mere absence.

The question of "negative facts" has been subtly argued, but I think the argument is won by the side which insists that a negative fact is always some positive fact incompatible with a positive hypothesis. It follows that a proposition compatible with any positive consistent proposition cannot be factually false.

It can also, I think, be shown that the admission of merely negative facts has embarrassing consequences. It is the basis of many skeptical arguments. Thus, "Your body might be exactly like mine, except that in mine there is consciousness, in yours no consciousness." If this is logically possible, nothing can show that it is false. But is it logically possible? Must not a particular mode of consciousness, like everything particular, exclude various otherwise possible things, some one of which must be there as the positive side of its absence? If your body is without a human mind, then it has something positive which mine lacks. For instance, it may be more predictable, more automatic in its action. But there seems to be nothing whatever which could constitute the positive side of the "absence of deity."

Note: We are not saying that God excludes nothing, but that His mere existence excludes nothing. By a free act, not necessitated by His individual existence, He may exclude many things; but imperfect individuals always exclude certain things merely by existing, no matter how they act. Our existence depends on a special environment and is incompatible with others. This is an imperfection.

If contingency inheres in all specific or exclusive predicates, it follows by no logical rule that non-contingency cannot inhere in a non-specific predicate. And if specificity or exclusiveness is the very meaning of contingency (as it is if merely negative truth is impossible), then what does follow is that non-exclusive predicates are either necessarily exemplified or else logically incapable of existence.

We shall call "contingent" those concepts whose exemplification or non-exemplification can only be contingent, or which are capable both of being and of not being exemplified.

We now state our second form of ontological proof.

Major premise: All contingent concepts are specific, exclusive, or restrictive with respect to the possible, in that their being exemplified is incompatible with some positive possibility (e.g., that men exist is incompatible with the world's having certain positively describable characters which would make it uninhabitable by human beings).

Minor premise: The concept of perfection is non-specific, non-exclusive, non-restrictive, its exemplification being compatible with the existence of any positively conceivable state of affairs.

Conclusion: The concept of divinity or perfection is not contingent. Either its exemplification is impossible or it is necessary. Since nothing is strictly impossible unless it is inherently contradictory or meaningless (this point will be defended in Sec. XIV), the choice is not between theism and atheism, but only between theism and positivism. "God" is without coherent meaning, or divinity exists necessarily. This at least simplifies and clarifies the issue.

X. *The Epistemic Proof*

Anselm said of God that He "exists so truly" that He "cannot be conceived not to exist." Some reply: even granting that His non-existence cannot be conceived, still, He may in fact not exist. Thus they first admit the hypothesis that they could not be conceiving a certain state of affairs, and then, without withdrawing the admission, assert that the state of affairs may yet exist, which implies that they have conceived it. Is this logical?

With ordinary contingent things, one may conceive their

existence and also their non-existence. Hume, to be sure, says that we conceive anything, if at all, as existent; but he is speaking somewhat loosely here. Since the existent is, or is embodied in, the individual, and finally the particular, and since empirical or contingent individuals, as well as particulars, transcend clear grasp in thought, it is as much a problem how we conceive their existence as how we conceive their non-existence. A commonplace of current philosophizing is that to understand an empirical proposition is to have some notion of what would count as experiential evidence for or against it: to understand a negative existential judgment, then, is to imagine, or otherwise represent, an experience or series of experiences which would be incompatible, at least in terms of probability, with the form of existence in question.

Ordinarily, there are two ways in which the non-existence of a thing could conceivably reveal itself in experience: first, minds such as the human may be conceived to experience the world as (probably) exclusive of a certain form of existence; and second, some superhuman or divine mind may be conceived to have this experience in a more conclusive form. A perfect mind, by definition, must have its valuations include all reality, and therefore must be aware of any exclusion which this totality effects from itself. But there is one exclusion from existence which no perfect knowledge could know, and that is the exclusion of perfect knowledge itself. This not only makes the alleged possibility of the non-existence of perfection a unique case, since it alone is by logical necessity unknowable by perfect knowledge, but in addition, it renders the definition of perfect knowledge contradictory. For "that whose scope of knowledge and valuation includes all possibilities" yet excludes one (alleged) possibility. The only way to remove the contradiction is to deny the possibility, by taking the existence of perfection as (impossible or) necessary.

But we must go on to note that not only must the allegedly possible non-existence be unknown to perfect knowledge, it must be unknown to any knowledge. For the supposition of a mode of experience "incompatible with the existence of perfection," whether absolutely, or even merely in terms of probability, is logically inadmissible, since perfection involves the unlimited capacity of self-maintenance, no matter what else exists. To say that from X the non-being of Y follows, is to say that Y, if it existed, would depend for its existence upon the fact that X did not. Our neoclassical (and indeed also the classical) definition of perfection excludes any such dependence. The particular states in which perfection exists depend, to be sure, like all particular things, upon what else exists, but that there are some such states, by definition, cannot so depend. The "non-existence of perfect mind" is thus, by analytic necessity, absolutely unknowable by any mind whatever. (This is a good example of the fallacy of inferring "trivial" from "analytic.") But the absolutely unknowable is nothing. How could you know that it was something?

Excluding the possibility of non-existence leaves us the choice: necessary existence or nonsense. The nonsensical could not be known either as true or as false, since it is not a coherent assertion. So let us look at "Perfection exists." Could it be known as true? An existing perfect mind could know its own existence. That seems clear enough, if it could know anything. But it is also demonstrable that an imperfect mind could know the existence of a perfect mind. For anything other than the perfect must, by the definition of the latter, depend upon the latter for its existence. But if x depends upon a, than "x exists" must entail "a exists", from which it follows that the latter proposition could be known from the former. (We are not trying to show how the entailment is to be discerned; we are only saying that there must be such entailment, and hence in principle it must be possible to discern it.) The same relation of one-way independence of the perfect from the imperfect which makes it a contradiction that the *non*-existence of the perfect should be known by the imperfect makes it not a contradiction that its existence should be thus known. Such knowledge must be logically possible. But logical possibility of knowing the truth of a proposition, coupled with logical impossibility of knowing its falsity, is one of the clearest implications of "necessary truth."

Anselm was in this respect exactly and demonstrably right: the perfect cannot be conceived not to exist; though there is, at least on the same level, no impossibility of conceiving it to exist. Perfection, therefore, cannot have the modal status of contingency; and the test just considered does not assign it the status of impossibility. A thousand scholars, relying on their predecessors or contemporaries to have looked into the matter with due care, may say otherwise; but the logical relations of concepts are what they are, not what they are said to be.

XI. *The Ten Marks of Contingency and the Omnibus Proof*

The critics of the Argument generalize the admitted contingency of ordinary existential statements to cover all affirmations of existence. What ground is there for such an induction? The contingency of ordinary sorts of thing is not a law of nature, but of logic. (Otherwise, we might think it at least conceivable that we should encounter a necessarily-existing elephant.) It is the logical structure of the usual judgments which makes them contingent. But this structure is not simply that of existence, the mere form, $(\exists x)fx$. For as we have seen, this does not of itself tell us that and why the vacuous case, "nothing is an f," must be logically admissible for any and every value of f. The generalization that is needed concerns the logical principle whereby the vacuous possibility is universally included. If it could be shown that this principle is inherent in any use of the existential formula, and if Perfection could be fitted consistently into the same pattern, or else shown to be self-inconsistent or meaningless, then and only then would we have the right to speak of having refuted the Ontological Argument (and not merely some particular formulation of it).

Contingency, we have said, means arbitrary selection, not between something positive and something merely negative, but between certain positive possibilities and others that are equally positive but incompatible with them. Such selection seems to have ten aspects, all of which are exhibited in ordinary non-controversial cases of contingency. At least three of the ten (3, 6, 8) were fairly well indicated by Anselm. I need hardly add that none are taken into account by the best-known opponents of the Argument.

An individual which exists contingently is of such a nature that it:

(1) By existing prevents some other things (otherwise possible) from existing;

(2) Depends causally for its existence upon some, but not all, other individuals (thus upon those coming before but not after it in time);

(3) Could conceivably be known to exist by some imperfect minds and by Perfect Mind (if this be itself conceivable), and it could also conceivably be known not to exist;

(4) Depends, for the details of its actual qualities, upon some other existing things (this qualitative dependence not being limited to things [as in (2)] without which it could not exist);

(5) Is itself a cause required for the existence of some other things;

(6) Includes in its actuality the actuality of some other things as parts or constituents (in a very general sense), and its potential states include some of the unrealized possibilities of the universe;

(7) Falls within some quantitative and qualitative limits essential to its individual identity, including limits as to number and kinds of parts;

(8) Has, or can be conceived to have, a beginning at some time and an ending at some time;

(9) Can be defined or identified as an individual only empirically, and only by some other individuals (not, for

instance, by those entirely before it in time), rather than universally or by mere universal concepts;

(10) Is "good" for some legitimate purposes only.

In all cases "some" is meant to include the meaning, "not all." Thus there is arbitrary selection among the possibilities; something else instead might have existed characterized by a different selection. Let us see (in incomplete, sketchy fashion) how this selection implies and is implied by contingency.

1. If an individual X of a certain kind by existing would prevent something positively conceivable from existing, then the non-existence of X must itself be conceivable; but if X would prevent anything and everything positive from existing, then since all thought must have some positive content, the non-existence of X must be necessary; while if X would prevent nothing positive from existing, its non-existence, being without positive content, must be meaningless and its existence necessary if conceivable at all. Thus contingency means partial exclusion of the positive.

2. If an individual X could exist only thanks to the existence of certain other individuals, then unless these exist necessarily, X cannot be necessary. But if an entire set of individuals could be necessary, why should not any set be necessary? Moreover, if those upon which X would depend are conceived as its causes, then, if causation involves an element of creativity, there must be an additional element of contingency in the coming to be of X, besides that involved in the existence of the causes. And if causation is thought not to involve an element of contingency, then contingency is a blind miracle, with no explanation whatever. (The only positive account of contingency is in terms of creativity.) An individual dependent for its existence upon no others must exist entirely of its own power, and what then could render it contingent? An individual existentially dependent upon all others can only be conceived definitely as an event with all others before it, an event without issue (for nothing depends upon what

comes after it). This is a doubtful conception, and certainly has nothing in common with ordinary contingent individuals. Thus contingency means partial dependence upon other individuals.

3. If the existence and the non-existence of a certain sort of X are both logically capable of being known by some minds, including perfect mind if that be conceivable, then both must be logically possible, and the thing contingent. If only the non-existence, or only the existence, could be known, then there is at least no epistemic meaning in the one case for existence, and in the other for non-existence, so that the thing must be either impossible or necessary. Moreover, since a thing's existence cannot be known by its predecessor in time, nor its non-existence by its successors (we should not have known the fact had our ancestors not existed), only a primordial and everlasting thing could be knowable by all, either as existent or as non-existent. But what could make a thing knowable as primordial and everlasting if not self-existence or necessity? (If its non-existence be possible, it cannot be known that it will always exist.) Thus contingency means, in epistemic terms, partial knowability, equally as existent and as non-existent.

4. If a thing depends for details of quality inessential to its being *that* individual, "gen-identical" with itself throughout its history, and depends in this manner upon some other individuals only, there must be an arbitrary or contingent reason for the selection of the particular set of other individuals upon which it thus depends. Should, however, the individual inessentially depend either upon absolutely all other individuals or upon absolutely none, this could only be explained, not by an arbitrary accident, but by some positive or negative necessity. For here there is no selection, no making of ad hoc exceptions to a rule, but simply the absolute rule itself. Contingency means partial or arbitrary inessential qualitative dependence, rather than dependence versus independence. Because this was not understood, the supposition gained wide acceptance that the necessary individual must have no qualitative dependence. It must either have none, or all;

what it must not do is to depend upon some others only for its inessential qualities (if it be thought to have such).

5. If an individual is a cause upon which some but not all other things depend, then there is arbitrary selection, hence contingency, in the determining of the "some". But if all other things depend upon a certain X, then the non-existence of X would mean total non-entity, which is nonsense; therefore the X must be necessary. If nothing else depended upon X, it must be a last event, without consequences, a dubious idea at best. Once more contingency is intelligible only in terms of partiality, incompleteness, this time of causal indispensability to other things. Only the necessary can be completely, universally, indispensable (or universally anything).

6. If an individual includes in its actuality that of some other things (as constituents) and in its potentiality that of some other things (as potential constituents), then it can only be accidental which other things are thus included. Moreover, its own non-existence must be possible, for should something be actualized whose potentiality was extrinsic to its own, this could very well include its own failure to exist. A world without us is not our potentiality, but the potentiality of there being no "us." By contrast, if *all* possibility is a thing's own potential possession, then, whatever possibility is actualized, the thing must exist to possess this actualization. (Complete) modal coincidence entails necessary existence; partial coexistensiveness with modality entails contingency.

Suppose an individual thing has no unrealized intrinsic possibility. Then, too, it must be necessary, but it must also be abstract and not really an individual actuality. Modal coincidence, universal potentiality, is therefore the more adequate conception of the necessary being.

7. If in the specification of the sort of X one must include quantitative and qualitative limits, say between certain maxima and minima, or the predominance of certain colors, then obviously arbitrary selection is at work. Why not some other sort of

individual, with other limits, occupying somewhat the same role in the world? Wherever men are in the world there might have been other sorts of animals, or inanimate objects; instead of a flower of one color and shape, another of different sort. Every contingent species of thing has its range of qualities and quantities, and each individual instance its narrower range. Such limits are achieved more or less by accident, and in unstable, uncertain competitive fashion. Where no such limits are relevant, contingency has no clear meaning. It does not follow that what exists necessarily must have actual infinity in every respect; what follows is only that no particular finitude must be essential to its identity as that individual. An individual capable of somehow possessing *any* finite qualities and quantities can exist no matter what selection of these is effected. It is particular and essential finitude that makes ordinary things contingent. Partiality with respect to quantity and quality explains contingency, not bare finitude or definiteness. Here again tradition made a huge error of careless analysis. In consequence it identified God with the wholly indefinite, which means in aesthetic terms wholly devoid of definite contrast, hence of beauty. "Formless, all lovely forms thy loveliness declare." But God must not merely "declare" or "manifest" Himself in definite forms, He must possess them actually in His own actuality; He must be the God of this actual total creation, not the God He might have been had He possessed a different total creation. (True, He would still have been the same individual God, but not in the same state of actuality.)

8. If a thing can begin or end in time, it cannot be necessary. (Anselm had this point particularly in mind.) Kant indeed rejects this criterion of contingency, saying that a thing might be necessary just for a certain time-stretch. But this only shows his non-comprehension of process as creativity. Nothing can be necessarily produced unless it be a feature of process as such, and then it could never fail to be exhibited by process, and is not really "produced" at all. The contingent is the fragmentary, that which is localized in space-time. Fragmentariness is quite different from

"finitude." Here too there was much traditional confusion. Being a mere part is not simply to be "finite," which only means, "less than" the actualization of all possibilities (including incompossibilities?); whereas to be fragmentary is to be less than all that is in fact actual. The necessary individual in his contingent de facto state cannot be less than all that is in fact actual. The entire actual world now is still only a fragment, for it is content of the divine knowledge, which is unimaginably more than this content. Also the entire actual world now is potentially only a fragment of the creation to come. God, however, is potentially inclusive of this coming creation. Remaining "Himself," He yet will endlessly acquire new content. Tradition thought to make God necessary by denying endurance to Him, substituting sheer immutability and uncreatedness. This is acceptable if one speaks only of the "primordial nature" of deity, the abstract essence, perfection as a property, rather than of the actual Life in which the essence is progressively embodied. Contingency means arbitrary, precarious endurance, not endurance per se. It means a partial, fragmentary share in the creative process, not a total participation in it.

9. If an individual is identifiable as an individual, not merely by certain, but by all, cognitive individuals, or through universal concepts (only so could it be identifiable by all individuals), and yet is capable of non-existence, then there could be such a thing as a "merely possible individual" (for its concept would individuate it, even were it not to exist). With many contemporary philosophers, I regard "merely possible individual" as an absurdity.

Possibilities are never wholly individual, but at most *infima species*, and even this notion has no absolute meaning. Hence the contingent is incapable of individual identification by mere concepts without empirical reference.

10. If a thing is good for some but not all purposes, there is possible motivation for thinking of its existence, and also for thinking of its non-existence. If, however, it is good for no conceivable purpose, there is no motive for thinking of it, and it

could not be thought of. If it is good for all purposes, then there is no purpose in thinking of its unreality, and this could not be thought of. Partial relevance to purposes is another character of the contingent.

We see then that there is contingency where, and only where, there is arbitrary selection among positive possible kinds of thing, causes, effects, limit, knower, purpose. So we have ten ways in which ordinary things exhibit characters logically equivalent to contingency. These characters are not entailed by the mere formula $(\exists x)fx$; hence we need not be astonished to find that some existential judgments do not exhibit the ten characters, and so classify themselves as noncontingent. This is the case with "perfection exists," or $(\exists x)Px$. The argument may be outlined as follows.

(1) Perfection cannot by existing prevent anything positive from existing, and so its own non-existence could have no positive meaning, hence no meaning. (2) It cannot depend upon anything else for its own existence — not that it could exist solitary, but that its existence is entirely neutral as between alternatives of particular existence other than its own (which is hence not really "particular"). (3) Its existence could be known both by itself and by any cognitive thing on a sufficiently high level of consciousness (since anything must require the Perfect as primordial condition of its own existence); but as we saw in section X, neither the Perfect nor anything else could know the non-existence of the Perfect. (4) Since the Perfect (neoclassically defined) must derive some quality from each and every other thing (in knowing the quality), it must, in some phase of its actuality, come after anything else you please; hence it must be everlasting, and this necessity of existing forever is intelligible only if its non-existence is impossible. (5) Upon the existence of the Perfect all other things must depend, for it must be the supreme form of creative power; hence its non-existence would mean that nothing was even possible, which is absurd. (6) Perfection being defined as universal modal coincidence, actuality

in general must be whatever is included in the actuality of the individual whose essence is perfection, and possibility must be whatever is included in its potentiality; hence the possibility of its non-existence would be the contradiction that this non-existence would be a potential state of itself. (7) Perfection is not defined by any quantitative or qualitative limits, or number or kinds of parts, but by a universal mode of relationship to any and every limited quantity, quality, or set of parts, namely that of totally including, possessing, all such properties and parts as may be actual or possible, in the objects of its actual or potential knowledge and valuations. Hence its own existence requires no one limit rather than any other. (8) Perfection could not conceivably begin or end in time, since even the possibility of this is a denial of Modal Coincidence. (9) Perfection is the only abstract property whose instances must all be connected with one another by genetic identity or personal order to constitute a single life; hence it is the only self-individuated property, or a priori individual. (10) Perfection is good in its existence for all legitimate or self-consistent purposes; for their possible fulfillment is the same as its possible possession of that fulfillment; hence the denial of this existence serves no purpose and is possible only verbally; yet, in spite of Wittgenstein, its existence can be significantly affirmed, for to recognize the eternal ground of all possible values does serve a purpose, that of making more conscious the universal ingredient of all satisfaction whatever, thus yielding a serene joy sought ardently in many religions, for example in Buddhism. (See Chapter Twelve.) Also we can infer from the affirmation, together with some contingent truths, certain further contingent truths, such as, God, who necessarily exists as infallible, must have complete and permanent understanding of me and all my values. Or, God, who necessarily exists as worshipful, is worthy of *my* worship.

Incidentally, if "the necessary proposition says nothing," then, unless the quoted statement is contingent, which it seems it can scarcely be, it too says nothing. No wonder "philosophy is not a doctrine but an activity!" If it be replied that the proposition says something about our linguistic practice, and hence is in the "metalanguage," then it is to be observed that metaphysics too is about something at least analogous to language. For words are, perhaps, above all our human way of being aware of the contrast between the abstract or universal and the concrete or particular. The animals have primitive, sublinguistic means of doing this, and the question arises, "Is there no superhuman and supralinguistic way of experiencing the contrast in question?" Metaphysical, or at least necessary, realities, we have repeatedly said, are abstract; but must we human beings flatter ourselves that we possess the highest possible mode of realizing the abstract as such? The neoclassical view is that God Himself has such a mode. The divine valuation is then the truly universal language, and its necessities are the necessities.

The contemporary realization that logical necessity is a matter of language is both under- and overemphasized in the literature. It is made too much of when it is taken to imply that there are no limits to the arbitrariness of the basic rules and primitive concepts of the language we adopt; and it is made too little of when people shy away from the Ontological Argument because it seems to pretend to settle the entire theistic question in one little step. Only within a language can it do this; one may always debate at length about the language itself. It is sloppy procedure (and I am not exempt from this criticism) to attack or defend the Argument without specifying the language within which one is operating. But if ordinary or standard language will do to attack the Argument, it should have some validity, when used, as I have been using it, to counterattack. There may, however, be features without which a language is incompetent to clarify its own procedures. I believe (see Chapter Five) that a non-theistic language is incapable of escaping from fundamental dilemmas as to its own meanings. Yet this the Ontological Argument alone cannot establish.

Our ten principles of contingency all serve to connect neoclassical perfection with non-contingency. With some qualification, they also connect classical perfection with the same modal status. The qualifications are that "(6)," the clearest and most cogent connection of all, is reduced to a weaker form through the denial of intrinsic potentiality to the divine, "(6)" thus becoming merely one more case of non-selectivity; and that "(4)" becomes also weaker in the following respect: true enough, if an individual derives quality from nothing else, it avoids selecting among possibilities, but then we have the anomaly that the perfect, according to "(5)" is that upon which all depends. Therefore, by the temporal test of causal dependence, all things must come after the perfect, which must be primordial, but since "(4)" classically interpreted means qualitative dependence upon nothing else, we cannot by the same test say that the perfect is also everlasting, or comes after every temporary thing. This is non-paradoxical only if the Perfect be abstract; for the more abstract something is, the less it derives its character from other things and the more universally they derive theirs partly from it. Arithmetical truths are in some sense primordial and independent, and what does not manifest them? But God is not classically regarded as a merely abstract entity.

However, it remains true that the classical theist disposes, even though in paradoxical fashion, of ten marks of non-contingency. Thus Anselm was right, ten times over as it were, even on his own classical ground — except (a most serious exception to be sure) that he had no remedy, and could have none, for the Logical-type difficulty and other antinomies in the classical idea. Here was his sole essential mistake.

In the light of the ten criteria of contingency, the old reductio ad absurdum counter-arguments are not impressive. The criteria will rule out as not necessary every individual property save perfection in the strict theistic sense. If "perfect island" qua "perfect" must necessarily exist, and yet qua "island" must, by the ten criteria, be contingent, then this shows, not that the criteria are wrong, but that "a-or-the perfect island exists" is self-contradictory or meaningless, as Anselm hinted (and, it seems, too subtly for his readers). Can you refute a mode of argument by showing that, when applied to a self-contradictory or nonsensical concept, treated as though it were cognitive and consistent, the argument yields unacceptable results? And who would seriously think that the concept made sense?

An inanimate physical thing, with an external environment (the meaning of island) cannot possibly "serve all purposes"; but a perfect being, defined as having intrinsic value coincident with all intrinsic value, hence a subject "enjoying all actual values actually and all possible values potentially," is one to whom any achievement whatever will contribute all the value it has, and in whose immortality the achievement will be immortal. Thus any purpose could look to the perfect something for its chances of lasting fulfillment. Where else could it look for strictly permanent results? To use the same word "perfect" in connection with island, dollar, or devil is to drop everything definite in the meaning of the word. Nor is the word "perfect" necessary for the Argument (Anselm did not use it), since the definition just given above, or one of the various equivalent definitions, is all that is necessary — or the concept of the worshipful, the possible object of total devotion. Those who speak of the jobs which words are set to do might consider the job which the word "perfect" has been set to do in the Argument. (Would such petty quibbling as this topic has seen have been tolerated, I wonder, in protheistic writers? It is this sort of unfairness which, more than anything else has made it seem my duty to think with prolonged concentration about the Ontological and other theistic arguments.)

XII. A Theory of Existential Modality

Against our ten intelligible criteria of modal status, the opponent must urge his one, to me at least, blind and unintelligible criterion, "existential vs. non-existential." The criterion is unintelligible because if any thought is not about the existent, I know not what it could be about. The criterion is also blind or merely dogmatic, for it is hardly evidence against the Anselmian who deliberately rejects the criterion, to declare 10,000 times: "Nonetheless, the criterion is correct, all existential judgments are contingent." That individuals other than the divine exist, or fail to exist, contingently is but one side of the very contrast Anselm was making between the supremely or uniquely perfect and less exalted things: the contrast that, while they exist only in the imperfect contingent manner appropriate to their imperfection, perfection exists in the unique manner appropriate to it, i.e., secure against any possibility of failing, or having failed, to exist. Moreover, that the divine uniqueness is modal is exactly what we should expect from the fact that modality appears in its (neoclassical) definition, i.e., as coincidence or coextensiveness of the individual's actuality with all actuality, and of its possibility with all possibility.

However, although no non-divine individual can exist necessarily, the neo-Anselmian, who has revised the concept of divine perfection, will not make the "existence of perfection" the sole necessary existential judgment. Obviously, the more indefinite "something exists" will also be necessary. But further, "Some imperfect individual exists" will, according to the criteria, refuse to be put under the "contingent" heading. However, this proposition asserts no definite individual, but only the non-emptiness of the vaguest possible class of contingent individuals. I defy the critic to show any absurd consequence of accepting "Some imperfect individual exists," as necessarily true. If it were false, only a perfect individual could know this! And there are objections even to that. Nor does the necessity of some imperfect individual or other destroy the existential independence of the perfect individual; for this independence is neoclassically defined, not with reference to the mere general or abstract truth of there being other individuals than the perfect, but rather with reference to any particular other individual, or set or special kind of such individuals. The coincidence of the perfect Something's own actual values with all actual values, and its potential values with all possible values, so far from implying that there are no other individuals, rather implies that there must be such, both to furnish a contrast of imperfect with perfect, and to furnish a set of non-inclusive values to be exhaustively embraced in the inclusive Value. All this is likely to be clear enough to anyone who has begun to grasp the neoclassical idea.[21]

Can there be any greater logical difference between propositions than these, that their exclusion of positive possibilities is (a) limited or partial or (b) unlimited and absolutely infinite or (c) zero? By what intuitive leap can one know that differences so vast, and indeed (as is analytic) infinite in the most absolute sense, have no bearing on the modality of the propositions? "Nothing exists" excludes everything positive, and so must be false; and "something exists" excludes nothing positive, and must be true. Let it then be shown that "Perfection exists" excludes something positive. If not, what good reason can be given for classing it as contingent?

Our theory, then, is: the modality of a statement depends not upon whether or not it refers to existence (implicitly at least it must do so) but upon whether or not it is significant and consistent, and upon what, if anything, it denies the existence of. If it is significant and consistent, and neither implicitly nor explicitly denies the existence of any sort of thing, nothing could make it false; if it is not significant and consistent, or if it denies the existence of any and every sort of thing, nothing could make it true.

The nine criteria other than exclusiveness yield, I believe, results entirely consistent among themselves and with the criterion. If such proves to be the case as others examine this matter, it will give strong confirmation, I submit, to our view.

The reader may be wondering if the ten criteria of contingency

[21] For other examples of non-contingent existential judgments, see my essay, "Metaphysical Statements as Non-restrictive and Existential," *Review of Metaphysics*, XII (1958), No. 1, 35-47.

are logically independent, rather than diverse ways of saying the same thing. Since we are in the realm of the absolutely necessary, presumably the criteria are not independent. Is "2+2=4" independent of "5+7=12"? But it remains reasonable, I submit, to put more trust in the criteria, or criterion, because it, or they, is or are capable of so many clear-cut and superficially distinct modes of expression, all leading to the same conclusions in particular applications.

Our criterion of exclusiveness is in striking accord with the logic of science as expounded by one of its most notable theorists, Karl Popper. As Popper says, the primary question in science is not what agrees with or verifies our statements, but what conceivably could or actually does refute them. And what refutes them is always a positive existential statement, what he terms a "basic" statement, of the form: "here is such and such."[22] If the theory being tested predicts that, under the given conditions, instead of the such and such there should have been something else, incompatible with it, then the theory is, in so far, refuted. Popper also says that particular positive statements of a certain form cannot be tested, for instance (my example), to test "in the universe is a planet exactly (within some margin of error) ten percent larger than the earth," we should have to scour the universe with impossible thoroughness. Still, we might by luck hit upon such a planet, and thus verify the statement. And we can, perhaps, in some sense imagine what it would be like to survey the universe as thoroughly as one can survey a room, and so to discover the universal absence of a specified thing, as we do that of elephants from our house. But statements which forbid no conceivable positive thing are not merely untestable by us, they are untestable absolutely, in principle, and by any mind. To observe that they were false would literally be to observe nothing. And nothing could not be observed, even by deity. Not to see, and not to see anything positive, are the same. (Even blackness is

[22] See his *Logic of Scientific Discovery* (New York: Basic Books, 1959), pp. 40–42, 101–102.

not nothing.) A statement thus unfalsifiable absolutely is not merely metaphysical (and thus, as Popper insists, beyond the scope of science), it is also incapable of being either true or false — unless it is true by necessity. Since it cannot in any significant sense be false, it also cannot merely happen to be true, but can only be necessary — or else nonsensical.

An interesting and fair test of our theory of modality is the application of the ten criteria to the actual divine states, which, as we have argued, must be contingent. The result of the application is consistent with this requirement, since by all ten tests the states are contingent, and that without any prejudice to the sense in which the states are "perfect." For example, each state may be strictly omniscient of the correlative world-state and of all preceding divine and world-states, and of the potentiality for future states; yet, tested by any of the ten criteria (for example, by the 10th), the state will fall on the contingent side. Thus any divine state excludes some conceivable legitimate purpose which another possible divine state would have fulfilled. Since this other state was possible, the mere existence of God is not exclusive, even though the actual state is. Again, any actual state is within some quantitative and qualitative limits, for it is the knowledge of a world with such limits; whereas there might have been a state knowing some other world with other and wider limits, instead of this world with its limits. Thus the state, but not God, is essentially qualified by the limits in question. And it, but not He, is contingent. Similarly, on the other hand, any state depends on previous states for its existence and qualities, but on subsequent states for neither, a pattern of partial dependence which is characteristic of the contingent. On the other hand, some but not all other states (the subsequent ones only) depend upon the given divine state — again the partial indispensability characterizing the contingent.

This is, so far as I can see, the first theistic scheme with anything like a clear and consistent logic. We hear about philosophy being concerned with logic; but the most important test case for this, the treatment of theism, has of late not generally been done by logical analysis, but rather by assuming that Hume, Kant, or Aquinas had already made the analysis!

XIII. On Giving the Theistic Case Away

One implication of the Anselmian Principle is that a believer who grants to empiricists, as so many are doing today, that the existence of God is logically contingent, has unwittingly admitted, as Findlay almost alone among empiricists and positivists seems to have discerned, that the divine existence is logically impossible. (It seems not to have been noticed that Findlay herewith justifies, by rather careful reasoning, Anselm's Principle!)

When the idea of logically necessary existence is given up by theologians, strange things may happen. One writer, Professor J. J. C. Smart, goes so far as to say that the necessity of God is simply his being required for our religious life. In the same way (I comment) water is necessary for fish, and the firmness of the rock at which I desperately clutch as I slide down the cliff is the intensity of my need that it be firm. An interesting explication, unabashedly anthropomorphic. To be sure, I have caricatured the doctrine. For we are also told that the divine necessity is like the necessity of some theory in physics to explain the known facts. But this is not really any better. For the laws of nature, as Boutroux pointed out long ago, are contingent, and there can never be any guarantee that they may not change, at least in some vast stretch of time, into very different laws. In all this we deal with creatures, not the Creator. Has not Smart here unwittingly fallen into idolatry, by thus treating God as though He were a mere chance product of the creative process? [23]

Is such anthropocentrism or idolatry the suitable outcome of "Analysis"? Actually, it is not Analysis, in particular, that is responsible, but the generally perfused habit, shared by so many, of duplicating, largely without fresh inquiry, the Hume-Kant reduction of all existential statements to a single modality,

[23] *New Essays in Philosophical Theology*, p. 40.

whether they be partly, wholly, or not at all exclusive of positive possibilities. This extreme trust in the judgment of two great men of the Newtonian era, an era in whose intellectual assumptions basic errors have been found, must, so long as it lasts, prevent philosophers from discharging their one indispensable technical function, that of clarifying the purely positive or non-exclusive, hence necessary, judgments of existence and value (for of course the same distinctions recur in regard to value). This clarification is, I suggest, our job, and before proclaiming to the wide world that doing it is logically impossible, might we not, for once, seriously ask ourselves, "What is the logic of contingency"?

Is non-necessity really a "leap from thought to reality," as though there could be any bare thinking that exists on its own, dealing with nothing? Or is it essentially, and in the first instance, the creative leap from something actual to a *new* and partly unpredictable actuality? In the latter case, must there not be universal traits of the creative process which are other than its precarious or chance products, but constitute the power, the something, presupposed by every creative option, and therefore on both sides of every alternative that is more than merely verbal? The proof that we rightly conceive this universal trait, power, something, is that we succeed, if we do succeed, in so thinking of it as not to negate any possible specific product whatever, i.e., we think non-exclusively about it. We must then be conceiving, not a contingent alternative, but the Creative Alternativeness itself, to which it is contradictory to suppose an alternative. Where have the philosophical Newtonians, and their followers long after, considered such a theory with any patience or care?

If anyone asks what Creative Alternativeness could be like, we may ask him what he has been doing all his life. Yet the rise of human creativity is itself only one of the contingent options or products. The metaphysical question concerns the universal of which this is a special case. To ask how to get from the thought (if clear and positive) of such a universal of universals to the knowledge of its reality is nonsense. It is realized in anything whatever, including any thought as real.

Findlay's suggestion that the ultimate Ideal, just because it is that, cannot be real, but should be viewed as a *focus imaginarius*, is in a certain sense quite compatible with neoclassical theism, which views the divine Ideal as an aim at perpetual creation of new values, new even in and for God, an ideal which cannot be exhaustively realized, since the possibilities open to divine and non-divine creativity are absolutely infinite, and their exhaustive actualization is self-contradictory. But the divine existence is nonetheless modally all-inclusive or perfect, in that it is bound to be actualized in some contingent particular reality whose actuality defines what is co-actual with it.

Why does Findlay not see that the conception of divine perfection has as much right to be taken seriously as the dogma that "modern analysis" has shown the untenability of "necessarily exists?" [24] Findlay makes it clear why he does not see this. He conceives perfection in the classical manner only. I agree with him that an "idea" so riddled with antinomies cannot be used to upset the empiricist dogma. But until the neoclassical idea, which in essence is centuries old, has been considered, nothing has been settled about the availability of the Ontological Argument. For (a) the neoclassical idea springs directly from the very conception of worship or total devotion from which Findlay takes his departure, but in construing which he forgets, or does

---

[24] This point is strongly made by G. E. Hughes, in his reply to Findlay. See *New Essays in Philosophical Theology*, pp. 56–57; also *Mind*, LXIII (1949), pp. 67–74. Hughes, however, does not mention the type problem, and he concedes too much in granting that existential statements cannot be analytic nor necessary existence a predicate. Of course the necessity must not result from "arbitrary conventions of our language," if it is to be significant. But this notion of arbitrariness begs the main question. Any language without conventions making existence in some cases analytic will, as I am trying to show, make nonsense out of theism, and in addition will not give an intelligible and consistent account of modality.

not clearly see, what such total devotion means, and follows rather the guidance of classical metaphysics; and (b) the neoclassical idea is simply the classical one, except for the removal of those very features which generate the antinomies to which Findlay refers (that God qua concrete must yet be the predicate goodness or perfection, and so forth). These paradoxes or contradictions arise, as we have seen, from the denial of contingency and relativity to God. You cannot establish anything about the new idea of perfection by showing the paradoxical character of the older idea, from which it differs in just the ways which are relevant to the paradoxes! The implications of the neoclassical idea have been investigated with some care. But it is not to be met, even in hints, in the pages of Kant or his rationalist predecessors, or in Dewey, Lewis, Moore, Russell, Wittgenstein (so far as I know), or Wisdom. The intellectual world is not so small as some perhaps would like it to be.

XIV. Replies to Some Objections

We are told that logical necessity "relates concepts to concepts, not concepts to existing things." We have here a fallacy of ambiguity. Of course necessity cannot relate concepts to particular existing things. But please note, "exemplified property," "unexemplified property," "necessarily exemplified property," are all concepts, not particular existing things. Necessity can perfectly well relate the concept "perfection" to the concept "necessarily exemplified property." And this is exactly Anselm's Principle! What is missed by the critic is that God is not a "particular" existing thing, though He can exist only in what is particular, in actual "states." God is not a "particular individual," as this phrase is normally used, meaning one with a particular, limited, partly exclusive role in the universe. Particular individuals are never relevant to all others, nor are all others ever relevant to them. We "do nothing" for George Washington; and our remote descendants can do nothing for us. But God does something for everyone, and everyone does something for God. He is the union (not identity) of universal and individual; He is in His bare existence the non-particular individual. He is, to be sure, also particular, but not in His mere existence and individuality, rather, in the states in which His eternally identical and unparticular individuality exists. *That* He exists is non-particular; only *how* He exists, or in what state, is exclusive or particular. Since individuality is always more abstract than actual states, it is not a contradiction that in this one case it should be so completely abstract as to be wholly non-particular, and yet uniquely individual. For this abstract character cannot be embodied in more than one coexisting sequence of states. Hence it defines but one individual, without possible fellow. The truth that perfection cannot be, in itself, particular is also directly clear from its definition: for to any particular state of actuality there must correspond a state of the perfect which fully possesses that particular actuality. Now whatever is correlative to every possible particular is no more a particular than is particularity itself and as such.

The necessity of the existence of perfection is simply that a "predicate so general that any possible state of affairs would embody it" is necessarily embodied, and this is analytic (like every metaphysical necessity). Does this make it a mere consequence of our language? No, in this sense: either there is, or there is not, "a predicate universal to all conceivable positive possibilities"; and either it is, or it is not, correct that all possibilities must be partly positive. I think the second or negative alternative is in either case counter-intuitive. From these two premises, it follows that the analytic necessity mentioned above does refer to something, and something which necessarily exists. If we should fail to have a language in which all this could be said, this might be no more significant than the fact that the lower animals have no abstract language at all! It would depend upon what other restrictions such a language would impose. Here are doubtless problems which only many good logicians discussing together can adequately deal with.

A recent writer illustrates once more how many parts of this "elephant" can be seen by various persons while scarcely anyone succeeds in beholding the elephant itself.[25] The writer referred to maintains that while God cannot be logically necessary, He can be indispensable in the sense that everything depends for the possibility of its existence upon God and He upon nothing else. Now I submit that any entity without which nothing is even possible must in some sense be referred to by any proposition whatever, since not to refer to it would mean having no referent at all. But then any language whose rules do not require the affirmation of this entity is inconsistent or is one whose rules are incompletely explicated. The universal element in all reality, actual or possible, must be implicated in any meaning whatever. That such an element must be abstract the writer mentioned does not remark. (He has abundant precedent for this omission). But a rule requiring that the element be affirmed cannot beg any question of fact, by the simple meaning of "universal to all reality, actual or possible."

An objection of Kant's is that if God's reality can be deduced from our idea, then our idea must be God Himself. Yes, in this sense: that in so far as we know God, He is included in our knowledge. But then, as we have seen, the necessary is included by definition in anything whatever.

However, God merely qua "necessarily-existing individual" is not God in His concrete actuality, but is merely the abstract necessity that there be some such actuality. The particular actuality itself is not deducible from our idea. In addition, how "far" do we know even the abstract necessity spoken of? Enough to make some correct statements about it, if we are lucky and are not making some mistake. But we are not able to make all statements that are true about it. I suspect that the whole of pure mathematics would be involved, for example, since God cannot be ignorant ever of the logical principles from which mathematical truth follows. So I see no great force in Kant's objection.

[25] T. Penelhum, *op. cit.*

We are told that "existence adds nothing," and thus a merely possible perfection need not be inferior to an existing one. Right or wrong, this is irrelevant, since "existing" here means either, "in contingent fact," and this could not be, or necessarily, in which case the failure to exist means the impossibility of existing. But the necessarily non-existent is either meaningless or inconsistent, and an inconsistency is less than a necessarily-existing perfection! "Perfect" must refer to less even than a logical possibility, or else to more. Exactly this is what Anselm discovered.

Kant insisted (Counterargument 5) that logical consistency is not enough to establish ontological possibility. This seems another irrelevancy. For if the logically possible is not really possible, this is because of the presence or absence of something whose absence or presence is a necessary condition of the existence of the thing. But no positive or negative condition can be relevant to the existence of perfection, for conditioned existence is an imperfection.

Although the objection is not directly relevant, I believe that exploring it further will be illuminating for some aspects of our topic. If, for the existence of f, condition C must exist, this condition itself must be logically possible or, contrary to hypothesis, f will not be so. Is C also really possible? If it is, then f is really possible; if not, this can only be because some further condition C' is not met. Now we have a regress. And what about the entire regressive series? Is it really possible? If not, we seem to have a contradiction; for a new condition looms outside the series supposed to contain all conditions. For this and other reasons I question the validity of an ultimate distinction between logical and real possibility. Suppose that a law of nature forbids a certain logically conceivable thing. Is this thing then really and forever impossible? Only if there is no real possibility that the law should change. The logic of induction lends not the slightest warrant to the notion of a law valid for infinite time, yet supported only by a finite sample; and for this and other reasons I should reject as metaphysically invalid the notion of an eternal law of nature which excludes something logically possible. Such exclusion is proof enough that the law is contingent and not eternal. Real possibilities narrower than logical can be accepted only for limited time, not for all time. In this way we can treat any exclusive or specific state of affairs as something that nature or God might once have produced or may yet produce. But we cannot conceive God Himself as such a mere product. Once more we see the uniqueness of the concept of perfection in its relation to possibility.

An objection of Kant and others, based on the more careless of Anselmian, and Cartesian, formulations, is that, although we cannot deny a thing's properties while affirming the thing, we can deny both the thing and its properties; hence, even supposing existence to be included in perfection, we could still deny the perfect something and its existence. But when we deny that a property characterizes anything, we still have to provide the concept of the property with *some modal status* or other, or else admit that we are not discussing the proposed subject-matter at all. Of course we can stop explicitly conceiving God, whether as existing or not; but so can the lower animals avoid conceiving God. It may still be true (as Descartes said) that *when* we conceive God, we find but one modal status, that of necessary existence, appropriate to the conception. It may also be true that implicitly we are always conceiving God (and the animals are always feeling Him). The idea that Anselm can be refuted by the contention that we can cease knowingly to think about the question he put is one of the more bizarre of the many oddities which have accumulated about this topic.

Kant (in his discussion of the cosmological proof) thinks of God asking Himself, "Why should I not have failed to exist"? ("Whence am I"?), and he describes the dizzy feeling this thought gives him. But this vertigo seems scarcely necessary. God would see Himself as the ground of all possibility whatever. The question, "What was the ground of my existence"? would be merely contradictory, except so far as the answer would be, "*I* am." And if the argument is, "We have no idea how one being could furnish the ground of all, including its own, possibility," this amounts to saying that we have no idea of perfection. We are back at the positivist position. Kant misled thousands by his blurring of the distinction between saying, "there may not be an idea of perfection," and saying, "there might not be anything perfect." If the idea is not logically possible, then there could not be anything perfect; if it is possible, then there must be.

And please note, perfection is definitely of a higher logical type than ordinary predicates, since it is a law by which any predicate on the usual level is embraced in the actuality embodying the perfect individual. If x is red, then the perfect must possess all the value and actuality of x and its redness. And if x could be, but is not, red, then the perfect individual is potentially in possession of this being-red of x. Since we pass thus to a higher type, why must the usual modality of contingency obtain?

Contingency is found wherever one goes from the abstract toward the concrete. "Something exists" does not entail "Animals exist," this does not entail "Foxes exist," and this does not entail, "Fox here with torn left ear exists." Any step toward concrete particularity is logically a non-necessary one. But, likewise, any step from the particular to the specific of which it is a particularization, or from the specific to the generic of which it is a specialization, is logically necessary. Thus, when we reach the most abstract and universal conceptions, we arrive at entities which are entailed by any statements whatever, and this is precisely what necessary means. Now consider: "something exists," "something could or might exist," "something perfect exists." Are not these all on the same level of abstractness, by any reasonable test? To know what is meant by "terrestrial animal," one must know this planet as an empirical fact; but to know what "exists" means requires no more knowledge than knowing what "could exist" means, that is, no particular empirical facts at all, rather than any others. (Of course some empirical facts or other are needed for any meaning, even in mathematics or pure logic, but not necessarily any particular set of facts rather than any other.) If now we look at "perfect" as we have defined it — "coincidence of one individual's actuality with all actuality, and its potentiality with all possibility" — we again find nothing empirical.

A possible refutation of our theory at this point might be this: a proposition such as "only ten individuals exist" lacks empirical concepts, yet it certainly is not necessary. However, there is a question about time: *when* do the ten individuals exist? All dating is empirical. And if one replies, "always," then this makes the proposition necessarily false. Reality could not be bound forever to an arbitrary number. (Only God could verify such a thing, and according to neoclassicism He could not do so. For "all the future" is knowable only a priori and in its necessary features, the rest involving indeterminacies.) And if the critic substitutes "sometime," we may still insist upon the "when." For either one speaks of the whole of time from the empirical standpoint of a certain now, all events before and after and including that time, or one speaks of the whole of time in a purely abstract way, *sub specie aeternitatis*. But then only a necessity or impossibility concerning the abstract nature of process as such can make any such assertion true. The creative view of process, inherent in neoclassical metaphysics, does not allow the conception of "all events" as a final totality. Thus the attempted reductio ad absurdum of our criterion of non-contingency — absence of empirical concepts — should not be accepted. If I have not justified this view of process in an already overambitious essay, neither have the critics of the Argument and of metaphysics justified their contrary views. Hume and Kant were but human. They too faced the difficulty, perhaps impossibility, of proving or disproving in definitive fashion. They eventually found, to be sure, an indulgent public.

It is sometimes said that only the laws of logic can be strictly necessary. But there are two interpretations of these laws, a theistic and a non-theistic. The theistic interpretation is that 'p v $\sim p$' — for example — means, "Either the perfect knowledge has the truth of p, or it has the truth of $\sim p$, among its data." Alternatives, in other words, are *either* merely alternatives of "existence," taken as a term incapable of further elucidation, *or* they are alternatives of divine existence, as the presupposed common medium of all reality. This "either-or" itself may be conceived as a divine alternative, in this sense: Either divine knowledge includes as datum some imperfect mind which (falsely) supposes that "existence" is intelligible in non-theistic terms, *or* divine knowledge does not include such a datum.

Necessity itself has a theistic meaning: p is necessary if and only if God in all His states and by reason of His very essence experiences what it affirms; p is contingent if in some state God may not experience what it affirms. Here, as always, necessity is the abstract common factor, with respect to which many things can be treated as equivalent. In all His states God experiences His own existence and that of some world of imperfect things, also (presumably) something corresponding to "$2+2=4$", since this follows from purely logical notions illustrated in any experience or object of experience. A language in which the logical laws, or the analytic alternatives, cannot be stated exhaustively in theistic terms is one in which theism itself cannot be formulated. Such a language would in this respect be acceptable to some persons; but then they must not claim to have adjudicated, within that language, the status of an Argument whose conclusion they have debarred themselves from formulating.

At this point we may deal with the 14th Counterargument, that the necessary being is simply reality, hence not what religion means by God. Taken in extension or denotation, "divinity" and "reality" must indeed coincide. Reality can take any form, from atom to angel (in whatever sense there can be angels), but so can the divine knowledge. It can be perfect knowledge of atom, or perfect knowledge of angel, and so with whatever you please Thus the absolutely infinite flexibility of "reality" as such is fully matched by that of "divine knowledge." Yet this knowledge is the property of an individual! No property of an imperfect individual can have any such flexibility. All individual elasticity other than the divine has a breaking point. Were there to be such a breaking point for the divine flexibility, then the requirement to "love nothing additional to God" could not be kept. In the very thought of what lay beyond the limit in question we should break it.

Does it follow that "divine" (so far as necessary) means nothing distinctive? It depends on what kind of distinctiveness is intended. There is here no factual distinction, but still a conceptual one. In conceiving the absolute flexibility of reality as property of a conscious individual who includes all values by enjoying them as his own, we set up an analogy between our finitely flexible mode of consciousness and an infinitely flexible mode all of whose instances must have genetic identity with one another. This analogy, by definition, cannot restrict the possible forms of reality. The only way, therefore, to distinguish "divine reality" from bare "reality" is by viewing the former as the more fully conscious way of conceiving the same thing. And, after all, any concept, to have meaning, must somehow be related to experience. The bare word "reality," plus the requirement of "infinite flexibility," does not suffice to clarify the relation of the concept to experience. Only the idea of divine perfection can clarify this relation without sacrificing the flexibility in question. For "God" stands for Experience in its absolutely flexible form, through worship (conscious and unconscious) always relevant to any lesser experience.

Once more, God as necessary is not God in His concrete actuality. This actuality, in a particular instance, is not infinitely flexible, but is in each case determinate. It has, so to speak, a cutting edge, excluding from existence some things otherwise possible. But it excludes them freely, so far as the particular exclusions are concerned. God must exclude, but there is no particular thing which He must exclude. The difference is between "some" and "this" or "that." Similarly with "reality": not everything possible could ever be real, but there is no one possible thing which is impossible. Reality must exclude, but there is no particular thing it must exclude. To say these things in terms of God, instead of reality, does not change the formal pattern, but it relates the pattern to experience by a certain analogy. And it makes it sensible to say that we love the inclusive reality and that it loves us.

A critic will ask if, in introducing so empirical an idea as "love," we must not be tying down our concept, allegedly as unrestricted as "reality," to a particular form. I can only deny this flatly. Human love is a particular form, but the manner in which it figures as base of our analogy is logically non-restrictive, even though in psychological probability (in the way our imagination works) some restrictiveness may be more or less inevitable. Whatever is special or odd about human love is precisely what the analogy makes irrelevant. Finitely flexible love (inevitably with arbitrary limits of flexibility) is one thing, infinitely flexible love is another. It may be unimaginable, but we are here conceiving, not imagining. To say that love must be limited in flexibility is merely one of the many ways in which the positivistic alternative to theism may be put. But the standard ways of supporting the contention lose their coercive power once the classical idea of perfection has been dropped. We no longer have to combine the incompatible requirements: complete non-relativity or immutability, and relations of loving, with contingent things as relata. According to the neoclassical idea, what is eternally fixed or absolute in God is exactly the unlimited flexibility of His capacity to know and value, and thus to relativize Himself. He is immutably capable, to an ideal degree and in an ideal manner, of self-enrichment through anything that may become real.

Finite flexibility implies arbitrary limits, but absolute flexibility is no more arbitrary than reality as such. Nor is unlimited capacity to love, which (in its actual instances) would assume an appropriate form, given any object of love you please. Note that hatred does not admit such flexibility. Anything can be more or less hated, but hatred is a limiting attitude, self-centered and arbitrarily selective. Love means sharing in the reality of other individuals; hatred means a partial refusal to share. It cannot be coincident with reality. Nothing but conscious love can be so. It alone can share in all unconscious and conscious forms of reality.

Part of Kant's argumentation (Objection No. 3, Section III) ran: We can understand necessity only as conditional; but the unconditionally necessary seems to mean that the thing makes itself necessary, which presupposes that the thing exists, thus begging the question. The error here is in overlooking the abstract nature of the necessary as such. Necessary existence is not actuality, plus something, some necessity or other. It is nothing actual at all, but an essence, embodied in any and every total state of contingent actuality. Actualities include in their natures the possibility of not having existed, and they definitely exclude some possibilities. This is a richer idea, not a poorer: God *merely* as necessary is less than any contingent thing whatever, even the meanest. To worship the necessary is but a subtle form of idolatry. This idolatry was found tolerable only because one inevitably, though often insensibly, goes beyond the stated object of worship, the merely necessary. For God as necessary is God considered under an extreme abstraction, God as barely existing somehow, in some state of concrete actuality or other, no matter what. But God cannot be limited to His merely necessary being; He is the individual that could not fail to be actualized in some contingent particular form. This implies an immeasurable superiority; but what actualizes the superiority is God-now, or God-then, not just God at any time or as eternal, which is a mere abstraction. The necessity that there be some contingent actualization is inherent in the unique abstractness of the identifying divine individuality or essence.

It is not true that we merely presuppose God as ground of His own necessity, and so beg the question. For once more, $\sim N \sim Np$ $\rightarrow Np$; if the existence of divinity logically could make itself necessary, it *must* do so. Hence we need only presuppose that the divine existence as necessary is not impossible. Here Kant innocently plays a sophistical trick upon us, and that this has not been noted shows the extreme awe given this noble and brilliant, but (in the garden-variety sense, not in his own fancy meaning) rather "dogmatic" and rigid mind. The sophistry consists in confusing "possible," as meaning "capable of existing and also of not existing," with "not incapable of existing," hence "*either* contingently (existent or non-existent) *or* else necessarily existent." Aristotle long ago pointed out this confusion; Kant seems unaware, throughout his discussion, of the modal logic expressed in the Argument. He talks in terms of simple, not modal, logic. This does beg the question. To talk about necessary existence is *ipso facto* to enter the realm of modality. Kant says that the Argument pretends to conceive the mere possibility of God, and then deduces His existence from this concept, which therefore could not have been that of any such mere (unexemplified) possibility.[26] The Argument makes no such pretension. It works by exhaustion of the logically possible relations of ideas to things. Among these is the relation, "contingently unexemplified" in existence, also the relations: "necessarily exemplified," "impossible of exemplification," and finally "contingently exemplified." The first and the last, the Argument shows, are in a certain case self-contradictory: a perfection exemplified merely contingently would be exemplified by something imperfect, hence not exemplified; it follows that "contingent failure of exemplification" is here also contradictory, by the meaning of "contingent." Thus Anselm's Principle is established, and it remains only to adjudicate the issue between a priori theism and positivism.

[26] Professor Julius Ebbinghaus has kindly given me the benefit of his profound scholarship. Yet after careful reading of his explanation of Kant's meaning, I still wonder what Kant was doing in that passage, if not what I have stated above.

Empiricism (in its non-positivist form) shows itself incapable of dealing with this central philosophical issue. Logical analysis is final arbiter of the theistic question, except so far as the question eludes rational grasp altogether.

The air of paradox which may seem to haunt "makes itself necessary" is due not only to forgetting the abstractness of necessity but also to overlooking the equivalence of "unconditional" and "on any conditions you please." What "makes" God necessary? Anything whatever; just as, Np implies that any contingent proposition implies p. We need not, and cannot, simply "think away all conditions" of the divine necessity, if "condition" means, "something which logically requires the divine existence." For anything does so; and he who does not think something does not think. Think God, and that requires God. Think atoms, and they require God. Think the mere possibility of atoms: that, too, requires God. (To deny this is to assert the impossibility of God's existence. For, once more, what could be necessary to all things must be: $\sim N \sim Np \rightarrow Np$). There is no danger of thinking everything away, "leaving nothing which could be contradicted" by the non-being of God. For you cannot think everything away, and still be thinking. And if you think perfection, and yet think thereby not a contingently-existing (nor a contingently-non-existing) property, nor a necessarily-existing property, nor yet a self-inconsistent property which logically could not exist, what does your "perfection" connote? Nothing coherent at all.

If we set aside the irrelevancies and question-begging dogmas in Kant's objections, and clarify the residuum, we are left with this: that on the classical basis not only the positivistic, but also the logical-type objections are fatal. In other words, Kant met a somewhat muddled argumentation for an impossible positive conclusion with a muddled critique leading to an ambiguous negative conclusion. The classical idea certainly was not, and (in my opinion) could not be, established by this or any argument; however, what collapsed was not the Argument, but rather its alleged conclusion. Yet the real question of the religious object, arbitrarily identified with the classical idea, was left open, or, rather, had gained some support from the entire history of the controversy. For this idea alone, taken as true, is in a position to explain clearly and cogently the possibility of so many great as well as innumerable humble minds holding the various positions which they have in fact held. What some of these people grasped was that they were in the neighborhood of the most profound of all ideas. They mistook a near-miss for a hit. And others took the familiar stand that "a miss is as good as a mile," which in theoretical matters has not the same validity as in practical.

A rather strange contention sometimes made is that Anselm's argument requires that one be a (so-called) Platonic realist. I wonder. Anselm is trying to show that perfection cannot be a mere disembodied universal, and this demonstration does not require that universals may or do exist merely in themselves. In fact, Anselm did not believe in the self-existence of any universals. They all existed in the creatures, or in the Creator, who is not intended to be a mere property. Yet the matter is complicated. In a way Anselm is too nominalistic, so far as God is concerned, for his own argument. He does not show us, and as a Classical Theist he cannot show us, how a definable property, perfection (he does define it), can be distinguished from and yet logically entail an existent "having" the property. Or, if God does not have, but is, His perfection, then He is evidently the mere content of an abstract definition! Accordingly, the Argument requires a distinction between universal and particular instance. Here is one of the difficulties which only the non-Anselmian, neoclassical concept of perfection can remove. God is indeed His perfection, but only *qua* existing and always self-identical individual. God *qua de facto* actuality, i.e., God-now, relative to the world-now, *embodies* perfection, and is therefore not identical with it, being one of its exemplifications. What the property, perfection, logically entails is only the law: there must always be some perfect actuality or other, and any such perfect actuality must without fail possess complete memory of its predecessors and perfect anticipation of its successors (limited only by the principle that the creative aspects of process as such have unforeseeable, antecedently indeterminate, results). Thus any perfect actuality is a member of a class which cannot be empty, any member is God, and any other is also God — but as antecedent or subsequent to Himself, in the manner of a "personally-ordered" sequence of experience. Thus we escape the old dilemma: either God as actual is His goodness (and this is the contradiction that an instance is not an instance, or that the concrete is also wholly abstract); or else God is a mere instance (but then of course He exists contingently). We say none of these things: rather, God as actual "is" not His eternal perfection or goodness, but the exhibition of this abstract property in a concrete form; yet God merely as existing is something quite abstract, namely the property as inevitably embodied in some concrete actuality or other, and as such that no actuality outside of the one personally-ordered sequence can have it. Other actualities than those which are perfect "could" have been so only in that the one divine sequence could at any moment have been prolonged otherwise than it was in fact prolonged. It must be prolonged somehow endlessly, but not necessarily by just the actual states which occur.

An objection to the Argument, less often formally stated than informally felt, is that it is not common sense to try to find out what exists merely by analyzing our thoughts. To try to find out what contingently exists, certainly not. But if a property is such that analysis shows it to be incapable of existing contingently, then to deny that its existence is a necessity of meaning is to treat its existence as impossible, implying that its *non*-existence *is* a necessity of meaning! For anything definitely conceivable is either contingent or necessary, and if necessary, necessary positively or negatively (impossible); if contingency is shown by logical requirements not to apply, then nothing remains but to decide whether the thing's positively necessary existence is or is not conceivable. For if it is conceivable, then its denial cannot be.

The argument from common sense is like saying, "Since ordinarily, or in common experience, wholes are greater than their parts, the mathematician cannot be justified in defining infinite collections as numerically equal to some of their parts." Hegel defended the Argument by saying that the prejudice against necessary existence is the fallacy of extending to the infinite what is valid only of the finite. An empiricist critic, who has reminded me of this, nevertheless insists vehemently that it fails as a defense, since the mathematical infinite is logically distinct from the finite not in respect to existence but only in respect to certain properties. But here all depends on how the analogy is taken. Common sense is found not to be a reliable guide as to relations of wholes and parts in the numerically infinite case. This is enough to show that we must employ common-sense prejudices with caution wherever we are dealing with ideas not customarily dealt with in everyday life — at least, not in contexts where accuracy and logical consistency are crucial for practical success. Critics of the proof have shown no such caution, but have given the usual way of thinking all the benefit of any doubts. Moreover, the mathematical infinite is not the theological infinite. Accordingly, even supposing (which I question) that the relation of the former infinite to existence is of the same modal type as that of the finite, it would not follow that the relation of the theological infinite, which is perfection, to existence must be the same. There is and can be no concept whatever more radically different from ordinary concepts than the idea of God. To assume as obvious that there is no modal difference is not intellectual inquiry, but is a sort of philosophical politics — defending or attacking a cause. We must ask, genuinely ask, what the relation is; and so long as the question is merely rhetorical, and we "know" what the answer must be, we are only pretending to ask, to inquire. Our primary intellectual job is not to attack or defend but to investigate logical possibilities and necessities — an investigation the eventual outcome of which may not have been foreseen by Gaunilo, Hume, Kant, or even Wittgenstein — but also perhaps not by classical theists like Anselm, or his astute critic, Thomas.[27]

XV. Does the Divine Existence Make an Empirical Difference?

Here is perhaps the place to face the positivist doctrine, stressed in Findlay's article, that significance or cognitive meaning referring to existence must "make an observable difference," must be conceivably disconfirmable, and so must exclude something. Here once more is a begging of the Ontological question. Alas, many theologians aid and abet this by admitting that the truth of "God loves all His creatures" ought to make a difference. I say it ought not and could not make a difference, for it is the

[27] Perhaps the strongest defense of the Argument by any classical theist seeking to answer modern criticism is found in Robert Flint's *Theism* (London, 1877), pp. 278–284. But this was before the development of the Theory of Types, and Flint shows no awareness of the identification of abstract and concrete which the Argument, as classically used, can neither avoid nor justify. For a learned and elaborate history of attitudes toward the Argument in the 17th, 18th, and 19th centuries see D. Henrich's *Der Ontologische Gottesbeweis* (Tübingen: J. C. B. Mohr, 1960). One of Henrich's conclusions is that Kant's main point was, we have no way of giving content to "perfection" over and above its mere "necessity," so that the Argument is the empty tautology: whatever, if anything, is necessary is necessary. Kant then was a positivist, denying that "perfect" or "divine" has cognitive meaning. This, we have seen, is a strong position, assuming the classical definitions. Henrich has no clear idea of the classical versus neoclassical issue. Even so, he does not treat the Argument as a mere sophistry. It makes sense, he holds, in terms of certain now not fashionable philosophical tenets (languages?). This of course raises the question, do *these* make sense?

An original and suggestive treatment of the Argument will be found in Paul Weiss's essay, "God and World," in *Science, Philosophy, and Religion: a Symposium* (New York, 1941), esp. pp. 406–412. See also his *Modes of Being* (Carbondale: Southern Illinois University Press, 1958), entry "argument" in the Index.

ground not alone of this, but of any possible world, which also must express the divine love. To say less than this is idolatry, the positing of a possibility outside God altogether.

On the other hand, the neoclassical idea does not imply that God, but only that His bare existence as "all-loving," makes no difference. In His contingent actuality God loves, not merely all creatures, but the very creatures which happen to exist. Since these are contingent, so is His love for them; for they could not be loved as individuals were there no such individuals. However, it is still true that "God loves me" makes no difference expressible by asking, what would have been my fate had God not loved me? For I should have had no fate and should not have been — period. But there is yet that in God which makes a difference to me, and which is a contingent matter, knowable, if at all, only empirically. God loves me in a particular concrete way, which is not deducible from any mere concept like "perfect love" plus the fact of my existence. If I knew this concrete divine love for me, I should know a great deal about myself, and my prospects, which I do not know. And I should also know how omniscience evaluates my neighbors, with whose values mine are more or less interdependent; I should know what good or evil there is that I do not see in Communism, or what you will. Here indeed are questions of empirical fact. But here we must consider a logical problem: how far can any mind know the contingent valuations of a radically-superior mind? Not very far, by logical consequence of "radically superior." Here the traditional theological retreat into the impenetrability of the divine wisdom is simply good logic. But it concerns the concrete contingent qualities of God, not His necessary essence. It is not so much the abstract or necessary which we cannot grasp—mathematics might have taught us that — but the concrete and contingent in its fullness, whether divine or not divine. Our intellects are at home in the abstract, the concrete is an infinitely-receding goal.

The mere existence of God, then, cannot make an empirical

difference. However, it implies that there are divine actualities which do make differences, though these differences relatively transcend our powers of comprehension. Only relatively! We can, for example, infer from our scientific knowledge that God must intend nature to follow certain patterns, those which she universally does follow. To be sure, this adds no predictive power to our science, since we gaily proceed and must proceed to make inductions with or without conscious belief in God. However, it does enable us to understand what it can be in nature that gives her a reliable structure, and indeed, enables a coherent world to exist at all. And moreover, it justifies our trust in induction, in this way: it is a reasonable inference that the laws of nature express the divine will, and that we shall serve God best by doing our best to learn these laws and apply them in our lives. "Providence" can scarcely mean less than that our powers are in principle adapted to the world and ought to be trusted enough to make their vigorous use possible.

The basic significance of the divine existence is not to tell us something particular about the world, but rather to tell us what it means to be particular, and why anything in particular matters. To be particular is to be a definite item in the divine consciousness, hence imperishably appreciated for all the intrinsic value which the particular actually has. Here too, theologians often give far too much away if they are to retain a good case. "God" is not *a* meaning, but *the* meaning and *all* meaning, focused or integrated in the most adequate way. What makes a difference is not that God exists, for there is no alternative, but that *we* should know and admit the necessary truth of this. To this admission there are indeed alternatives, subjective ones. Such knowledge and admission make all sorts of differences. But they are all differences between implicit and explicit knowledge and admission. Implicitly everyone knows (or at least feels) the divine existence. (No believer can without contradiction claim less than this, for it is a consequence of the conceived dependence of all meaning and truth upon the divine existence.)

XVI. The Barthian or Fideist Position

That Anselm "presupposed faith" (Objection 18) is true enough. But here, too, let us be careful. The "fool" who denies God's existence thinks he knows what this existence would mean — at least some of the fools do so think. Against them the Argument is valid, to the extent that it forces them (if they are logical) to shift their position from empirical atheism to positivism. Moreover, the believer gains something from the Argument. For without it he might fear, in moments of unbelief, that the idea of God perhaps represents a fictitious state of affairs, which we believe because it would be nice if it were true, although unfortunately it happens not to be true. This fear Anselm showed to be groundless. It could not "happen" not to be true. Either no conceivable state of affairs could make it true, or any conceivable state of affairs must do so. The problem of unbelief is a pure problem of meaning and self-understanding, not of "what the facts happen to be." Knowing this is a real aid to belief. It reduces the question to one of sincerity, clarity, and self-understanding, in depth, of our own thought.

Nor is this all. That such vast multitudes have thought the idea of God significant is some evidence that positivism is in error. Not perhaps in itself very strong evidence, considering the confusion between the classical (with its paradoxes) and the neoclassical conceptions of God. And yet the fact that so many have been so sure that they knew what they meant by the religious idea, in spite of the rather obvious antinomies in most theologies, is least puzzling if we take into account the ease with which classical and neoclassical concepts may be confused, also recall that the classical is the simpler concept and therefore naturally the one considered first ("Seek simplicity — and then mistrust it"), and if, finally, we see that the positivistic objections tend to lose their force in relation to the more subtle conception. We could then say that believers have obscurely and somewhat confusedly apprehended a genuine, logically-possible idea (which by its own logic turns out to be a necessarily-embodied one). Is this not what we usually find with widespread fundamental notions?

Karl Barth's reasoning in the book previously referred to (footnote 12) is not offered as an objection to Anselm's proof, but as an interpretation of it. Unlike many interpretations, it is extremely attentive to the textual indications. It would be presumptuous were I to attempt to correct his scholarship with respect to Anselm's meanings. He admits that there is some "methodological unclarity" (pp. 56–57) in the *Monologium* and *Proslogium* as to whether the theistic proofs are or are not significant for any but believers. Barth cleverly "finesses" the issue by suggesting (p. 74) that perhaps Anselm doesn't quite believe in the unbeliever's unbelief. One never knows—God is great, and may have revealed Himself, or may at any moment reveal Himself, to the self-styled unbeliever. Barth even suggests that there is only a hair-splitting distinction in the practice of a theologian between the rightful theologizing which remains always on the ground of faith, and the utterly erroneous kind which pretends to derive theological conclusions from neutral premises. This is a bit puzzling: there is a great gulf between the two procedures, and yet scarcely any perceptible line at all in practice.

The correct theological procedure is explained in this way (p. 69): one shows the logical or rational connection between a particular bit of faith, this or that proposition, and all the rest taken as granted. Thus the criterion of success is coherence. But then the question I see is, what about unfaith? Can it exhibit comparable coherence in its basic life-principles and ideals? I do not believe it, and I think the comparison can be made on neutral ground, in whatever sense there is any neutral ground. But this is a large issue, which I hope to deal with in a later work.

With respect to the Argument, Barth makes the distinction between the first (simple or non-modal) form and the second or modal form (my phrase), and points out, what must strike any careful reader of Anselm, that whereas the simple argument appears briefly in the second chapter (which is less than two short pages) of the *Proslogium* and once in the *Reply* to Gaunilo, the modal version is presented, not only in chapter 3 (and by implication in 4, a page beyond) but in variant forms over and over again in the Reply. Thus we have strong textual, as well as (if our reasonings have been at all sound) strong logical grounds for taking the modal argument as the essential one. And Barth objects vigorously to the assumption of Gaunilo, followed by almost all the world, that the simple argument is *the* argument. Rather, Barth declares that if one version is to be ignored as superfluous it should be the first or simple version. The eminent meaning of "exist" which alone is compatible with divinity and by which contingency is excluded is the key to the entire reasoning. Here surely he is right. In general Barth takes a dim view of Gaunilo's procedures and influence through the centuries. The irrelevancies and gross misconceptions of the famous monk (who has some claims to the status of the most overrated thinker in history) are itemized at length in Barth's book (pages 83–96, 103 f., 105, 124, 127, 135, 146 f., etc.).

Barth agrees essentially with Malcolm, Findlay, and this author that Anselm's main point is that even the thinkability of non-existence is excluded by perfection, or by the formula, "that than which none greater can be thought" (pp. 150–186). The formula itself, according to Barth, is a piece of revelation (pp. 80–81). There seems to be some analogy between this and my adaptation of Tillich's proposal to define "God" through the idea of worship, or unrestricted devotion. To be capable of non-existence is to be unworthy of worship, and so not God, since the term stands for the object of worship. It follows that the denial of theism is equivalent to the assertion of its impossibility. For, once more, if contingent existence is logically excluded, so is contingent non-existence. Worship is either a revelation of necessary truth, or it is a confusion, affirming what could not be true.

Does the Argument presuppose faith? It presupposes enough understanding of what it is to worship to grasp how worship regards the worshipped. But it at least simplifies the philosophical problem of theism by showing the sense in which God could neither exist nor fail to exist — i.e., as a mere matter of positive or negative fact. Empirical atheism is ruled out on logical grounds, leaving only the positivistic form of unbelief to evaluate, in comparison to theism.

Barth shows in this work (so far as I have discovered) no awareness of the relation of the Argument to the ways of construing "none" in "none greater can be thought" — (1) no individual other than God, (2) not even the same individual in another state. That is, he either remains on classical metaphysical ground or leaves the matter ambiguous. Apparently I am alone in taking this distinction between the two views of divine perfection as the sole way of resolving the dilemma: God cannot exist contingently, for contingency of existence is an imperfection; but also God cannot exist necessarily, for the necessary is abstract and inactual, the mere common factor of possibility. The neoclassical view, by construing the excluded "greater" as another individual, leaving open the possibility of greater contingent states of the same individual, not only resolves the dilemma, but also removes various other antinomies. Since these are the strongest grounds for the positivistic negation, it is by no means clear, to me at least, why the Argument does not acquire a certain force, even on neutral assumptions (in whatever sense one can speak of neutrality here).

I should note that for Barth "faith" means the whole Christian complex of beliefs; whereas I am discussing only the contrast between acceptance of the God of worship (complete devotion) and the non-acceptance of Him.

It is curious that Kierkegaard, also a sort of fideist, recognizes the distinction between "factual existence" and "ideal being," and argues that only the latter can be necessary and that God must also have factual reality.[28] This is in agreement with our contention that the full concrete reality or actuality of God cannot be necessary. But Kierkegaard apparently overlooks one logical point here: it may very well be necessary that God have some factual existence or other. For factuality as such is an abstraction, not another fact, and all factuality must express God. Kierkegaard has another important insight: that "God is not a name but a concept." Only God could do the general sorts of thing God does: the abstract principle of His actions is self-individuating and we have here a unique union of universal and individual. Kierkegaard insists, however, that we cannot identify the actions of God in the world of mixed good and evil, order and apparent disorder. But this is what the ontological argument shows to be unnecessary, if we only want to know the bare existence of God. For any world will do, since by his modal coincidence, God is the ground of possibility itself. We have to choose, first, between the necessity and the impossibility of worship and its object. In this choice one finally, at some point, appeals to faith or intuition, there is no evading that. (Concerning this I shall try to say something in my systematic metaphysics.) So far Kierkegaard is right. But I do not see why we cannot distinguish two steps here, first making the choice just mentioned, and then, if the decision is positive, trying as best we can to sense something of the particular factuality of God in our world, what it means to Him, and what He as *its* God means to us. (Here we shall always be in abysmal ignorance.) Kierkegaard speaks as though, if the Argument fails to perform the second step also, it accomplishes nothing. This seems excessive. Similarly excessive, in my opinion, is the "Absolute Paradox" that God and man are absolutely unlike and therefore God is absolutely unknowable to reason. "Reason" has produced this paradox, even though there is something like it in religious feeling, and reason can also

[28] Sören Kierkegaard, *Philosophical Fragments*, trans. by D. F. Swenson (Princeton: Princeton University Press, 1936), pp. 32–34.

correct it where it needs correction, as I am confident it does. (See Chapter Four.)

The possible utility of the Argument for secular theory is not limited to its availability as an argument against unbelief. For the elimination of empirical theism, along with empirical atheism, can be an immense gain for philosophy, when and if it learns to take advantage of the clarification thereby effected. It is really empiricism itself which is at stake; and this no doubt is one reason for the frequently more emotive than intellectual handling of the argument. A methodological cause is in the balance here. But since empirical knowledge is science rather than philosophy, it ought not lightly to be assumed that philosophy is logically driven to espouse absolute empiricism. It would thereby condemn itself to relative futility. Perhaps we are obligated to take this rather heroic course. But how ironical to do it if we are not obligated, if a more resolute intellectual integrity would lead us to restore the promise and importance of philosophy as inquiry into the necessarily existent, that is, into those (highly abstract) traits of reality which are non-contingently embodied in some actual instances!

XVII. Did Hume and Kant Refute the Theistic Proofs?

I wish to challenge my colleagues: What refutation of the Argument have I not refuted — or at least, shown to be as problematic as the Argument? If my tenfold Ontological Proof is essentially in the wrong, let it be pointed out just how and where it fails. If this cannot be done, then I hope philosophers will be so candid as to admit to their students and associates that, so far as they know, the ontological Argument for God (the God of worship and total devotion, not "the absolute," or *Actus Purus*) has not in principle been refuted. It has at most been shown to turn on some difficult and not as yet wholly clarified — perhaps even, not wholly clarifiable — issues in the logic of modality and the theory of language in its cognitive use. And what philosophical argument is in better case? [29] And so, why not tear out of the textbooks those passages in which the Argument is treated, with authority and finality, as a mere sophistry? (Kant set the fashion, by his dogmatic barring of the path of inquiry in the "all labor's lost" passage which closes his famous discussion of the Ontological Argument in the *Critique of Pure Reason*.)

And should one stop there? If the Argument can be put in something like ten definite and logical ways, all missed by the objectors, what of the other types of theistic argument, which, according to Kant, are intimately connected with the ontological? These too, as I shall, I trust, have opportunity elsewhere to show, are open to radical revision, and as revised they also elude the standard objections, and support the neoclassical, not the classical, idea of the divine or perfect.

I conclude: Kant and Hume refuted, not *the* theistic arguments, but their own, admittedly weak, versions of some arguments for a substitute for theism. Consequently, the entire episode appears to have been in a sense an irrelevant detour, save as an object lesson in how not to proceed in order through reason to find out if it is possible through reason to know the divine existence. To find that out (and have we not an inescapable obligation to try, since we have been assuring the world for a long time now that we had already done the job?), should we not start afresh, albeit inspired by the courage of these men and their determination to think with the greatest clarity and honesty of which they were capable?

[29] See Henry W. Johnston's fine book, *Philosophy and Argument* (University Park: The Pennsylvania State University Press, 1959). Everett W. Hall's *Philosophical Systems: a Categorial Analysis* (Chicago: The University of Chicago Press, 1960), covers somewhat similar ground in stimulating fashion. I am in better agreement with my lamented friend's conclusions than he realized (the sentence he puts in quotation marks and attributes to me — on page 27 — expresses nothing I have ever thought, and I believe nothing I have ever said or written, though I understand why he supposed that I had said something of the sort), and I think this last of his books is also the best.

CHAPTER THREE

The Wider Context:
Theism as an Integral Philosophy

"All existences are Buddhahood."
                    DOGEN (Japan, 13th Century).

"On the tablet of the universe is no letter save thy name;
By what name then shall we invoke thee?"
                    JAMI (Persia, 15th Century).

THE GREEKS held that concrete particulars are essentially unintelligible, objects of mere opinion, not knowledge. As men often do, they made their own limitations the measure of things. Since we can have clear, definite, certain knowledge only of abstract forms, they said that it is these alone which are worth knowing. So Aristotle's God does not even trouble to notice what is going on in the world; He contents Himself with the bare "thinking of thinking." I see in this view an attempt to make a merit out of our human limitations. Science has achieved its great advances by taking the concrete seriously, and by contenting itself with probability instead of certainty. Even science, to be sure, has had to deal with the concrete somewhat abstractly, ignoring all but the measurable and perceptually identifiable of its characteristics. But it views the abstract as means for the exploring of the more concrete, not vice versa.

Since to God the concrete is an open book, the theist cannot think about these matters as the Greeks did. For the theist wishes to see the creation, if in any way possible, as God sees it; therefore, he must try to understand the concrete as such and to see what it is which we miss through our human restriction to more or less abstract modes of dealing with the world.

Both God and the world can be viewed more or less concretely. Every concrete thing is in its fullness and uniqueness an unfathomable mystery, and in God all mystery is compounded, since God knows and thus contains all things, including all mystery. This mystery of God, however, as we have already noted, is not in the mere concept or essence of "divinity," but in God as an actuality — not the abstract principle of His knowing, but the actual knowing. Of this we know next to nothing. The mere essence of deity, however, is the principle of all principles, and is really the entirety of what we can know a priori about reality. Those who deny any such a priori knowledge are insofar quite right to reject theism; for as Comte said, any non-empirical knowledge or metaphysics can only be an abstract or desiccated quintessence of theology. Compared to theistic ideas, non-theistic basic principles differ solely by virtue of their inferior clarity or greater ambiguity. They are obscure, rather than mysterious, and their opacity is due to our own mistakes.

Unfortunately, the inherent advantages of theism are often thrown away by the acceptance of concepts which are subtly atheistic, as well as opaque or confused. One such concept is that of substance — not, of course, the mere word, but the pattern of thinking for which the word has almost always been used in technical philosophy. This pattern is destructive of the idea of God in the following ways:

(1) If a human individual is absolutely and perfectly one entity, strictly identical numerically from birth to death — or even

for infinite time! — then deity cannot in this respect transcend the human. Numerical identity seems not to admit gradations; if a man is in all circumstances simply the same person, then God can be no more truly identical with Himself. This makes light of and in effect denies the monstrous breaks and shifts in our self-identity — complete breaks, apparently, in deep sleep, enormous shifts from virtually mindless infancy (or existence in the womb) to adult consciousness, from sanity to delirium or virtually-mindless intoxication, etc. Having rendered harmless these creaturely aspects of non-identity, we can then exalt God only by saying that not simply is His "numerical identity" absolute (like ours) but His qualities or states all collapse into one timeless quality or state, without real distinction or succession. In taking this step we do not exalt the identity of God, we merely make of it a self-contradictory blur of notions. Neither "identity" nor "quality" has any recognizable reference where all diversity is denied.

(2) In viewing self-identity as mere numerical oneness, with at most a plurality of qualities, a single noun with many adjectives, we leave it wholly unclear how the many created substances can be "in" God. So we perhaps go to the opposite extreme from "pantheism" (in the sense which takes God to be the mere totality of non-divine things), and take Him to be not even this totality, but something wholly independent and exclusive of it. This makes pure paradox of the divine knowing, since perfect knowledge, at least, must include its objects. It also makes a conundrum of "serving God," since nothing we can be or produce will literally make any difference at all in Him. It helps not at all here to say that God is immanent as well as transcendent; the relevant question is whether the world is immanent in God.

(3) If I am simply one with myself through time, just a single entity, then when I know myself this must be an absolutely different thing from knowing other substances. Knowing becomes either identity, I know myself because I am myself, or

sheer non-identity, as when I know you. And so with loving, or taking an interest in, myself and others. Spiritual categories are not here used to explain self-identity; for that has been taken as irreducible, as an ultimate principle. Since the principle is vague or ambiguous, one tends to fall back upon physical analogies and metaphors. The soul is breath, God is a great sun or an overflowing fountain. Substance philosophies have been tinged with materialism from the beginning. At the crucial points in the argument, it was not concepts like love or knowledge which tipped the balance, but either some physical analogy (which meant analogy with things taken as primitive physics took them, usually wrongly) or else some supposedly self-evident technical concept like that of the numerical identity of substance. The remedy for this is, partly, to think in terms of events, happenings, or acts, rather than of enduring individual things to which events happen. The endurance can then be constructed from relationships, such as remembering and loving, found in the events.

(4) The religious meaning of death and immortality was misconceived in substance philosophies, as will be shown in Chapter Nine.

The most important result, perhaps, of these aspects of substance thinking has been the dangerous "individualism" of our Western world. Of course there is a noble individualism, but it is very evident that there is an ignoble one. By comparison with Buddhism, wherever this is genuine at all, the ignoble side in our individualist philosophies is nearly always apparent. Also, the immense ethical drive in communism cannot, I am sure, be understood until we see that it means in some respects a higher spiritual level than our official philosophies attain. Communists teach a philosophy of the common good. We either teach or do not make clear that and why we do not teach a philosophy of "enlightened self-interest." And all four features of substantialism mentioned above help to make this denial of the Great Commandment, "love thy neighbor *as* thyself," more or less inevitable. The Buddhist "no-soul" doctrine, which would, I presume, sound shocking to most pious Christians, makes it possible literally to love the other as oneself, i.e., as not another substance.

In the language of events, the whole puzzle begins to clear up. Absolute numerical unity belongs only to the momentary self, all past and future experiences are numerically other; however, with some we may have relations of intimate or wholehearted sympathy or good will, and whether or not these belong to the "same" physical organism, embody the same personality traits or ego, etc., is a secondary question.

The Buddhist-Whiteheadian view also enables us to transcend the communistic paradox that the group is more real than its members. Logically this is without clear sense. Ethically it is dangerous, as most of us in this part of the world realize. Nothing is real but individuals — on the human level, conscious individuals. Groups are not such individuals. But neither are egos, as single entities there for sixty years. No such ego is ever literally "conscious of itself." The self-now is the individual subject actually enjoying the present consciousness; later selves will enjoy it so far as they remember it; past selves did enjoy it only so far as they anticipated it. Any "timelessly the same" self, birth to death, is a mere abstraction. It does not literally do or know anything. But what is more concrete, and the inclusive possessor of value, is not the group, as a super-substance identical through time. It can only be the divine Self-now as inheriting our momentary selves, Itself to be inherited by subsequent divine selves. A kind of neo-trinitarianism can be worked out from this — with, however, an infinity of Holy Spirits, rather than just one. There must indeed be a kind of "begetting" in the divine life.

Theism should take its stand and not let itself be dictated to by bits of philosophy which had no origin in religious insight. The concept of creative becoming has a religious origin, for it is the generalization of the divine "fiat" back of the world. Not the

Greeks but Philo had this idea; he only failed to generalize it beyond man. Augustine went back to the Greeks and exempted even man (after Adam) from creativity.

Theists should decide what it is they worship. Is it "substance," "soul," "immortality," "the absolute," "creation *ex nihilo*?" This last phrase adds scarcely any spiritual insight to the idea of creative fiat, but dangerously hampers its generalization into the idea of a creation of creators. For if we too in our humble way create, then God's action in the world now does have "materials," for we have partly made them. "But, at the beginning . . ."? Ah, is it the idea of a beginning which you worship? Do you exalt God's power by deciding that He has created only a finitude of past time? Whence this passion for limiting God by explicit negations? We forbid Him to be infinite in the temporal span of his sphere of action. At the same time, we also forbid Him to be finite or limited in any way at all in His own actuality, as though the merely unlimited might not be the formless and valueless, the greatest limitation of all! I sincerely believe that our inherited religious doctrines are a mélange of self-worship, worship of humanity, worship of "substance," and other tags of Greek philosophy, and — some genuine worship of God!

Another example, closely related to substance, of a non-theistic and confused conception is that of mere matter. Mere matter must mean the zero case of mind, that is, of sentience, memory, and the rest. If God is mind with absolutely infinite capacity (not absolutely infinite actuality, for that is contradictory), then the zero of mind would be the zero of the presence or manifestation of God. Leibniz was among the first in the West to see that this contradicts theism, but some of the Hindus, Chinese, and Japanese saw it in a vaguer fashion long before.

I find in this antimaterialistic implication of theism a confirmation of its correctness. For by what criterion that will survive analysis can one distinguish the zero of mind (and hence, of the presence of God) from the zero of reality (See Chapters 5,

THE LOGIC OF PERFECTION

8, 13). Descartes proposed a clear-cut honest criterion, "extension." But since he did not show, and no one can show, that mind is in every aspect inextended, the criterion fails. Other criteria differ by being less clear and forthright. It is for this reason that I am unimpressed by the fashionable notion that mind has emerged from mere matter. First show me the mere matter.

I also question if "emergence" as here used has any legitimate meaning. It is not that particular qualities, including qualities of feeling and thinking, cannot emerge unpredictably, or be created. But since any quality, to be known, must become a quality of experience in some form, sensory or affective, mind as such cannot be a mere species of quality; rather, it is the universal correlate of quality, and of quantity as well. It follows that the analogy between any known instance of emergence and the alleged emergence of mind is tenuous in the extreme. Let us take, for example, the emergence of life from lifeless matter. Unless we assume that the lifeless means the mindless, which is the question at issue, all we have to go on here is that out of certain relatively simple physical structures more subtle and complex structures arise. Spatio-temporal configurations alone are involved in the known or non-controversial aspects of the occurrence. In what way is this like the appearance of whole new categories of awareness, feeling, desire, and the like? Starting with the notions of structure and of process as involving an essential aspect of creativity or novelty, we can predict that new structures will keep arising, the novelty varying in degree or extent. However, that something which is not merely spatio-temporal configuration, but the enjoyment, awareness, of configuration, should arise, this is on the premises not only unpredictable, it cannot even be stated without introducing a whole new language, and indeed, without introducing language itself, as entirely new and unpredictable.

Many will say, you forget that mind has been shown to be simply structure and behavior; hence the emergence of mind is merely the appearance of somewhat new modes of behavior.

Here is a nice dilemma. If mind is just behavior, then there is no emergence of mind from mere matter, there is only mere matter, though sometimes it is more complex, and moves about and transforms its shapes in especially elaborate and intricate ways. This is one horn of the dilemma: mind really vanishes from the problem, and so does its alleged explanation. There is nothing to explain — except mere matter, which three thousand years have felt to be a riddle, and most physicists still, I suspect, take to be one. The other horn of the dilemma is, mind is not merely behavior; but then there is simply no analogy at all between its alleged emergence and any established case. The known cases involve either forms of behavior arising from other forms, or forms of experience arising from other forms, as in the development of each individual as he is himself aware of this development. Before we can talk scientifically about experience arising from mere material stuff or process, devoid of experience, we must be able to specify the sort of observations which would falsify the statement, "mind or experience in some form is everywhere." For millenia many have believed this proposition; what scientist has any notion of the factual test by which it could be falsified?

That the human type of mind is everywhere is indeed open to factual falsification. Certainly birds do not think or feel just as men do, still less, by all analogy, frogs or amoebae, a fortiori, not molecules. But that they neither think nor feel in any way whatever, complex or simple — what intellectual content does this have? It is an infinite negative which even infinite observation might still not suffice to justify. For an infinity of forms of conceivable feeling might be absent, and yet feeling might be present. Simple infinity is not enough to exhaust the possibilities of feeling and thinking.

If the absence of X in a situation S is not to be established, then neither is its emergence in S. We must content ourselves with the emergence of species of mind, not of mind as such.

Similar remarks apply to creative freedom. Specific forms of freedom, such as the human, emerge, but creativity as such cannot significantly be so thought of. And the effort to think it is anti-theistic; for since God is conceived of as infinite creative capacity, the zero of this capacity which determinism posits must be the zero of the manifestation or presence of God. Again, by no criterion can this zero be distinguished from the zero of reality itself. (See Chapters 6, 8.) Physics has been coming closer and closer to the realization of this point, which in itself, however, is logical. The logic was first laid bare by philosophers, e.g., Boutroux and Peirce.

Theism is not an adjunct to a world view; fully thought out, it is the most coherent of all explicit world views. To make it incoherent, as dualistic or deterministic systems have done, is an unwitting betrayal. The intellectual and spiritual demands of our time cannot be met in this way. God, if anywhere, must be everywhere, nothing must be the mere opposite of God. If the least particle is "wholly other" than God, then "God" is nonsense. For the word means that nothing could possibly be other than a form of the presence of infinitely creative mind.

I shall give one more example of what this means. Not only does theism exclude even the logical possibility of a zero case of mind or creative freedom, but it excludes the zero case of participation of mind in other mind or, in the broadest sense, "love." God is infinite love; the zero case of love could only be the total absence of deity. Once more, no criterion is available for such an absolute negation. No animal is absolutely non-social, without indications of sympathy. And nothing could conceivably tell us that an atom has *no* feeling for the feelings in its particles, or in another atom to whose presence it responds. To retort, as some would, "but no criterion could tell us that the atom does feel," in the sympathetic or participatory way in question, is open to three objections:

(1) To detect positively and definitely the faintest traces of feeling is a task for unlimited mind, not for such as ours.

(2) Wherever experience is most vivid and clear, careful observation reveals that it has feeling, not an insentient something, as its datum. A toothache, or the memory of an emotional experience in the nearest past, are only the most obvious examples. We can know cases of "feeling of feeling"; in order to know cases of feeling (or experiencing) mere non-feeling, we must have absolute introspective clarity, and this would be superhuman. The positive, not the absolutely negative, is alone accessible to us.

(3) God could detect the least traces of feeling; whereas the notion of God detecting the sheer absence of feeling in a positive reality would mean that God could know something absolutely without loving it, and this conflicts with the idea, implicit in all theism, that universal love of the creatures is His very essence.

Sooner or later, I believe, theists must acquire the courage of their conviction. They must reject all anti-theistic theories of matter and mind, and take the consequences. Then men will begin to see that the recognition of God is not a mere verbalism, or a mere sentimental glow. They will also begin to see that God in His abstract essence is not one more thing, but the reality by which all things whatsoever, actual and possible, are in principle intelligible and also, in the larger context and in some way, beautiful.

The secret of all intellectual advance, overlooked or reduced to triviality in many theories of science, is the drive to uncover the hidden beauty of the universe. The greater the scientist, the more likely he is to feel this. Theism is the hidden principle of all these hidden beauties, a principle not necessarily so very hidden, after all. How hidden it is depends in part upon philosophy and theology, aided no doubt by the inspiring discoveries of science, which keep showing us how much grander the real universe is than even our most hopeful dreams.

"A world in which all things show the presence of freedom and love" may seem too pretty to be true; but since freedom is the source of risk as well as of opportunity, "pretty" is scarcely the word. "Sublimely beautiful" is more appropriate. And what in intellectual history justifies us in expecting the truth to be as tame as our market-place common sense? From that standpoint, the astronomer and physicist are stark mad. What, the moon falling perpetually toward the earth, like an apple, and the earth toward the sun! Billions of tiny animals making up the human body! Atoms in an "excited state"! Matter created and destroyed!

Perhaps there is no very radical difference between the man who says that to attribute feeling to inanimate nature "is to attribute human traits to the sub-human," and the man who says, But surely the earth is not like a falling apple, or surely solid matter is not full of waves and motions swifter than sound, or surely if a paramœcium is an animal it must have eyes and ears like a rabbit, or surely a bird cannot feel "territorially" possessive. (An ornithologist objected to the use of this term because birds have no legal concept of ownership.) At what point does the refusal to generalize concepts "rashly" or beyond good sense become merely the inability or refusal to generalize — period?

You may reply, it is the point beyond which no further predictive power is achieved. Yet metaphysical universals by very definition and intention are not predictive. And does any prediction follow from, "There are (or at least logically could be) parts of nature which neither as wholes nor in their parts have feeling"? Dualistic or materialistic metaphysics in this sense makes no testable prediction either. So why assert it? For, in addition to predicting nothing, it lacks conceptual unity, since it puts together two kinds of physical thing, and covers the duality with the idle phrase, "emergent quality." No explanation is or can be given as to why mere matter should produce mind, or why mind needs mere matter. (The need cannot be in order to have objects, since experiences can be and are objects for other experiences, e.g., in memory; and since abstractions, such as numbers, or the idea of "object," can also be objects.) The psychicalist, on the other hand, can explain all known facts about the empirical world so far as anyone can, and explain them economically by a single principle, love or creative participation as capable of many degrees and kinds. He has the same predictive power, and by far the greater conceptual clarity and beauty.

The theist has something more; he has the key to facts and the key to values in a single idea, since participation, i.e., love, is traditionally recognized as in some manner the supreme ethical standard. To find the key to facts and values in the same principle is, I submit, an intellectual achievement than which none could be greater. In this respect, what rival could theism have? Its serious rivals are the pseudo-theisms, the idols to which the name of God, or the attitude of worship, has, with insufficient caution, been attached.

Here is a reason for "theological rancor." We theists can scarcely doubt that the primary theoretical enemy is in our own ranks. As Blake put it, once for all, "Your vision is my vision's dearest enemy." Where else could the enemy be found? Among the communists? Not if it is an essentially theoretical enemy we are speaking of. Let communists cease appealing, like the Popes of old, to force or material power to settle theoretical and spiritual questions, and we shall see whether they can stand on their own feet intellectually. In mere skepticism? It is belief which drives the world. Science itself is faith in the inexhaustible beauty of truth. Who but the theist has the key to that beauty?

Lest this advantage go to his head, the theist should be reminded that it profits him little to know that theism is the key to the world's beauty unless he can be sure that he has the key to theism itself. An ugly, illogical mess, which is what many theists as well as atheists see in the views of various other theists, is not, for practical purposes, the key to much of anything. We must, with patience and good humor, submit the possible forms of theism to every test that seems relevant, and try to face honestly the indications that some of these formulations, including certain much venerated ones, fail to pass them. Meantime all theists should mitigate their rancor, partly by bearing in mind that life is much more than theory, and that the man who says Lord, Lord, like the man who never says Lord, or whatever we think the right word is, may or may not be serving the Lord's cause; partly also by taking into account the verbal elements in all controversy and the open question how far human language and mental operations are capable of achieving simply right results in fundamental matters; finally by applying the injunction to love one's neighbor as oneself even to theologians and philosophers.

But what of the view that a certain Church is infallibly right in religious matters? I find this a most puzzling claim. For the doctrine of infallibility is either a theory, and then like any theory it can be doubted, and can hardly be proved by infallible reasoning to be correct, or it is itself a mere pronouncement by the authority said to be infallible. But by what infallible method does one choose the authority, or even know that there is one? I have never been able to see how, by a rational argument that God might be expected to furnish us with a strictly reliable guide to His existence and nature, and another argument supporting a certain choice as to which of the claimants to this role is the true guide, we could have more than at best a fallible knowledge that the said guide is infallible. Or do we have an infallible intuition to this effect? And do we infallibly intuit that we have this infallible intuition? Perhaps I am merely confused in all this, perhaps there is some way through this labyrinth. But to me it seems more reasonable to accept human fallibility as covering all human institutions whatsoever.

If anything important is infallibly known, I should think it is the appropriateness of love, or the transcendence of mere selfishness, as the ideal of action. In this, I do have almost the sense that we could not be mistaken. And for me it is no long step from this to the acceptance of belief in divine love. But I have to admit that short as the step is, it is strangely barred by the most amazing entanglements of historical doctrine and controversy. The history of theology is something I could never have imagined; it is indeed "a world I never made." But the history of atheism is also strange, especially in its recent chapters. That is the odd sort of creatures we are — at least, to one another.

If, according to a consequent theism, all reality must exhibit the presence of deity, this applies also to language as a reality.[1] One way in which language can exhibit deity is by having implicit or explicit rules which validate Anselm's Principle, the necessity of the divine existence. Any language whose rules do this may be termed pious in principle; a language which treats all existence as contingent is impious in principle. For, as Findlay showed, if it needed showing (and apparently it did, since the truth is not even yet taken into account in the literature): to deny Anselm's Principle is to deny the logical possibility of God's existence. Thus there can be no religiously neutral language, except through vagueness in the rules of existential assertion. Our official philosophical language, in spite of its pretended neutrality, has been so taken as to be almost overtly impious, in seeming to imply the contingency of all existence. The move next in order is to face the decision more consciously and squarely, should it or should it not be so?

I believe it to be to the advantage of theism that this austere alternative should be dealt with as honestly as possible. I have enough faith in the wisdom of belief to think that the sharper we make the implications of worship, the better it will be for the future of religion and of mankind. The theistic question — it seems necessary to say it again and again — is not one more question, even the most important one. It is, on the fundamental level, and when all its implications are taken into account, the sole question. Linguistic analysis which fails to grasp this is not, whatever else it may be, analysis of the basic metaphysical idea. Whether and how we conceive the God of worship, in His

[1] Ian T. Ramsey, in *Religious Language* (London: SCM Press, 1957), pp. 59–60, says that "the word God presides over the rest of language."

necessary, eternal aspect, this is all that is left when empirical accidents of the world, including language as accidental, are set aside. Philosophy as a non-empirical study has no other subject-matter. Here Comte and Anselm come into a strange agreement.

If philosophy is not the rational element in religion, then it is an assortment of implicitly independent specialties (logic, linguistics, history of ideas, theory of fine arts, etc.). Or it is the cultivation, by more or less rational methods, of the theoretical side of the art of living. But living for what? Be the aim Nirvana, the Classless Society, the Welfare State, Self-realization, the query is never silenced, what good is it, from the cosmic and everlasting perspective, that one or other or all of these aims be attained for a time on this ball of rock? (And if one does not view the matter from the wide perspective, why raise the theoretical question at all; does reason accept such limitations upon its own scope?)

Only through a relationship to the Everlasting Itself, it seems evident, can the query concerning the aim of life have an answer which avoids giving rise to a still more ultimate query.

CHAPTER FOUR

Three Strata of Meaning in Religious Discourse[1]

"Primary words do not stand for things, but they intimate rela-tions. . . . Men wish to regard a feeling (called feeling of de-pendence . . . more precisely, creaturely feeling) as the real element in the relation with God. . . . Yes; in pure relation you have felt yourself to be simply dependent . . . and simply free, too, . . . both creaturely and creative. . . . We take part in creation. . . .

The man who prays . . . knows that he has—in an incom-prehensible way—an effect upon God, even though he obtains nothing from God. . . . And the man who makes sacrifices? I cannot despise him, this upright servant of former times, who believed that God yearned for the scent of his burnt-offering. In a foolish but powerful way he knew that we can and ought to give to God. This is known by him, too, who offers up his little will to God and meets Him in the grand will. 'Thy will be done,' he says, and says no more: but truth adds for him 'through me whom thou needest.' . . . Magic desires to obtain its effects without entering into relation. . . . But sacrifice and prayer are set 'before the Face,' in the consummation of the holy primary

[1] The first half of this essay appeared originally in *The Southern Philos-opher*, III (1956).

word that means mutual action: they speak of Thou, and then they hear." M. Buber, in *I and Thou*, trans. R. G. Smith, Pp. 3, 81, 83.

A common doctrine is that religious statements are not meant "literally," but "symbolically." Descriptions of God, for example, are held to use words in unusual ways whose meaning is not obvious from their ordinary use or meaning. I wish to argue that two kinds of predicates are applied to God, and while those of one kind are symbolic, those of the other are not. We need to distinguish between formal and material predications. To compare deity with a rock, a king, a shepherd, or a parent is a material description, that is, one in terms of a concrete species of entity, a particular part of the psycho-physical universe. Such predications are not literal, for God is not just another ruler, together with human kings, or another parent together with human parents.

But there is a radically different sort of predication concerning deity, in which no one part of the universe more than any other is involved in the comparison. Rather, in such predications, deity is compared to any concrete being you please other than Himself. This non-material mode is illustrated when one speaks of such negative properties of God as "non-corporeal," "non-temporal," "non-relative," and so on. Here no material difference between rock and man, or rock and sand, or one man and another, comes in, but only purely abstract and general philosophical categories, such as space, time, becoming, relation.

I wish now to emphasize my conviction that the formal predicates of deity are not exclusively negative, and accordingly, some positive properties of deity can be connoted by non-symbolic designations.[2] I have spent, and I hope not wasted, much of my

[2] An ingenious attempt to rescue the negative theology by modern linguistic interpretations is given by Ramsey, in the work already referred to (see footnote to p. 31). I think he is very kind to this tradition, and I hope

life exploring the positive formal characterizations which seem compatible with the religious meaning of the term "God." This religious meaning is well indicated by the phrase, "supremely worshipful." If one is conditioned by early training to react negatively to certain words, like relativity or contingency, then of course one cannot worship God and also call Him, in any respect, relative or contingent. But this negative evaluation of relativity and contingency seems to me a confusion. Is the relative or the contingent as such essentially bad or mediocre? On the contrary, all the beauty of the actual world seems to consist in its relationships and its contingencies. A "good" man is not, compared to a bad or inferior one, any less relative or contingent; but rather, he is more adequately related to other things and richer and more harmonious in his accidental qualities.

To be sure, it is not good to be too dependent upon, or relative to, any *one* aspect or part of the total environment, or too sensitive to merely momentary changes. But such excess of sensitivity consists in an imbalance between our response to some things and persons and our response to the remaining things and persons. The wise and strong respond to each stimulus for what it is worth, in comparison with other available stimuli; they do not fall on this man's neck and then turn coldly away from some other who has as much or more to offer, or whose claims for attention are quite as legitimate. Also, the wise person balances the stimuli of the moment against the background of past stimuli and past decisions of his own, and against the ultimate ideals of life. Balanced appropriateness in one's relativity to other things or persons, not non-relativity, is the mark of wisdom and goodness. The non-relative or merely inflexible person, who will not be influenced, who will not or cannot adjust to the actual situation sensitively and quickly, need not be especially admired. Yet according to many metaphysicians and theologians, from the

he is prepared to be as kind or kinder to the neoclassical technique, even though it is a less conspicuous strand through the centuries. See *Religious Language*, Ch. 2.

Stoics and Philo down to our time, such inflexible persons ought, it seems, to be deeply revered.

There is another confusion we need to clear away. This is the failure to distinguish between relativity, or dependence, with respect to an individual's existence or personal identity and dependence merely with respect to the concrete state or experience of the individual, granted that "he" exists as that very individual. For instance, one does not depend for being, and for being oneself, upon any particular state of the weather, though one does depend upon it for some of the details of one's experiences, assuming that one goes out, or looks out of the window, or even hears a weather report. To depend for very existence, or individual identity, upon changeable factors is indeed a mark of mediocrity; and no being so characterized could properly be worshipped. A sufficiently radical change in the weather would destroy your personal existence or mine; and this is one mark of our not being truly worshipful. But in simple logic there are two ways, and not one way only, of conceiving independence with respect to existing-as-oneself.

The usual way, on which classical theism wagered everything, is to suppose the existentially independent to have no need to adjust to changes, to be indifferent or neutral to them all. But there is another way. This is to identify existential independence with an invincible power and will to achieve self-consistent adjustment to any changes whatever. We human beings adjust successfully to a wide range of diversities, but there comes a point beyond which we cannot achieve adjustment, and accordingly, we lose consciousness, or sanity, or life itself. Is there any rule of logic telling us that the mere idea of "adjustment" means the possibility of failure? By that principle, the mere idea of "existing" should imply the possibility of failing to exist, and then God could not exist unless contingently. Since nearly all theologians have held that God's very existence cannot be contingent, we face the question, is His necessary existence or absoluteness to be conceived as an infallible power to harmonize relativities in Himself, to respond coherently to diverse stimuli, or simply as the absence of relativity, of power to respond to other beings? This dilemma, I hold is between literal alternatives. No concrete difference among things is in question, only the categorial difference between the contingency of the proposition asserting your existence or mine (or an elephant's), and two categorially or formally opposite ways of interpreting the necessary truth of the proposition, "divinity exists" (or, if you prefer, is real). In either interpretation such necessary existential truth is as literally necessary as contingent existential truth is contingent. Nor is it merely negative; for necessary truth is definable as the common factor in all possible truths. All-pervasiveness with respect to the possible *is* necessity. And the very idea of God as creator implies that not only was this world so much as possible solely because of the creative power which produced it, but also "other worlds" were or are possible only in that the same power would have been, or would be, adequate for their production. The divine power is thus conceived as, by definition, all-pervasive with respect to possibility. To be possible is to be a possible-creature-of-the-creator. Accordingly, the creator, as such, is constituent in every possibility.

I am not saying (with some proponents of the Ontological Argument) that the divine existence must forthwith be conceded, since it is necessary; that would be going too fast; I am saying rather: *either* the divine existence must be conceded, *or* we must reject the conception of God as meaningless or absurd. For what it cannot connote is an unactualized potentiality of existence; since its very meaning is that all power or potency is derivative from divine power taken as real. This is both compatible with and implies the contingency of ordinary existence to which Anselm's critics so irrelevantly and monotonously point!

Are such general categories as "Existence" symbolic or literal?

THE LOGIC OF PERFECTION

Philosophers certainly construe them in different ways, and thus their meaning is not to be made ostensively obvious in the same fashion as the meaning of "rock" or "king." But neither are such concepts, when applied to God, symbolic in the sense in which "divine shepherd" is symbolic. For "necessary existence" takes no account, in its meaning, of the difference between one non-divine thing and another. Rather the contrast, necessary-contingent, sets up a dichotomy between God and everything else. True enough, necessary existence is a different kind of existence from contingent existence — Anselm's great discovery, widely misunderstood — but can anyone understand "contingent existence" and not know what the contrasting term is? The two sides of such a contrast seem inseparable. It is quite different with true "symbols." The sense in which God is "ruler" is not categorially definable, even by negation, since "divine ruler" assumes the idea of God, and "superhuman ruler" is insufficient. "Ruler of all things" is more helpful, since here we do use the category of totality, but it still does not tell us what *kind* of rule can apply to all things. Necessary existence, however, is literally definable, for it must mean *either* non-capacity for contingent properties *or* (as I hold) an invincible capacity to achieve, a certainty of possessing, some contingent property expressing the identity of the being — regardless of what other beings exist or fail to exist. Here there is nothing material, and so nothing symbolic.

I should now like to point a moral. The denial that divine predicates can be both positive and literal (e.g., "common element of all possibilities," or "relative to all things") has derived from a misconception, not simply of God, but, implicitly, of the creatures. God must, it is thought, be non-relative, because relativity is bad, which implies that when we compare creatures as good rather than bad we compare them with respect to the number of things they escape being relative to. But this is contrary to what we really do in evaluating creatures. I believe that every basic error in theology similarly reflects a correspond-

138

ing error in the conception of the creatures. If we have (un-wittingly) a non-literal, i.e., vague, ambiguous, inconsistent, notion of creaturely "existence," "dependence," "relativity," or "better" and "worse," then we cannot arrive at positive literal ideas about the divine existence, independence, absoluteness, or goodness. But if we are literally correct about the creatures, per-haps we can be so about certain formal, positive attributes of deity.

If God is formally describable as ideally and infallibly relative, rather than as simply non-relative, then the contradictions to which many writers point, between the formal properties of God and the non-formal ones, do not obtain. He can be loving, in the sense of adequately sensitive to the needs of others, rather than (self-contradictorily) both responsive to their needs and wholly devoid of intrinsic relatedness to them. The dogmatic refusal to consider positive formal properties of God has saddled theology with the impossibility of making even decent symbolic sense out of such religious terms as love or purpose, all implying relativity, without covertly abandoning the formal negations. Admittedly, the divine sensitivity is not just one more case of sympathetic response to need; yet that which distinguishes it from the human form is not to be found in the direction of sheer insensitiveness, mere neutrality or non-relativity. Atoms are much less variously and richly sensitive, less relative, more "ab-solute," than men. Is not the divine sensitivity inconceivable to us because of the richness of the divine relationships to the crea-tures (not simply between persons of the Trinity!) and their balanced integration into one life, rather than because of com-plete poverty in such relatednesses? Again, is not God incom-parably complex in His total reality, rather than incomparably "simple?"

Besides obviously formal and obviously material ideas about God we have descriptions whose classification depends partly upon one's philosophical beliefs. To say that God has awareness,

THE LOGIC OF PERFECTION

feeling, memory, sympathy seems to be a material statement, for do not some rather than all creatures have these qualities? Yet, according to panpsychism, psychical concepts are categorial, universal in scope. However, even so they must be different from the purely formal concepts, for example, contingency, which has a single literal meaning applicable to all cases, the meaning of excluding some positive possibilities. But in what sense, for instance, is "feeling" of a frog the same thing as "feeling" of a man? Here there seem to be innumerable differences of degree, and of specific kind. Frog feeling is "analogous" to human feeling, rather than the same. Much more, then, is divine feeling merely analogous to creaturely feeling. I think here the old term "analogical" is best, rather than "symbolic." God is symbolically ruler, but analogically conscious and loving, and literally both absolute (or necessary) in existence and relative (or contingent) in actuality — that is, in the concrete modes of His existence. True, His relativity is not the same in scope as ours, for He is relative to all things, and we are relative only to some. But the point is, that "all" and "some" have here their literal logical senses; whereas who can say literally how divine love differs qualitatively from ours? Quantitatively, yes, for He loves all creatures, we love only some. But how does He love them? Here we have no literal grasp, for we cannot love anything as God loves each and every creature.

There is another way of showing that the analogical concepts differ from the literal, on the one hand, and the formal on the other. Contingency and relativity apply not only to individuals but to groups of individuals, and not only to concrete, but also to more or less abstract entities. Only the completely abstract is non-contingent or absolute, everything less abstract is contingent and relative; but in order to feel or remember, an entity must be quite concrete, as well as singular. Groups do not feel, except in so far as their members do, but whatever existence they have is contingent and relative, like that of their members. Similarly, abstract common qualities of specific groups do not feel; but they exist contingently. Thus, even assuming panpsychism, the most general psychical terms, though universally applicable to concrete singulars, and in this sense categorial, are not purely formal in the same sense as the other categorial terms. To apply them to things, one must know on what level of concreteness the things are.

And yet there is a strange sense in which the analogical concepts apply literally to deity, and analogically to creatures. We say that human beings "know" various things, but then we have to qualify by adding that this does not mean the possession of such evidence as to make mistakes impossible. What then does it mean? The entertaining of beliefs which by mere good luck happen to be correct? This is an odd meaning for "know." So we must mean that men have evidence, falling short of absolute proof, that certain beliefs are true. But how far short of conclusiveness can the evidence be, and still entitle the beliefs to be termed "knowledge"? We see that the term "know" in the human case turns out to have a rather indefinite meaning. In the divine case, the matter is simple: God, as infallible, has absolutely conclusive evidence concerning all truths, so that if knowledge is possession of perfect evidence as to the state of affairs, then God simply knows — period. No such plain definition will work for human knowledge. In this sense, it is the theistic use only of psychical conceptions which has literal meaning, a meaning from which all other meanings are derived by qualification, diminution, or negation. So, instead of the old "negative theology," one might propose a new "negative anthropology."

It is the same with love. If this means such things as appreciating the qualities of others, caring about their weal and woe, wishing them well, or what you will, then either one has to admit that in no case of human love is it simply true that one does these things, or one must leave their meaning extremely vague. A human being appreciates the qualities of this or that other person—except the qualities he does not appreciate, through some limitation of his own; he cares about the other's weal or woe, with similar exceptions; he wishes him well—except so far as (perhaps unconsciously) he has impulses to wish him harm, whether from envy, rivalry, fear, or what not. But God appreciates the qualities of all things—period. There is no envy, rivalry, fear. He wishes all creatures well—period. He cares about their weal and woe—there is no material qualification or negation. That God cares about "all" is purely formal, and positive. True, God "cannot" wish the weal of one while disregarding (as, to a greater or lesser extent we always do) the woe of others; for no woe is ever merely indifferent to God. (But this is a double negative—he cannot not regard—and so it is positive.) There may be those who think otherwise, who suppose that God can wish well to the sick child in such fashion as literally not to care about the woes of bacteria causing the sickness. But such persons, in my opinion, are thinking anthropomorphically about God, who must always relate Himself to absolutely all creatures. This is often forgotten, but it is a formal requirement of the idea of deity.

It is obvious enough, but widely overlooked, that if we allocate to ourselves divine properties, such as literal, simple knowing or loving, then in so far we have nothing left with which to characterize deity. Could this be part of the secret of the "negative theology?" We say, for example, that "memory" is unworthy to be attributed to deity, "forgetting" how infinitesimal is our remembering compared to our forgetting. To remember is "to be aware of the past"—who but God could literally be so? We are aware (with any degree of clarity) of but tiny scraps of the past, and these are constantly coming and going, into and out of our consciousness. God, however, is aware of the past, *simpliciter*. He remembers—period. No mere creature can do anything of the sort.

Again, we say that it is not enough for God to be everlasting,

He must be simply devoid of becoming altogether. And one reason we think so is that we have blithely attributed everlastingness to ourselves, at least as a possibility, without really facing the question of whether or not such an absolute property as infinite duration is appropriate to creatures so limited in every other respect. And even those who do not regard themselves individually as immortal are likely, consciously or not, to take it for granted that at least our species is immortal, again without serious consideration of the reasonableness of this belief. We shall never see clearly what "God" means until we see how problematic if not absurd are all such ascriptions of infinity to ourselves. Man endures for a while; God endures.

There is an opposite way of so conceiving the creatures that God becomes inconceivable: that of denying to man, or some of the creatures, even a bare minimum of excellence under some category. Thus we may say that all human love is really pure selfishness, there is no such thing as love; and so the way is barred that should lead to the idea of divine love. Again if we say with Hume and his countless followers that there is no intrinsic connection between any state of experience and any other before or after it, or that causality is merely the fact that this follows that, then the idea of God causally affecting all things would merely mean that what goes on in the world happens to be what God thinks, or resolves, should go on. There is no rational way to God if we have denied even the inferior version of causal power which is all that, in the creatures, could represent the divine power. If, on the other hand, we exaggerate causal influence by making it mean absolute determination of effects, including volitions, then too we have deprived ourselves of any analogical basis for the idea of the creative power of God. We should have to put some cause behind the supreme volition and hold that this supercause absolutely determined the divine action, so that precisely this world had to be created. And then all evil must be good, since it proceeds necessarily from the divine perfection. The way to avoid this difficulty is to admit that action always has some leeway, in spite of causality, or because of the proper meaning of "cause." It is then consistent to ascribe supreme leeway or scope to the divine creativity.

In the foregoing discussion I am indebted to a lecture by Paul Tillich. But I think also that his own procedure illustrates how true it is that a correct view of the creatures and of the supreme creator-creature must develop together. Tillich denies that contingency and novelty can apply literally to God. Yet he rightly holds that God must be all-inclusive. If then the creatures are literally contingent, there must be divine constituents which are literally contingent. But in truth Tillich never reaches a clear notion of the root of contingency in creativity; he speaks sometimes quite like an Augustinian determinist. He never clearly envisages the issue between classical and neoclassical views, whether of God or of the creatures. And the idea of a God who responds lovingly to the world is lost in the indifferent absoluteness of "unconditioned" being. I think Whitehead's God is closer to Christianity than this.

If the position I have been taking is correct, the desire of the best men for clear knowledge about themselves cannot be satisfied without facilitating the attainment of what some of them do not consciously desire, clear knowledge about God. If it could be satisfied save on this condition, then atheism would be in a very strong position. But history is strewn with misconceptions of man serving as barriers to an intelligible conception of deity. The present scene is still strewn with them. Communism is one example; it is very shrewd in some respects in its anthropology, and very blind in other ways, and its blindness here is closely connected with its blindness concerning God. It tends to worship national power as a quasi-deity, confused more or less with party and Marxian dogma, and it cannot face honestly and with rational modesty the limitations of human nature which characterize the nation, the party, the dogma. It faces individual death bravely, but never mentions collective death. Yet what meaning would remain to the whole enterprise in that event? Its dialectical notion of cosmic history is a confused version of providence, as often remarked; its theory of historical determinism is a confused compromise between the dream of absolute cosmic regularity and the admission of human creativity. And so on. But all these mistakes in slightly different form are older than Marxism, and some of them are found in theological traditions also. We have pretty much all been at fault in confusing the issue of theism. History is still young. If we collectively survive the atomic phase, we may yet do far better.

In one respect communist theory is closer to true piety as I understand it than are the ideas of many well-meaning Christians. The communists do realize that ultimately the individual is contributory to what is beyond himself: that his fulfillment is in serving, for a time, an enduring Cause. The Cause is misconceived, but at least it is not Self. Unless we make haste and learn this lesson, a partial moral, and in a sense religious, superiority will continue to give the communists their dangerously great appeal. God cannot be "seen" steadily, and without confusion with self, by those of us who, however subtly and innocently, accept for ourselves roles which are proper to God — for instance the role of being finally recipient of values, rather than, finally, ourselves contributory to the treasury of achieved goods. To say to God, "I shall serve Thee forever — on condition that Thou serve me forever"! is that really so pious?

Individualism has a noble side and an ugly side. In our tradition the two sides have never been adequately distinguished. We are in great danger partly for that very reason. Individualism is right in holding that a person is not a mere means to a collectivity, for this has no realization of value save in its members; moreover, all creation of value is individual, and the uniqueness of each individual is his central value, his most basic contribution to the greater Cause. But it does not follow that he makes this contribution by enjoying infinite duration in some transcendental community. For in that case, he contributes forever and above all to himself. And then "enlightened self-interest" is given transcendental justification. Is it any wonder that sacrifice in the national safety seems hard to elicit just now? We have too much of the feeling, all things ought to serve Me. Ought they? They ought to serve the Supreme, who serves each and all to be sure, but in their time and place. He, however, is to be served evermore. Or, He is to be served.

The individual is demeaned if he serves only a collectivity, which is not even a definite consciousness, and does not begin to know him in his concreteness. But he is not degraded if by promoting the welfare of the collectivity he serves God, who is conscious and knows us all. To clear the way to the idea of God we need to get rid of all rivals to Him as the ultimate recipient of the fruits of our labors. In our brief time, of course, we do receive such fruits, the privileges of living for the highest and sanest of all ideals; but God receives the fruits both in our time and everlastingly. This is His privilege. How can this be understood if we have put ourselves in His place?

It is also unlikely that we shall effectively "see God" if we refuse to make any effort to look upon our neighbors as we look upon ourselves, that is, in terms of needs, capacities, thoughts, and feelings. The crass materialism which many of us betray by evaluating other people, not in terms of what they feel, think, and do, but almost exclusively in terms of some external marks of color, bones, hair, sex, wealth, or the physical location of some of their ancestors, is hardly calculated to make the divine perspective upon the world intelligible. We have scarcely begun to see the infinite implications of loving the other "as oneself." In some ways the Buddhists have seen this more clearly than Christians.

It comes to this: the inaccessibility of God to the rational mind upon which atheists and many theologians so nearly agree is correlative to the inaccessibility of our own natures, hidden beneath self-serving illusions about them. Piety may be more than modesty concerning our human estate, but it can scarcely be less than that. Have we not tried to make it less, in our very theologies and philosophies? The question at least deserves scrutiny.

But so does the correlative question: do we honor deity by denying to ourselves and the creatures generally even the most modest analogon to the divine attributes — for instance, some genuine, however humble, capacity of creation, some little leap beyond the causally inevitable, or some little simulacrum of the divine participation in the lives of all, some slight measure of sympathy or love? If God is all in all, in some sense everything, we must be something of this everything, not bare nothing. We have no divine attribute in its fullness or infinity, but yet we are not zero in comparison to any attribute.

An all too negative theology made God the great emptiness, and an all too negative anthropology made the creatures also empty. I suggest that nothing is only nothing, that the divine attributes are positive, and the creatures' qualities are between these and nothing.

CHAPTER FIVE

Two Views of the Logic of Theism

(Criticism of John Wisdom on "Gods")

I N HIS essay on "Gods,"[1] Professor Wisdom contends that the affirmation, "There is a God," is not, in our time, intended as an experimental statement. It does not predict observable facts — apart perhaps from facts about a future life, which are confessedly left out of the discussion. The question of divine existence is also said to be something like the questions: Granting all the facts of X's behavior, can he be said to have exercised reasonable care? Do flowers feel? Is this picture beautiful? Is this house haunted? Is the garden tended by an always invisible gardener? To believe in God, it is further suggested, is to have "feelings of awe before power, dread of the thunderbolts of Zeus . . . feelings of guilt and of inescapable vengeance, of smothered hate and of a security we can hardly do without."[2]

How close is this to the meaning or logic of theistic statements? According to much careful thought in modern philosophy and theology (a list of names would be long, beginning, say with Socinus and coming down to Whitehead and some other

[1] In *Philosophy and Psychoanalysis* (New York: Philosophical Library, 1953), pp. 149–168). Also *Proceedings of the Aristotelian Society*, 1944.
[2] *Ibid.*, pp. 164–165.

recent authors [3]), "God," not in any extraordinary sense, but as the term occurs in ordinary piety, refers to a being conceived as having two aspects: an abstract, eternal nature which is strictly necessary, and a total concrete, *de facto* actuality, containing both the eternal nature and successive accidental qualities. To illustrate: according to this doctrine, the two statements, "God is all-knowing," and "God knows that Analysis, as actually practised, is inadequate," represent two logically different classes of statements, and the referent of "God" in the two cases is not simply identical. The second, but not the first, refers to deity as possessing a certain contingent predicate, inasmuch as there might have been no such thing as "Analysis," and then God would not have known it (as something "actually practised"). He would, nevertheless, and in any possible case, have been all-knowing; and thus the first statement above is necessary, not contingent. For, and here we come to the technical point which Wisdom, as I think, misses: theists, whether or no they have made the distinction just explained, have almost unanimously viewed God as, in His eternal essence (which includes the attribute of omniscience), existing necessarily, as *ens necessarium*.

"Necessary" means, without alternative possibility; "existing necessarily" means, without possibility of non-existence. In spite of Kant, there is no hopelessly baffling mystery about this. The divine power is conceived, even in ordinary piety, as constitutive of possibility itself — this being the meaning of "creator of all things" — and there can be no such entity as the possibility that there might not be possibility. Even the theologians who have rejected the ontological argument have implicitly or explicitly admitted that though we may not be able to use the divine necessity as ground for our belief, God Himself is to be conceived as knowing Himself to exist necessarily.

Professor Wisdom may think that any conception of "neces-

[3] For illustrative passages from many of these, see C. Hartshorne and W. L. Reese, *Philosophers Speak of God*, Ch. VII; also Introduction.

sary existence" is nonsense, but to ignore it is to beg, or fail to understand, the theistic question, which concerns the status of an allegedly necessary and yet existential truth. How can such a claim be evaluated?

The claim poses no question of "fact" (in the convenient sense of contingent truth), therefore not of anything like, "He exercised reasonable care." The only possible rational evidence must come from category-analysis. This, I think, was the intent (somewhat obscured) of the old theistic proofs, which our author dismisses as "medieval." [4] In their old forms, they will scarcely do, but in principle they still are the issue, which is not to be decided on a mere ground of dates or of fashion. If the categories, the essential or most universal ideas, are fully intelligible when interpreted non-theistically, then indeed "God" is philosophically meaningless, or contradictory. But are they?

Consider, for example, the question of "matter," which Wisdom is fond of discussing. Apart from theism, we may choose among the following: matter is a surd to all experience, with properties which no experience, however constituted and interrelated, can have; matter is "permanent possibility" of human experience; or finally, the "panpsychist" theory, matter is experience on various subhuman levels. The first of these views makes matter an unknown X; the second is a monstrous anthropomorphic paradox, which also commits the illicit category shift of answering the query, What is physical actuality? by talking about psychical potentiality; the third generalizes the concept of other mind sufficiently to include lowly forms like atoms: but thereby it generalizes the familiar paradox of other mind — How could I really know the feelings of another without making them my own feelings, and how could I do that without swallowing up the other's individuality in my own? In a theistic context, the panpsychist theory can be strengthened, as follows: I can, in a certain deficient fashion, embrace the feelings of

---

[4] Wisdom, *op. cit.*, p. 156.

others, so that, to take an example, what for one of my pain cells (or its cortical terminus) is the entire quality of life at the moment, for me constitutes relatively the merest speck of feeling in my total experience; and this relegation to unimportance of the cell's feelings, as in my feelings, safeguards the distinctness of both. However, it does not enable me to do full justice to the "other mind" involved. My feeling of the cell's feelings is deficient; the inner complexity of the cellular life at the moment is not accessible to my conscious introspection; I feel it, but not vividly and distinctly. However, to speak thus of a "deficient," is to suggest an adequate or sufficient, form of inclusion of the feeling of one subject in the feeling of another. This sufficient form can only be divine. God can accept our entire feelings into His own life, where they become mere items, and yet do justice to their complexity and intensity; and He can do this because His own complexity and intensity have no upper limit. In other words, in Him sympathetic participation or love is limitless, whereas in us it is drastically limited. Wisdom quotes the text, "God is love," to support the equation of the divine with love as it is in us, a limited degree of identification with others; and he points out that non-identity, otherness, is also necessary.[5] True enough; but the ideal form of love, which alone literally is God, is in no danger of losing its distinctiveness, since this consists in the unique fullness of its appreciations of others.

Accordingly, the question of privacy is answered: to God all emotions and impulses are fully open to enjoyment, inspection, and comparison. We thus eliminate the paradox: "How can your feelings (not just your behavior) be like or unlike mine, since the comparison can never take place"? It can take place—in God. And the "argument by analogy" gives us good justification for supposing that the verdict of the comparison is, *close similarity in normal cases*. What the argument by analogy cannot, and only theism can, do is to furnish the *meaning* of the comparison.

[5] *Op. cit.*, p. 168.

Perhaps I may now dare to state the following contention: Language is bound to generate paradox if one attempts to purify it of all theistic implications; standard language is essentially theistic. It takes for granted that one does not mean (exclusively) by "your feelings," "your observable behavior," nor by "plants existed before there were mammals," "*if* mammals had been there, they would have perceived such and such." Normal language does not suppose that truth consists in (though it may for us be established by) conformity of beliefs to actual and possible observations by localized beings like ourselves. What then can it consist in? Perhaps in conformity to what is experienced by an omnipresent "observer," having "other minds," not simply through their perceived behavior, but as internal possessions, directly revealed — somewhat as occurrences in our bodies are revealed to us through pains and pleasures, but in the divine case with incomparably more distinctness and completeness. Again, by "the past," one appears to mean, not merely what we remember, or could recall, nor yet what monuments and other traces might enable us to infer, but what unlimited or cosmic memory can nevermore forget.[6] "The moving finger writes . . . nor all thy piety nor wit shall lure it back to cancel half a line." Deny such theistic implications of language, and paradox immediately appears.

In "a security we can hardly do without" our author refers, I presume, to the childish emotional state of wanting the course of life to be controlled at each moment for the special benefit of each one of us. Such universally preferential control I regard as a logical impossibility. But there is another kind of security

[6] See MacIver's vigorous rejection of the idea that the historian can permit the truth to be defined in terms of the humanly accessible evidence. A. Flew, *Logic and Language*: Second Series (Oxford: Basil Blackwell, 1953), pp. 199–203. MacIver suggests an implicit appeal to a "Recording Angel," or an electric recording device. Yet the latter could give but a schematic outline, and the former differs only rhetorically from divine memory.

whose absence I take to be likewise logically impossible: It must always henceforth be true, and in some appropriate way, however humble, significant, that we have lived as we have lived, and have not lived as we have not lived. The need to be able to have some slight understanding of this prospective, necessarily indestructible truth and significance is rational, if anything is. That the proposition is in some sense analytic does not mean that ordinary secular common sense and prosaic imagination can enable us to realize much of its import. Only theism furnishes the clue to this import, theism itself being in a broad and nontrivial sense analytic, since it is the elucidation of the full bearings of unavoidable word uses, categorial meanings, including the meaning of "God."

Once more, part of the evidence is found in the paradoxes of non-theistic philosophizing. It is, for instance, a paradox to assert that we can reach absolute objective certainty; for when and where can human mistakes be strictly impossible? Yet, as Professor Wisdom says,[7] it is also paradoxical to view certainty as unattainable; for then what is the point of the notion? But, in normal good sense, "we can never be absolutely certain" means, "we can never be omniscient or infallible (as God is); we should remember that we are mere creatures, limited by a localized body, etc."

True, even we can reach virtually absolute certitude if we assert virtually nothing. Experiencing several colors, I say, "I experience qualitative differences." How could I be wrong? But I am also not very significantly right. This tendency toward an inverse correlation between significance and certitude is the mark of our human mode of knowing. It contrasts with and thereby implies the idea of another mode — the divine — in which certainty is not similarly purchased by vagueness. In conceiving this other mode we have analogical support from our own experience. (This remains true even though many theologians have indulged

[7] *Philosophy and Psychoanalysis*, pp. 42–46.

in inconsistency in their use of such analogies, and thereby brought discredit on their whole enterprise.) Thus we get rid of skepticism about the possibility of knowledge (for assuming theism it becomes reasonable piety to trust that our powers are not useless or condemned to mere frustration); but we are equally released from the unhappy need to *define* "reality" *simpliciter* as that which man may know, with all the ensuing temptations to explain away whatever appears inaccessible to man. As though the blind should develop subtle theories as to the unreality of visual qualities; or as though we should suppose either that a frog's feelings must be as vague as our justifiable notions of them are bound to be, or else that they must consist solely of humanly detectible bodily actions or dispositions thereto! Instead, reality is definable as that which God knows, though we may or may not be able to know it — according to our likeness or unlikeness to God. To understand all this, we must know God in some sense or fashion; but we need not know, or be able to know, all that is true of Him, or all that He knows.

In this way we escape the paradox of a public language which pretends that feelings are merely changes in somatic structure and position, without falling into the contrary paradox (so powerfully attacked by Wittgenstein) of an ultimately private language of feeling. To God there is no mere privacy, since all experience is expressible in terms of His own participation in it. The question then is, "Can we participate in (and analogically conceive) divine experience, not sufficiently to be divine ourselves, but sufficiently to know what we mean when we say that, for example, a man born blind cannot know what normal sensations (as measured by divine participation in them) are like, though the rest of us can know, if only probably and approximately, what other men's sensations are like (by the same measure)?" It is not that we thus become more certain about other minds, but that we understand better what we mean by our degree of uncertainty, or of high probability.

It is the same with the appeal to God as "ground of induction." We do not thereby decide the question, "Shall we make inductions"? (we must anyway), nor do we raise their level of certainty; but we become more conscious of what it means to be certain or uncertain about events which have not yet occurred, or about an Order of Nature. For we become conscious, in some measure, of *what* it is that orders occurrences, so far as they are ordered, and perhaps also leaves them to some extent appropriately free, and hence partly chaotic.

The appeal to God need not, we have seen, be concerned with "security," in the obvious or conventional sense. But further, there is a ground of insecurity and tragedy in the eternal nature of deity, in that (as we shall argue later: Chapters 6–8, 13) He is necessarily, not merely contingently, concerned with free or self-determining creatures — *some* such creatures *or other*. Also, since knowledge of other minds involves sympathy, there is no "punishment" which God could inflict upon us in which He would not Himself participate. So much for the emotions which Mr. Wisdom (too mindful, perhaps, of Freud or Nietzsche) associates with the idea of God!

All questions concerning things as public, private, knowable, ordered, physical, mental, good, evil, have one meaning if "God" or some equivalent term (suitably defined) is introduced into the discussion, another, if not. This difference in meaning is one of degree of intelligibility (up or down); for the alternative, that the existence of God should be an hypothesis which might or might not fit the facts, is self-contradictory, since the conceived perfection or eternity of deity (whether as classically defined, or as redefined in Socinus, Whitehead, Montague, Hartshorne, and others) is incompatible with such contingency of existence. The customary flat rejection of Anselm at this point has not clarified but confused matters.

One mark of a contingent statement, as we have seen (Sec. XII, Chapter Two), is its exclusion of positive alternatives. "The garden is tended" excludes the flowers growing wild; "John occupies this space" excludes Henry's occupying it (at the given time). But what does "God watches over the world" exclude? That the world grows wild? The difficulty is that whereas untended or wild flowers are recognizable entities, the kind of world which would be wild is by no means obvious. How much disorder would enter into its wildness, and yet leave it still a world, or a definite state of affairs? This is the question of the argument from design, whether a "world not ordered by God" is anything but a contradiction, anything more than an "unordered but ordered" system of things. Wisdom's sense of the unreality of God is, I suggest, a misreading of the non-exclusiveness of God (taken simply as existent). God in His necessary existence (His accidents are another matter) excludes nothing, and His "non-existence" has no conceivable factual meaning, unless it means, "no world at all." But no world at all is something no one, unless God, could experience! So how does it furnish the meaning of the divine non-existence? There is, I hold, no such meaning; the sole appropriate object of doubt here is whether "the divine existence" is not also meaningless. If it has meaning, then, since there is no alternative, the divine existence is necessary. It is not one among the facts of existence, for it pervades all facts, actual or possible.

The contingent accidents of God, like all contingent actualities, do exclude positive possibilities. However, we can know these accidents only in such modal forms as, "God knows that it rained yesterday," which obviously excludes a cloudless sky all day yesterday. All such statements presuppose the necessary existence of God as "knowing whatever there is to know," and this of itself excludes nothing whatever, except the negative formula, devoid of consistent meaning, "there is no all-knowing God." It is devoid of meaning, once more, since no conceivable experience could illustrate it. By contrast, "there is an all-knowing being" is quite capable of experiential illustration. In the first place, God can be aware of, experience, His own existence (while He could not experience His non-existence); and in the second place, we can be aware that the world has an Orderer, since it is ordered, and since this comes to the same thing ("a set of things whose only order is their own mutual adjustment" can be shown, I believe, to define "chaos," if none of the things has pre-eminent influence over the others); and finally, we can be aware that it is only consciousness and knowledge which constitute power to order, and only eminent consciousness and knowledge which can do this pre-eminently. Or, we can find that our experiences, in still other categorial aspects, are made more intelligible by conceiving them theistically.

It is very true that, as some define "theism," experience is not made more intelligible by it. But this does not establish a negative fact, "no God" of the hypothecated nature; rather it shows that the alleged hypothesis has no clear and consistent meaning. For instance, the fact of evil, taken as contingent, refutes no form of theism which makes sense even when we forget this fact. For the hypothetical all-arranging God whose power or goodness is supposed to be impugned by the evils of the world *could* only be a God with no genuine individuals to deal with, thus without a world, good or bad. Individuals cannot, absolutely speaking, be arranged, they must arrange themselves, evil or no evil. This is analytic—"individual" means this. And what is "power" if exercised over nothing save the absolutely powerless (i.e., over nothing)?

Until we see that these questions are pure matters of meaning, we shall waste our time in their discussion. To this extent contemporary positivists are precisely right: we are here concerned with meanings, not contingent facts. But that we are therefore not in any sense concerned with existence, but only with language, is a non-sequitur. The non-factual aspect of existence is not essentially linguistic. One way to put the theistic question is to ask, Must there not be eternal and necessary meanings or thoughts?

What can in no case be known through mere meanings is not

existence but actuality, the concrete "state" in which something exists. Here the opponents of Anselm are in the right; even the divine actuality must be contingent. But this actuality is *how* God exists, in what concrete experiences and acts, it is not the mere truth that He exists. The latter is the least common denominator of all possible contingent divine actualities — a class which cannot be empty, though it has no necessary members, just as "true contingent propositions" has none, and yet cannot be empty.

Since the "existence of God" is a categorial topic, it can be assimilated to notions like the "feeling of flowers" only if such notions are completely generalized, and so made to coincide with panpsychism, or some similarly universal theory of what is meant by "physical reality". But one may not discredit theism by a supposed analogy to belief in haunted houses, say, or to any particularizations of the view that, in principle, concrete realities are composed of experiences, or sequences of such. No one says that all houses, by the very meaning of "house," have ghosts. Such particularizations as ghost stories are candidates, promising or not, for the status of scientific fact, and in so far are without logical analogy to theism, which is no particularization whatever, but a theory as to the meaning of any and all possible particularizations (that they are forms which the divine experience may take, or have as data). Regardless of all particular images and emotions ("guilt," "revenge," "awe"), regardless of all particular fancies and superstitions, and even of psychoanalysis, there remains the sheer logical issue concerning the meaning of the expressions, "categorially specifiable individuality," "necessary being," "categorially inclusive experience," or (to employ more ordinary language), one "to whom all hearts are open," i.e., by whom all mere privacy of feeling is overcome. Being a question of universal meanings, this is a purely philosophical question.

The noneternal or accidental predicates of deity, referred to previously, are indeed to be conceived as matters of fact and transcendent or "metaphysical" fact, in two senses: (1) *that* there are some such facts or other, some divine accidents no matter what, is necessary truth (or else nonsense), just as it is no accident that "accidents happen," and no mere fact that there are facts; (2) precisely *what* divine accidents there are is knowable by men only in an infinitely inadequate fashion. For these contingent predicates of deity consist in the all-inclusive experiences which God has of successive stages of the cosmic process. Obviously we cannot distinctly participate in such experiences; and if we knew those which were actual, we would know all things. But what we thus fail to attain is not knowledge that God "in fact" exists, for this is categorial nonsense; rather, we fail to know *how* God exists, how He in fact feels and thinks, about Mao Tse-tung for example. We can explore the truth about the individual named, and then infer, since God sees truly and values rightly, He must see and value Mao Tse-tung thus and thus. But the infinite "more" of "perfection" or adequacy which distinguishes the divine vision of truth and value from ours, we naturally miss.

What we can do, and our author does not do, is to inquire how the various alternative conceptions or pseudo-conceptions (for they cannot all make sense) of divine attributes, taken as necessarily realized in some total divine actuality, succeed or fail in clarifying the meaning of the fundamental categories — causality, matter, or other mind — as such, and not merely in their factual illustrations. Any possible world would, if it existed, be tended by this Gardener, supposing the idea of the Gardener to make sense at all.

In blunt outline the answer to the question, how do we rationally know God, is this: we find Him in all of our fundamental meanings, and if we try to purify them of involvement with deity we find that nothing unequivocal is left. All begins to dissolve in paradox.[8] Unless we are forced to conceive God Himself

[8] For an example which I find horrifying, see R. L. Goldstein's view that it is only a verbal convention if we say that a drop of blood of a diseased person really contains microorganisms rather than that the microscope transforms the drop into a medium containing the organisms. I may

THE LOGIC OF PERFECTION

in equally paradoxical terms — which might be called *the* question of philosophy — we are bound to stand by our meanings, God and all. The question is not, shall we affirm the (necessary) reality of deity; but rather, can we do so, and know what we are saying? For if we can, then we must.

have missed the point, but I cannot help thinking that it is not a verbal question but a factual one whether God enjoys the lives of the tiny organisms in question or does not. Strangely the author had raised the question earlier as to whether or not we are within some great organism for whose sake we exist. He calls this a metaphysical question, and says it is similar to that about the microbes. That whatever exists is within an inclusive life is to my mind no possible fact but a necessity — or nothing. But that we and the microbes are both within that greater life, this is a factual matter, not a linguistic one. For we might neither of us have existed at all, and then we should not have been included in the greater life. See Goldstein's essay, "Language and Experience," in his *Constructive Formalism: Essays on the Foundations of Mathematics* (Leicester: University Press, 1951); reprinted in *Philosophy of Science*, edited by A. Danto and S. Morgenbesser (New York: Meridian Books, 1960), p. 97.

CHAPTER SIX

Freedom Requires Indeterminism and Universal Causality

"Being . . . is undeducible. For our *intellect* it remains a casual and contingent quantum that is simply found or begged. May it be begged bit by bit, as it adds itself? Or must we beg it only once, by assuming it either to be eternal, or to have come in an instant that co-implicated all the rest? Did or did not 'the first morning of creation write what the last dawn of reckoning shall read?'" WILLIAM JAMES, *Some Problems of Philosophy*, p. 189.

It is an old view, much defended in recent books and articles, that "freedom" in the moral sense is compatible with causal "determinism." The motivation inspiring such discussions appears to be this: moral freedom is an indispensable idea, strict causality is also indispensable, or at least science might need to assert it; hence it is important to show that the two ideas do not conflict. In addition, it is held that even for ethics we need insight into the probable results of our acts, viewed as causes, and that a responsible person is he whose acts are effects of a good character, while an irresponsible person is he whose acts spring from an unstable or bad character.

On two points one may well agree with the views just expressed. Moral freedom is certainly indispensable, and nothing could justify denying it: men do choose, and in some cases their choice is influenced by ethical principles. Second, it is true that, even in ethics, we require causality. But what I wish to urge is that the universal validity of causality is not the same as determinism. The point is simple: there is a deterministic definition and an indeterministic definition of "cause," and the difference does not turn upon whether or not "every event has a cause." It turns rather upon how causes are thought to be related to their effects, or antecedent conditions to subsequent happenings. Here is where determinism and the (relative) indeterminism I wish to defend part company. One may, if one wishes, use the word "determinism" for the mere assertion that every event has its cause or causes, and "indeterminism" to mean that at least some events have no causes, thus making the issue a choice between two absolutes (so far as these events are concerned), instead of a triadic choice between two absolutistic views and one relativistic view. But if this is done, then it is arguable that indeterminism is a doctrine no one defends, a fictitious position invented for purposes of controversy. By ostentatiously burning this straw man, deterministic writers frequently distract attention from the real opponent who is trying to defend something else. I have read scores of defenses of determinism (including under this description writings which maintain that determinism at least *could* be true), and how few of them there are which do not, at some point, solemnly commit this lifeless effigy to the flames![1]

Every event has its cause or causes; so far we nearly all agree. And to avoid quibbling, if anyone objects to the word "cause" as obsolete in science, let him substitute "antecedent conditions,"

[1] An exception is Charles Stevenson, "Ethical Judgments and Avoidability," see *Mind*, XLVII (1938), 45–57, reprinted in *Readings in Ethical Theory*, edited by Sellars and Hospers (New York: Appleton-Century-Crofts, 1952), especially p. 555. However, Stevenson cleverly, and perversely, tosses the burden of proof to the indeterminist, that is, the relativist.

so that the argument may proceed. But not every event — indeed some of us would say, not *any* event in its concrete actuality — is fully and absolutely determined by its causes. In other words, an indeterminist (as conceived in this article) rejects a certain definition of "cause," namely that it is a condition, or set of conditions, from which only one outcome is possible, or from which, in principle or ideally, the outcome is wholly predictable. To be substituted for this is a definition which, whatever else it includes, involves the following requirement: the cause is a state of affairs such that when granted something more or less like what happens subsequently was "bound to happen," or (if you prefer) could safely have been predicted. Given dry TNT, a confined space, and a lighted fuse, there will inevitably, or with practically infinite probability, be an explosion; but it does not follow, and indeterminism denies, that the exact details of the explosion, the behavior of each atom and particle, will be the only possible ones (in principle, uniquely predictable) under the circumstances. Read fifty arguments for the tenability of determinism (beginning, say, with David Hume, Part III of the *Treatise*), and there will perhaps be one or two that address themselves consistently to the issue as thus defined; and probably not one which shows much comprehension of the reasons which have led various philosophers and scientists, including Clerk Maxwell, Whitehead, and other distinguished thinkers, to adopt the indeterminist view.[2]

Our question, then, is whether causes or conditions determine happenings absolutely, or whether they merely limit more or

[2] To show that I am not thinking of straw men, or even of mediocre men, let us cite an illustrious contemporary example, Bertrand Russell. See Section IV of his brilliant "Elements of Ethics," in *Philosophical Essays* (London, New York: Longman's, Green and Co., 1910), reprinted in *Readings in Ethical Theory*, pp. 17–23. The distinction between relative and absolute determinism is missed, and the argument proceeds as though one had two absolutes to choose between, one of which no one could defend. (Russell would be somewhat more careful today.)

less sharply what can happen. "More or less sharply" will perhaps seem hopelessly vague. However, one may state the indeterminist or relativist view more subtly, as follows: events are always to an appropriate degree determined by their causal antecedents. And what is "an appropriate degree"? I think we can give at least a rough answer to this question. A human being, in full possession of normal intelligence, surveying wide alternatives of action under general conceptions whose very meaning is that they admit highly divergent possible instances, must dispose of a wider range of possible reactions to a given situation than there is reason to attribute to a molecule reacting to its situation. The scale of chemical and biological types of individuality, from atoms (or lower) up to man, may reasonably be looked upon, and by some scientists and philosophers has been looked upon, as a hierarchy of degrees of freedom in possible responses to given causal conditions (including among these conditions the past history of the individual). Inanimate nature involves the least scope of alternatives — and here the "more or less determined" means "more"; man involves the widest scope — and here it means very much "less." Thus we need not make man an arbitrary exception to the general principles of nature; he is but the intensive case of the general principles of creative action, of which causality is an aspect.

I have now betrayed my secret, in that word "creative." Moral freedom, as we all know, requires the exercise of rational reflection and decision; but what many philosophers fail to see is that this exercise of higher powers involves a creative leap beyond anything made inevitable or predictable by the causal conditions. The creative act is influenced by its conditions, and requires them, but it cannot (I wish to argue) be required or precisely determined by them — much less, even, than an electronic event according to the Uncertainty Principle. This aspect of creativity is what the determinist overlooks or denies. How shall we convince him of his oversight?

First, we may ask where the burden of proof lies. Truths in general are relative, not absolute; they are matters of degree, subject to quantitative limitation of some sort. Determinism, however, is an absolute, holding that conditions unqualifiedly restrict the outcome to but one wholly definite sort of event, entirely excluding any creative leap, any novelty not specifiable in advance, given ideal knowledge of conditions. It is somewhat amusing to converse with persons who tell you that they are suspicious of "all absolutes," and that they accept absolute determinism. They may not use the word "absolute" in the second case, but what does that matter, if they affirm the unqualified causal determination of events? Surely we know by this time that no accumulation of scientific observations could establish, even as probable, an unqualified regularity. Observation does not have that kind of exactitude.

Second, if process is not (in some degree) always creation, what is it? This was Bergson's point, still poorly digested in philosophy. If it is only ignorance of causes which prevents us from mentally seeing the effect in advance, then the entire character of "coming events" is real beforehand. Before events happen, they lack nothing except a totally transparent, featureless something called "actual occurrence." To some of us this is truly an absurdity. If becoming does not create new quality and quantity, new determinateness, then, we argue, it creates nothing, and nothing ever really becomes. (I pass over a possible counter-argument from "precognition.") A causal destiny, no less determinate than what happens, is just the happening twice over, once as already true but not yet real, and then as true and also real. But truth is "agreement with reality," in some sense, and if the truth is already there, then so is what it agrees with. How can there be a wholly determinate relation prior to its term? In short, creativity is an essential aspect of the idea of becoming or process. Conditions do indeed — condition, that is they establish and limit the possibilities for otherwise free or creative activity.

And this phrase "creative activity," or "creative becoming," only escapes redundancy because there are degrees of creativity, implying the zero case as a lower limit of thought, a necessarily fictitious entity, like "perfect lever," or "wholly isolated particle." Thus one may, in a relative sense, speak of "uncreative process," and at the opposite extreme, by a more violent exaggeration, of "wholly free" or causally undetermined action, where the creative leap is maximal, though in any real case by no means uninfluenced by its conditions. (Consider Kubla Khan, and the known sources for the images and ideas of Coleridge's poem, together with what is known of his antecedent poetic habits and character.)

Third, the conception of law now actually operative in the sciences is not a deterministic one. To be sure, many are still telling us that the Uncertainty Principle is irrelevant to the problem of freedom. It does not seem to occur to those reiterating this statement that the *dis*connectedness of basic principles is far from being an axiom of scientific method. Rather, something very like the contrary is axiomatic. What such people may have in mind is: (a) the human organism, viewed statistically, involves large numbers of quanta, so that any indeterminacy due to quantum laws must practically approach zero;[3] (b) the freedom of the electrons, if it be called that, is *their* freedom, not ours; (c) we know that we are morally free, and it is silly to suppose that we need quantum mechanics to justify this principle of everyday life; (d) indeterminacy as experimentally justified expresses only our ignorance of ultimate causes, which may in an undetectible manner fully determine even electrons. I grant all but the last point as probably sound. But as to the last, it must be said that many scientists and philosophers would reject the notion of unobservables which it involves, and that some competent investigators would go further, and hold that there is positive evidence that real randomness is at work, that the laws

[3] However, see J. C. Eccles, *The Neurophysical Basis of Mind* (Oxford: Clarendon Press, 1953), pp. 278–279.

are genuinely laws of chance. This is so (according to my under-standing) apart from the Uncertainty Principle, in the case, for example, of radio-active atoms. However, my main objection is that the four points together do not, even if granted, establish the irrelevance of quantum mechanics to the understanding of human freedom as a fact in nature. For it remains true that quantum mechanics explains the world not through causal laws which contradict the notion of creative leaps or unpredictable aspects of happenings, but rather through laws which are in principle compatible with that notion. The ground laws of the world, as we seem ever likely to know them, are thus essentially statistical, in the sense that their demonstrable exactitude is due to the presence of large numbers of similar events, and not to any knowable precise causal determination of the events taken singly. An exact regularity supposed to be hidden behind these statistical laws is at best irrelevant to scientific explanation. It apparently can have no technological consequences, nor any ap-preciable experimental significance. Thus the contention, so much and so long insisted upon, that science *requires* us to think purely deterministically, has been concretely, and probably defin-itively, discredited. Einstein and Planck resisted this conclusion to the last; but how many among the younger scientists take this resistance as more than a slightly pathetic example of scientific conservatism? Long ago Clerk Maxwell, who with Gibbs, Dar-win, Mendel, and Bolzmann was a founder of the statistical ap-proach which emerged in the second half of the Nineteenth Century, suggested what is now perhaps the prevailing scientific view, that the statistical notion of law is the fundamental one. Nearly a century ago this superb thinker calmly set out some of the essentials of this matter.[4]

[4] See the essay quoted in *The Life of James Clerk Maxwell* by Lewis Campbell and W. Garnett (London: Macmillan and Co., 1882), pp. 434–444, especially 438, 441, 444. That even classical physics was not rigorously deterministic has been held by high authorities, e.g., by Karl Popper, in "Indeterminism in Quantum Physics and in Classical Physics," *British*

A famous physicist once said to me, "The uncertainty principle is not relevant to the question of moral freedom — except [he added] by analogy." The exception is significant. For if submicroscopic particles are (for our possible knowledge, at least) somewhat indeterminate causally, and if the exactitude of the laws we verify is due to our dealing with large numbers of particles, why should we suppose that particular human individuals are subject to exact laws? A man is not identical with super-billions of particles. He is one human individual. Indeed, is not our very notion of unity, or individuality, based on our own experience as one? The statistical laws of particles can hardly tell the whole story of human behavior, for there is at least one more entity present in that behavior besides particles, namely the human personality, or the stream of human experiences. It is at best sheer assumption that the presence of the higher-level unity makes no difference to the behavior of the particles.[5] Quantum mechanics need not be thought the entire and exact truth concerning particles in organisms or in the human brain. Subsidiary principles are presumably needed, if human thoughts and purposes are not "idle wheels in nature," to use Whitehead's phrase. These subsidiary principles may be expected to reintroduce the merely statistical character of causal regularity at the higher or human level, so that the single human being will not be bound by the causal conditions to a single determinate course of action. (We shall consider presently the contention that particles are not existent entities.)

Fourth, we must evaluate a familiar deterministic tenet which

Journal for the Philosophy of Science, I (1950), 117–133, 175–195; also by Hans Reichenbach, *The Direction of Time* (Berkeley: The University of California Press, 1956), p. 95. See, too, H. Feigl's characteristically lucid account in "Notes on Causality," in *Readings in Philosophy of Science*, edited by Feigl and Brodbeck (New York: Appleton-Century-Crofts, 1953), pp. 408–418, especially pp. 411–412.

[5] That this difference is fully compatible with what we know of neural action is clearly explained by Eccles, *op. cit.*, pp. 271–278.

is that chance or randomness is one thing, and moral freedom quite another. Dice, it is caustically pointed out, are not free. However, that moral freedom is not the same as chance is no proof that it does not require an element of chance. Moral freedom, we have held, is a special, high-level case of the creative leap inherent in all process, the case in which the leap is influenced by consciousness of ethical principles. The leap itself always involves "chance" — meaning simply that the causal conditions do not require just the particular act which takes place. They make it possible, but they make other acts also possible. Moral freedom is chance plus something; no one (except a man of straw) identifies the two.

Fifth, the notion that ethics requires absolute determinism is an oddity in an age when relative standards of value (and relative almost everything) are commonplaces. Moreover, the contention is quite baseless. Ethics requires relative determinacy, and this is precisely what opponents of strict determinism are glad to affirm. For "relative determinacy" and "relative indeterminacy" say the same thing, with a mere difference of emphasis. (This is forgotten when it is sometimes said that determinism and indeterminism are equally erroneous. On the contrary, while the one affirms an absolute, the other by no means asserts the contrary absolute, but rather, it recognizes relativity.) No one would deny, though some popular proponents of indeterminism underemphasize and gravely neglect, the causal conditioning in behavior. For instance, with respect to the argument that responsibility involves character as a cause guaranteeing certain kinds of acts, all that any careful writer disputes is that the guarantee is absolute, or that the "kinds" of acts reduce, at a given moment, to just *one* precisely-determined course of action. Must ethics be more severe in its demands for law than even physics?

Consider the role of "motives," of which the determinists have made so much. A motive, in a human being at least, is always more or less general, e.g., the wish to "make a good impression";

and an act is never general but always particular. What spans the gap between the general and the particular? The character? But this is something general also: an established type of action, not a determinateness of agency with respect to the particular act now to be performed for the first time. The creationist holds that our very power to form general conceptions (in a sense in which these are beyond the reach of the other animals) is the same as our being not determined by irresistible impulse, habit, or antecedent character, to but one mode of acting in a given case. The openness to alternatives, the flexibility, of our response is the behavioristic aspect of our knowledge of the universal, as that which can be indifferently instanced by this particular *or* by that. Such instancing, by its very meaning, must have wide ranges of freedom. Freedom in the indeterministic sense is thus inherent in rational understanding as such, understanding through universals.

Let us now consider the following "paradigm case." "Suppose two young persons, normal, of opposite sex, with obvious congruence of background and nature, no available third person calculated to attract either, no obstacle to marriage, and no inclination to 'free love'; could not a psychologist (or perhaps anyone) predict that they will marry? And will such predictability deprive their decision of its freedom?" So determinists sometimes argue. But they fail to make the requisite distinctions. Does "predictable" mean with certainty, or with probability? If the former, then will any careful scientist accept it? If the latter, then, since probability only refers to what will happen in many similar cases, the individual case remains unpredictable. Again, it is one thing to say, "The two will marry," and quite another to foretell a single concrete action that either will take. Every act of either party might be strictly unpredictable, and yet it might reasonably be foretold that the marriage would (barring death or other accident) take place, for this only means that, whatever series of actions the two might perform, the abstract features of "proposal" and "acceptance" would be involved. And indeed, many writers tend to forget that the particular acts we feel to be free are concrete, while what is predicted is not. Moreover, it is common enough for people in such situations as we have imagined above to declare that it is fate or necessity, not free will, that has brought about their union, that they "could not have helped themselves." Granting this, their behavior may still have had moral character. For while they perhaps could not have avoided marrying, there are thousands, or an infinity, of ways in which this could have been done, so that at every moment they may have exercised moral choice. Moreover, their conscientiousness may have been such that had there been any cogent moral objection to the marriage, they *would* have recognized and yielded to it and thus have removed the step from the class of features "common to the real possibilities." Would it then have been excluded from all the possibilities, so that not marrying would have been inevitable? Even supposing this to be so, still, moral choice may have been involved farther back, in the creative acts, from infancy onwards, by which such a firm ethical character had been developed. When we feel morally responsible for an act, this need not mean that we think that, as we were the instant before, we had the psychological capacity to refrain from it. It may only imply that at some time previously we could have entered upon a different course from the one which led to the act. Until we learn to do justice to the subtle relativities of this problem, we shall merely beat the air (or each other) with verbal alternatives.

Sixth, the idea that to know is to be able to predict, so that any inability to predict must mean partial ignorance, is, I hold, untenable. The ultimate function of knowledge is not to foresee, but to create. The two are by no means coincident. We predict most perfectly astronomical phenomena where we have no creative control. We control most perfectly our bodily behavior, but how vague and uncertain are our predictions of this behavior! We must ask whether by "control" is meant settling things in advance, and once for all, or — step by step? To predict what is to happen tomorrow is to deprive tomorrow of the right to decide for itself. I predict where I shall be weeks in advance when I admit or establish a conclusive obligation or reason to be there; but in this case, I renounce the right to make the decision later on. I must already have made it. Is the goal of knowledge thus to put all decision into the present, leaving for the future the mere execution? But the life of decision-making is life itself. We should be dead, from then on. Does not science aim most basically at power, rather than foresight? Is the goal of psychology to be able to write the poet's poem beforehand by predicting it, to foresee, and thus make, the creative decisions, and their expression in speeches and laws, by which statesmen, or an entire people, resolve some political tangle? I suggest that, since creative activity is that which leaps unpredictably from its causal base, the proper function of psychology in regard to creation is to increase our freedom from the compulsions and fixations which often make behavior only too largely predictable. When therapy (or a good upbringing) has freed a man to the full use of his constructive powers, it is not for science to say how in particular he will use these powers. That would be sheer impertinence and redundance. Statistical laws applying to large numbers of similar cases, yes, but the numbers and the similarity are more limited than in physics, and hence the laws cannot be so precise. Where behavior is essentially unconscious or mere habit, as in the knee-jerk, or in all cases where the cells of the body act with no appreciable interposition of thought, there statistical laws applying to the numerous bodily parts may give highly predictable modes of action. But all truly individual activity, especially on high levels, means the impossibility of precise prediction.

The idea of predictability, when turned into an absolute, like so many other ideas when so treated, loses all sense. Scientific prediction is not an end in itself, whose absolute attainment is our goal, but rather (a point insufficiently emphasized in this article) we use prediction as a means of finding out errors or blind spots in our knowledge of the statistical possibilities open to creative action. Discovering, by verified prediction, the principles of atomic fission did not make the future of things on this planet more precisely foreseeable. What it did was to show us hitherto undreamt of, or inadequately discerned, potentialities for the future. Primitive man knew well enough in rough outline what he himself was going to do; but he knew very little indeed of what could be done by other men in other circumstances with other means at their disposal. What upset the expectations of the primitive Australians was the coming of white men, with their unpredictable ways. But who can fail to see that while the white men were not so unpredictable to themselves as to the natives, they were at least as unpredictable to themselves as the natives had been to themselves. Science probably decreases the predictability of human events, in the absolute sense of "predictable"; and the race to catch up by conditional scientific prediction seems a losing race. Moreover, the more power men acquire over nature, the more closely prediction is assimilated to social and political prophecy. If "we" could control the planets, who would predict their movements? Fortunately, to foresee the future is not the purpose of life. The purpose is rather to maximize the opportunities for good in the future; it is not to be able to say now exactly what use will be made of these opportunities. Deciding that will be the future; it is no task for the present.

A final consideration against determinism is that it confronts us with the dilemma: either admit with Hume that events have no logical connection with their conditions, or accept an unqualified rationalism, according to which temporal succession, if "real" at all, coincides with logical implication. Indeterminism enables us to explore a third possibility, which is that conditions logically imply not any particular subsequent event as their inevitable outcome, but only a class of "really possible" outcomes (excluding as impossible a vacuous outcome of nothing at all happening). The features which all the really possible outcomes have in common are then necessary, i.e., they are bound to be actualized whatever happens. This is the precise meaning of "necessary," namely, "common to all the possibilities." What is common to most of the possibilities is probable. Thus temporal succession is quite different from unqualified logical implication: yet there is implication. Something like what happens next was bound to happen — so far, there is "necessary connection" — but the precise particulars just do happen, quite without necessity or implication. To be sure, all this is no "answer to Hume," until or unless it is made intelligible how conditions can limit the scope of "possible outcomes" to a definite class, with traits in common. I have elsewhere tried to explain, following Peirce, James, Bergson, and Whitehead, how this can be understood.[6] The point here is that the sole answer to Hume which has not been refuted (it has rather been ignored) is one which, according to its leading expositors, implies indeterminism, or — the same thing — relative determinism.

In contrast to this relativism, contemporary thought tends to combine two oddly-associated absolutistic notions: (1) at each moment anything could conceivably happen next; but (2) if we are rational we shall expect only what the conditions and laws imply. We can think anything following upon anything else (thus, as the poet had it, lowing herds might "break from the starry skies"); but we ought not to think of anything but the one thing which is causally implied. Thus an idle unlimited freedom of conception is combined with a theoretical narrowing down of conception to a single course of events. In this view, events and the laws connecting them are absolutely distinct; the laws, though perfectly strict, are not characters of events, but — of what? They are, as it were, between events, not in them. This

[6] See "Causal Necessities: An Alternative to Hume," *Philosophical Review*, LXIII (1954), 479–99, especially 485–489.

merely separate reality of causal relations which Russell (following Hume) has done so much to fasten upon the learned world (partly by excess of reaction, perhaps, to Bradley's equally excessive monism) is in strange company with the unqualified unity of pattern asserted for the world process throughout time. Forget "laws," and events have simply nothing to do with each other; remember laws, and there is really but one vast complex event or event-system stretching into the remotest past and future. Thus we have absolute pluralism and absolute monism, equally by fiat or by magic. The two contrary and similarly excessive contentions taken together make the universe unintelligible. No wonder it is contended that philosophy can tell us nothing about reality: certainly it cannot when it is proceeding thus in absolutistic fashion, and in two opposite directions at once. What we need is a qualified or suitably relativized doctrine of the logical independence and dependence of events. The key notion is that events logically and precisely require the very antecedent conditions which they have, but not precisely the results which issue from them.

An English physicist, influenced by Wittgenstein, tells us that there is no such thing as physical, but only logical, necessity; yet he also claims that logical necessity is simply a relationship among our symbols (if I have not misunderstood him).[7] So then when an overtaken rabbit finds he cannot escape from but must go into the fox's jaws, this necessity derives from our way of talking about the world! Alas, I cannot make it out. I think there is physical necessity, and it is also logical. The logic, how-

---

[7] W. H. Watson, *On Understanding Physics* (London: Cambridge University Press, 1938), pp. 68–74. For an interesting comparison, showing, I think, that changes in intellectual fashions may be less than pure gain, contrast Watson's analysis of necessity with that given by Bernardino Varisco, in his neglected but brilliant and powerful book, *Great Problems*, trans. by Salvadori (London, 1915), especially pp. 158–175. Varisco seems to me to have gone fairly far toward neoclassical metaphysics, without quite completing the transition from the metaphysics of being.

ever, is that of events, and not simply of our thought about events. (God's thought, perhaps, but not essentially ours.) But there are also open possibilities in nature, and this is what determinism in its pure form denies.

To prevent misunderstanding, it should be said that my contention is not that we must either accept a certain brand of indeterminism or give up causal explanation and prediction. This last we cannot do, for every animal must have its expectations modified by past experience; and above all man must exhibit such modification. But it remains a genuine alternative whether we can understand an objective counterpart in nature to our capacity to predict (statistically or approximately) or must be content to exercise the capacity without further curiosity. Those who disparage such curiosity because we can make our predictions without satisfying it are forgetting, I think, that the wish to know transcends pragmatic needs and is a principal glory of our natures. In addition, such thinkers often suppose that the alternative to Hume can only be a strict rationalism according to which causal laws suffice to render events (ideally) deducible in all detail. The irony of this is that Hume himself held the rationalistic view! His skepticism attached not to the Newtonian or deterministic concept of causality, but only to our means of demonstrating it to be true of nature. That we should assume it as valid he had no doubt. Our cultural situation calls for very great doubt on just that score. Indeed, we have apparently much to gain and little or nothing to lose by adopting the properly qualified or relativized indeterministic theory. Creative freedom of individuals as such, with statistical regularities expressive of the influence of causal conditions, gives us what we need, whether in ethics or in science.

One of the most painstaking and detailed discussions of our topic is a posthumous essay, characteristically acute and learned, by Ernst Cassirer.[8] In view of the deserved prestige of this author

[8] Ernst Cassirer, *Determinism and Indeterminism in Modern Physics* (New Haven: Yale University Press, 1956).

and his extraordinary grasp of the history of science and philosophy, let us see what we can glean from him. Cassirer defends what he terms "critical determinism," which he sharply contrasts with mechanism, or the Laplacean conception of the complete predictability of the future, given absolute knowledge of the past. Absolute knowledge, our subtle author reminds us, is not a human affair, and if the knowledge is thought of as divine, then there should be no question of prediction, since a divine intelligence is to be conceived of, if at all, as a single eternal intuition of all times. (I have frequently defended a different concept of omniscience, as did the Socinians hundreds of years ago; their well-formulated and pointed arguments on this topic seem to have escaped our learned author's attention.) Critical determinism is the acceptance of the regulative principle that we are to look for "strict" laws, in seeking to explain nature. If, as Cassirer seems disposed to grant, the only strict laws we can find are statistical, that is, applicable to collectives, not to individual things or events, this does not abrogate the strictness of the laws or imply any compromise with indeterminism. (In other words, "determinism" and its denial are redefined so that one may remain attached to the former *word*, but give up the chief point which it has been used to express!) Moreover, he holds, where properties of supposed individuals elude observational detection (for instance, the simultaneous location and velocity of electrons), there simply are no determinate properties of the kind in question. The law of excluded middle has, it seems, no application at this point.[9] Nature is what she is humanly knowable as, nothing more. Nevertheless, there is talk of individual events, which must have definite properties, and it is hard to see how there can be collectives unless there are singulars. Yet these singulars, whether construed as single human perceptions, or as events independent of our knowledge, are in either case, as Margenau reminds us toward the end of his preface to the book, subject to no knowable laws except statistical ones.

[9] *Ibid.*, pp. 189–195, especially 190.

Before making a few further remarks on this issue, I shall relate for the reader's entertainment an incident which happened in my presence at a meeting of the Australasian Philosophical Association. A lively young man had read a paper dealing with the philosophy of science; at the close of his reading another lively and still younger man eagerly rose to put a criticism or question which, unluckily for him, he prefaced with the confession, "I don't know anything about physics . . .," whereupon the reader of the paper broke in harshly, "Then why do you talk about it"? Therewith that segment of the proceedings came to a dead stop; we never did learn what the criticism was to have been. Warned by this incident, I shall not confess to knowing "nothing" about physics; and it would be incorrect, since I have read works by many excellent authorities with some care, and conversed with others. At worst I could be said to know next to nothing. Yet who can resist talking about these things?

Heisenberg appears to have a strong case for his view that the mathematical beauty ("symmetry") of the laws stands or falls with the admission that what is described in them is neither the absolute incidence of particles, as observed or unobserved, nor the individual events of observation, but rather the statistical possibilities for the latter. This does not mean that the human mind has to intervene, for a machine can be set to do the "observing." But it does mean that what physics deals with as strictly lawful is not the singular actualities, observed or otherwise, but the potentialities of nature as expressible in innumerable cases of reaction, such as an experiment is. Attempts to reduce these potentialities to conceived actualities subject to precise laws have so far proved incapable of clarifying the theoretical structure or of leading to new facts. No one can be forbidden to seek an escape from this (to some persons unsatisfactory) situation. But a conclusive argument in the deterministic direction seems out of the question, and there may never again be even a strongly plausible one.

Von Weizsäcker told me once how he quit discussing philosophy with N. Hartmann after he learned that the latter refused to admit a distinction between actuality and real potentiality. Physics apparently needs just this distinction, which — as Peirce and James saw some time ago — is the nub of the determinist controversy. Not what does happen can be strictly lawful, according to the indeterminist, but only what can or would happen in sufficiently many cases.

The point is not, as I see it, the positivistic one that unobservables cannot exist, but rather that we can infer definitely as to what is beyond experience only through laws, and according to the "Copenhagen" view the only definite or actual facts in any way accessible to us are those of everyday experience. If we want to go further and "penetrate into the details of the atomic happenings, then the contours of the objectively actual world begin to dissolve, not into the mist of a new and still less clear conception of actuality, but into the lucid clarity of a mathematics, which expresses the lawful structure of the possible not the factual." [10] Real potentiality is thus the subject-matter of atomic physics, for "possible" here is not simple logical possibility, but is "objective." Deterministic philosophies, if they understand themselves, deny this objectivity. They want the rigor of law to apply to what actually happens, to facts, not to classes of really possible happenings or facts. The patterns of probability of atomic physics are then subjective devices for dealing with the actual. But it makes at least as good sense to view them as the very framework of law of the objective world, within which, with an element of chance and freedom (the only positive meaning of "chance," as Peirce pointed out), actual facts are born. Law is exhibited in

[10] See the splendid account, in which this passage is cited, by Oskar Becker in *Die Grösse und Grenze der Mathematischen Denkweise* (Freiburg/München: Verlag Karl Alber, 1959); also Norwood Russell Hanson, "The Copenhagen Interpretation of Quantum Theory," *The Philosophy of Science*, edited by Danto and Morgenbesser, pp. 450–70. The sentence of Heisenberg is to be found in *Daedalus*, Vol. 87 (1958), No. 3, p. 100.

this theory as a limitation upon chance, not its absence. And thus creativity can be given a pervasive role.

Is it not of some significance that one of the most distinguished scientific representatives of determinism today, the psychologist Skinner, has as his principal working conception that of the "probability" or "strength" of a mode of response in a given organism at a given time, a strength which can be increased or decreased? How can he fail to see that he is dealing with real potentiality, not with inevitable, singular facts? Surely a probability of one is here a mere limiting concept. True, he says the psychologist would be content to "settle" for psychological "indeterminancy" if it were no greater than that which the physicist has had to accept.[11] But why assume that the indeterminancy is no greater? If indeterminancy as positive (and every negative fact has a positive side) consists in creativity, then who would suppose an atom to be as creative as a human being? And I see no sign that Skinner has faced the absurdity of the psychologist undertaking to do in advance (i.e., predict) the "creative thinking" for facilitating which his book gives some admirable advice. Nor is there a necessary connection between the fine causal accounts in Skinner's work and his determinism. What he shows us is that (as all sensible people know) creativity has narrow limits, which can be shifted by stimuli in all sorts of ways which (also within limits) are predictable. As James Clerk Maxwell said, not without a touch of exaggeration, "if there is any freedom it is infinitesimal." I sometimes think of an individual's freedom as the fraction of which the numerator is the momentary experience of the individual, and the denominator is the past of the universe, so far as effectively involved. The value of this fraction is small, but still not zero. A pigeon so conditioned that it definitely will perform a certain act within ten seconds, or two minutes, has no creative options as to performing or not performing that act in that time. This does not mean it necessarily suffers

[11] B. F. Skinner, *Science and Human Behavior* (New York: The Macmillan Company, 1953), p. 17.

from any feeling of "compulsion" or that the act is in no sense voluntary, but it means that the act is not an example of creative freedom. And a man equally narrowly determined with respect to a certain act is in that respect not creative either. But this is quite compatible with indeterminism. A pigeon's life in the segment of time mentioned is immensely more complex, even though in slight and trivial ways, than the mere "act" describes; much more so a man's. If the creative leeway is cut off here, it can open up there, and when it has no opening the creature can cease to be, as an actually sentient or conscious individual — in deep sleep, for example.

It takes time to outgrow so deeply fixed a habit as determinism represents for many. But the working physicists seem already largely to have outgrown it. To some persons there is a kind of impiety in this, and in very truth determinism has been almost a deity to multitudes.

Cassirer shows this attitude clearly enough. He agrees that laws have been shown to be essentially statistical. But then he turns special pleader and urges that this is not "indeterminism worthy of the name." [12] "Real" indeterminism would be the doctrine that not merely are there alternative ways in which a singular event can happen, but there are alternative laws which nature might apply to a given case. Taking account of the ultimate time perspective, or of a possible succession of cosmic epochs, each with its own set of laws, this is not necessarily absurd. But, be this as it may, the usual meaning of determinism is that every event in

[12] Cassirer, *op. cit.*, pp. 118–119. W. H. Watson similarly neglects the fact of unpredictable events, burying it under subtle talk about language and symbolic levels. (*Op. cit.*, pp. 79–83). He has no notion of creativity as the pregnant meaning of freedom nor of the problem of objective chance, which in the end is unavoidable, since, in spite of Spinoza, the totality of facts cannot follow from any necessary premise, so that chance either comes into the world in a single cosmic throw of the dice, or piecemeal. For an admirably clear exposition of the basic role of chance in physics see W. G. Pollard, *Chance and Providence* (New York: Scribner's, 1958).

all details is unambiguously specified by its conditions and the causal laws. We shall see how Cassirer's indifference to the question of singularity avenges itself when he comes to deal with ethics. And it is clear that he has an ax to grind. He wants to make an absolute out of causal order and to drive the defender of relativity into the contrary absolute position, that there is no order, but only chaos. Thus the doctrine of the merely relative validity both of "order" and of its contrary are by fiat denied access to verbal expression. And in the process something else becomes relative indeed, namely the independence of physical reality from our knowledge! Nature is the lawfulness of human experience. To me it seems that nature is a sublime totality, of which humanity is but a very tiny and dispensable fraction.

In the final chapter, in which our erudite author turns to the question of ethical freedom, his bias becomes especially clear. Thus he repeatedly identifies the denial of strict determinism with "limitless indeterminism," with the assertion of action which should "simply fall out of the causal nexus," etc., thereby missing entirely the possibility of "appropriate" degrees of determinacy, proportional to the various levels of being. The vice of thinking in mere dichotomies here raises its ugly head. We are not surprised to find human freedom and worth practically identified with "reliability," stability of good character,[13] as though there were no such thing as creativity, whose measure is precisely its transcendence of any mere permanence or derivability by rule from the past. And what has become of the admission that strict laws apply to collectives, not to individuals or singular events? Is a human experience of decision not a singular — is it, as seems to be hinted, a mere collective of atomic occurrences? Cassirer refers us to the Kantian notion of a noumenal freedom not in space or time. One had thought that this idea, or rather formula, had been sufficiently criticized by now. He also refers to Spinoza almost as though there were no serious objections to metaphysical necessitarianism. He does not refer to the

[13] Cassirer, *op. cit.*, p. 204.

views of Locke, James, Descartes, Lequier, Renouvier, Boutroux, Varisco, Bergson, Peirce, concerning the untenability of determinism.

I entirely agree with Cassirer on one point, that the self-identity of individuals or substances through time is not the ground, but rather an aspect of, the interconnectedness and lawfulness of events. I also agree that electrons are probably not enduring individuals moving through space. But it does not follow that we are free to define the realities of nature simply in terms of humanly knowable regularities or laws. Nature is a stream of interconnected events, and both laws and "things" are functions of these events. Each event is a determinate, but not antecedently determined or predictable, act of concretion, endowed with its proportional spontaneity or possibility of partial self-determination. Lequier's great saying, "God has created me creator of myself" (not a contradiction, though a paradox), applies to every concrete unit-event. Ethical freedom is merely the kind of self-determination appropriate to events in which there is consciousness of a hierarchy of ideas, hence of alternative possible kinds of actions, not merely alternative details of actions all of one kind. A dog can only act doggishly; but it has a very different meaning to say that a man can only act humanly. For *we* choose not simply among details, but among categories, of actions, and under more or less conscious reference to a highest principle of good which transcends even the difference between man and other animals, and gives us obligations to the reality including all species.

Cassirer protests against the blurring of boundaries between sciences — for instance between ethics and physics.[14] It does not seem to occur to him that science has no intention of permitting man to be regarded as outside nature, and that biology is bound to conceive the scale of animal forms as a single problem. Nor does he see that, as various biologists have pointed out, it would be silly to refuse to take advantage of the fact that in ourselves we have the one individual piece of nature which we know in its

[14] *Op. cit.*, pp. 197–198, 205–206.

individuality from two sides: externally, quantitatively, and by behavioristic observation and test, and also internally, qualitatively, by immediate intuition — whether termed introspection or retrospection (short-run memory) is no matter. Here is our only complete clue, not to noumena out of time, but to concrete spatio-temporal reality. To hold that nature is what is knowable as absolutely determined by strict laws is to imply either that the qualities of individual experiences, whether human or subhuman, are thus determined, for which there is no scientific evidence at all, or else that there are no such qualities. Neither alternative seems to me defensible. What transcends our knowledge through strict laws is simply "experient events" (Whitehead), whether human or otherwise, in their concrete qualities. There is little in present-day science to even suggest exact laws applicable to such events taken singly. Cassirer is trying to have it both ways, to have his determinism absolute or strict, yet not mechanistic or Laplacean; but he can do so only by rendering ambiguous the notion of reality as applicable to individual events, without which "collectives" must remain unmeaning.

Our author's learning saves him from altogether overlooking the significant truth that it is only through the law of increasing entropy, a statistical law if there is one, that the direction of time can be construed in physics.[15] But the drift of his discussion tends to minimize the asymmetry of time. He would like to think of causal order as applying equally and in the same way to retrospective and prospective relations.[16] Thus he exhibits what I call the prejudice of symmetry, which was so neatly embodied in the old saying, "The cause must be equal to the effect." Logical analysis shows that symmetrical ideas like that of equality are derivative: thus "X is equal to Y" merely means that neither is greater than the other; while on the contrary "X is greater than Y" cannot be derived from the denial of their equality. The ultimate relations must then be non-symmetrical or directional. If

[15] Pp. 75–79.
[16] Pp. 63–64.

causality is ultimate, it must be so either in the form, the cause greater than the effect, or in the converse relation. Which is it? The answer is again given by simple analysis of meanings. In a causal transaction in which, from the set of conditions C issues a result E, we have first C alone and then C *and* E. Thus the total result of causation is in every instance an enhancement of reality, the creation of a new whole. The more comes from the less. This (crudely sketched) is Bergson's and Whitehead's idea of process as creation. Any denial of the creative aspect of process leads to antinomies. Thus, if it be said that when E is actual, C the cause has ceased to be, we face the contradiction of an alleged causal relation of E to C, although there is said to be no such thing as C to serve as term of this relation. And if it be said that from an ultimate, or eternal, point of view there is no such thing as "C alone," but only C as prior to E, or E as subsequent to C, then, since these two complexes are equivalent, one is defying the indications of logic that equality, a symmetrical relation, is derivative. I incline to believe that logicians will eventually, though some of them reluctantly, accept the theory of asymmetrical creativity as ultimate. But this acceptance, when and if it comes, will be a vast intellectual revolution whose consequences can only in part be foreseen. One foreseeable consequence is that absolute determinism will be definitively discredited. Another consequence must be that the doctrine of the timelessness of truth will be limited to necessary truths, and abandoned with respect to truths of fact, truths about particular events or any non-eternal entities. A tense or modal theory of factual truths, such as Aristotle, Lukasiewicz, Prior, have tried, not very successfully, perhaps, to work out, will then become an unavoidable task.[17]

[17] See A. N. Prior, *Time and Modality* (London: Oxford University Press, 1957); R. Taylor, "The Problem of Future Contingencies," *Philosophical Review*, LXVI (1957), 1–28. The best brief analysis of this subject that I know of is Paul Weiss's "The Semantics of Truth Today and Tomorrow," *Philos. Studies*, IX (1958), 21–23. See further P. Wolff, "Truth, Futurity, and Contingency," *Mind*, LXIX (1960), 398–402.

Cassirer is partly right when, to the notion of an electron as an individual making choices, he objects that physics has now discredited the notion of electrons as enduring individuals identical through time.[18] But as a philosophy of creativity sees the matter, he is partly wrong in supposing that this destroys the relevance of electronic indeterminacy to the question of free choice. For the locus of freedom is not in the enduring ego, but in the self here and now, the subject immanent to a unit-event. Cassirer with all his vast grasp of thought has never quite comprehended what a philosophy of creativity, really thought through, is about. The decider of a present issue is not simply identical with the self which resolved a previous issue, but is a new decider.[19] This is the only consistent way to maintain the notion of self-creation. It is the precise meaning of freedom, as transcendence of mere regularity or law. It is also the way to answer those, who, like Schopenhauer, argue that a self which has been created (no matter by what) cannot be free, for its creator must, by determining its character, have also determined its acts. For we are as we act and act as we are. The solution of the puzzle is to deny any *antecedent* character or cause sufficient to determine present action. My present self is not real until I act, and its becoming determinate *is* the occurrence of the act, not the cause of this occurrence. Effects are more determinate than their causes, causation is creation of new determinacy. Thus there could be electronic decisions even though no electron survives from one moment to another as the same.

Another point which Cassirer is too knowing to miss, but, as it appears to me, too biased to see clearly, is the connection between atomism or discontinuity and indeterminism. Let us start with the most striking case, a living organism. Such an organism reacting to stimuli is subject to a threshold principle. Below a

[18] Cassirer, *op. cit.*, p. 208.

[19] See my "Strict and Genetic Identity," *Structure, Method and Meaning: Essays in Honor of Henry M. Sheffer* (New York: The Liberal Arts Press, 1951), pp. 242–254.

certain minimum of stimulation there is no response; as one gradually increases the stimulus, abruptly a response occurs. This disproportion between continuity and abruptness can easily be spanned by a statistical law. From zero probability of response one goes toward a probability of one. Thus, viewed statistically, the disproportion between continuous increase of stimulus and abrupt emergence of response disappears. But who can imagine a non-statistical law here? In each given case, response occurs or not. This situation is not peculiar to living things: indeed, the point of quantum physics, in this regard, is that the problem of a threshold is general. Individuals are sensitive to their environments, but are they infinitely sensitive?[20] Rather there is an all-or-none law. Thus a quantum of light is either reflected or refracted by a prism; there are, as physicists say, only two "degrees of freedom" in the response, while the angle of incidence of the stimulus, or causal condition, is varied continuously. True, the angles of reflection or refraction vary continuously, but nevertheless the abrupt disjunction between going through the glass and returning from its unpenetrated surface is without parallel on the side of the conditions. There we have only continuous variation of angle. Again, suppose a ball rolled through a tube aimed from various angles at the sharp-edged top of a metal sheet. If the angle is at one extreme, a ball will certainly drop on one side of the sheet, if at the opposite extreme, on the other side. In between it becomes more and more uncertain on which side the ball will fall. Again we have an abrupt disjunction between two possible outcomes, and a sheer continuity on the side of the causal conditions. Once more, suppose a drop of water falling upon a knife-edged divide and rolling then into either of two oceans. The drop may split, to be sure, but not into an infinity of fragments, one for each possible angle! Here too, we have the problem of relating discontinuously variable results to continuously variable conditions.

[20] See Aloys Wenzl, *Die Philosophischen Grenzfragen der Modernen Naturwissenschaft* (Stuttgart: Kohlhammer, 1954), p. 104.

The disproportion is overcome by the continuity of probabilities; how else would it be overcome? It is not a question of our ignorance, but of the mathematical form of the situation. It is no accident that Einstein, with his Spinozistic bias, should have sought to reduce quantum mechanics to a mere corollary of field physics. He was trying to get rid of discontinuity or (as Heisenberg profoundly put it, individuality), with its implication of a creative leap. Cassirer had a different way of seeking to escape the implications of atomicity: he merely denied that individuals, so far as they fail to exhibit regularity of action, exist. The statistical states of collectives constitute the entire reality; definite members of the collectives, seemingly, there are none. Is this a genuine solution?

Cassirer makes one final effort to show that statistical laws are just as incapable of providing for a freedom of indifference, of open alternatives, as classical or "dynamical" laws. Not only are there statistical regularities in the number of suicides, but also, according to some authors, in each kind and method of suicide, down to fine details. Reference is here made to some resounding claims of Quételet and Buckle concerning the analogy between physical and sociological laws. Let us grant that "freedom of indifference" may not be the correct phrase; the various sorts of acts which could result from a given set of conditions, including those furnished by the individual's own antecedent character, are not equally probable. But it does not, so far as I can see, follow that there is a certain act which has a probability of one, and other acts but zero probability. And if it be objected that probability is merely relative to our knowledge, merely subjective, then I maintain, with many present-day physicists, that all of science must on that assumption be equally subjective. The very meaning of "law" is modal; the controversy over contrary-to-fact conditionals, or over dispositional properties, is still seething, and there seems no reason why it should not go on forever, or until objective possibility and probability are conceded. Freedom is choice among really possible acts, acts possible not only given the external situation but also given the pre-existing individual with his history and constitution; however, "really possible" need not mean "indifferently possible," i.e., equally likely. The whole mystery of probability lies here, in this weighting of possibilities. Popper, who is not a determinist, speaks of "propensities," and perhaps (I do not know) he would admit degrees of strength in these propensities.[21] He says propensities are something like generalized forces, and these certainly vary in strength.

The age-old experiment of absolutizing or "deifying" causal law was an aspect of another deification, that of deductive reason. Surely the derivation of necessary consequences is not the absolute function; this function is rather the production of valuable novelty, of real additions to the definiteness of reality. Not "reason," in the mathematical or predictive sense, but "creative love" (a theme for another occasion) is the symbol of supreme power. If the evil in the world seems to contradict this, it is perhaps because we forget that were there but one creative individual, its love must take the degenerate form of mere self-love, and since there are many individuals, then because plural freedom cannot be ordered (no matter by whom) save approximately and statistically, a certain element of disorder and hence of conflict is to be expected, even assuming a theistic interpretation. Absolute determinism and a certain alleged notion of "omnipotence" are of one family of doctrines; what a relief it might be if we could rid ourselves of both, as distortions which destroy the meanings of the terms they attempt to expound!

But let us end on a more positive note. The relativity and statistical character of the world order do nothing to diminish its majesty. On the contrary, only when viewed as a power inspiring, yet not individually determining, countless acts of partial self-determination, wondrously coordinated to make a coherent world in which frustration and confusion, though real, are sec-

[21] Karl Popper, "Philosophy of Science: a Personal Report," *British Philosophy in the Mid-century*, A. C. Mace, editor (New York: The Macmillan Company, 1957), pp. 155–191, especially 188.

THE LOGIC OF PERFECTION

ondary, while fulfillment and harmony are primary, can we adequately appreciate the "grandeur of reason incarnate" of which Einstein so nobly speaks.[22] Those who, like Cassirer, emphasize the mathematical definiteness of current science, in protest against loose talk about the indefinitely chaotic world sometimes supposed to be implied by it, are well-justified. Yet we should not forget that wholly exact regularities are known only where very numerous (Bernouilli's "Law of High Numbers") and closely similar cases of process occur; that, further, the higher the level of being, the fewer are the individuals (in general) and the more pronounced the individual differences; and that, finally, on the highest level known to us (apart from deity), that of human beings, a single individual can, through symbolic means, communicate to others something of what is unique to himself, not merely in details but in basic ideas and attitudes, and thus infect multitudes with his own creative novelty. Solely by keeping all these considerations in mind can we see steadily and as a whole the mixture of order and disorder which is reality. Thomas Jefferson said that without God the world would be a "shapeless chaos." The relative indeterminist or creationist only wishes to add: with God it must still be chaotic, but how wonderfully shapely a chaos!

[22] *Science, Philosophy and Religion: A Symposium,* edited by L. Bryson and L. Finkelstein (New York: Conference on Science, Philosophy and Religion in Their Relation to the Democratic Way of Life, 1941), p. 214.

CHAPTER SEVEN

A World of Organisms

". . . with the magic hand of chance." JOHN KEATS.

"I cannot think that the world . . . is the result of chance; and yet I cannot look at each separate thing as the result of design . . . I am, and shall ever remain, in a hopeless muddle."

"But I know that I am in the same sort of muddle . . . as all the world seems to be in with respect to free will, yet with everything supposed to have been foreseen or pre-ordained."

CHARLES DARWIN, writing to Asa Gray, 1860.

AN "ORGANISM" in this essay is a whole whose parts serve as "organs" or instrument to purposes or end-values inherent in the whole.[1] It is scarcely deniable that organs and organisms exist. A man is aware of realizing purpose, and he is aware of doing so through parts of his body. Hence he is aware that he exists as an organism. It follows that either nature contains two types of wholes, the organic and the inorganic, or all natural wholes are organic. We must choose between a dualism and an organic

---

[1] For further considerations relevant to the speculations in this chapter, see my contribution to *Philosophical Essays in Memory of Edmund Husserl* (Cambridge: Harvard University Press, 1940). For a defense of the speculative method, see Ch. II of my *Man's Vision of God and the Logic of Theism* (New York: Harper and Brothers, 1941). Also, "Anthropomorphic Tendencies in Positivism," *Philosophy of Science*, VIII, 184–203.

monism, since an inorganic monism would contradict obvious facts. Is organic monism possible?

It seems not, for just as it is evident that a man is an organism, so it is evident that a mountain is not, although primitive man sometimes thought otherwise. Science exhibits nothing in the behavior of the parts of the mountain to suggest that these parts serve a purpose whose realization is enjoyed by the mountain as a whole. But this fact does not prove that no form of organic monism is possible. There is no evidence that the parts of a finger serve any purpose whose realization is enjoyed by the finger. Not all the parts of an organism are organisms. Yet a finger may in two senses be viewed as organic: it belongs to an organism; and its own parts, at least on one level, the cells, are or may be organisms. That cells literally enjoy health and suffer from injury is a supposition that conflicts with no facts, while there are facts it helps to explain. The mountain, like the finger, may be part or organ of a larger organic whole, perhaps the entire universe as an organism; and the molecules (or if not these, the atoms) composing the mountain may, like cells, though on a still humbler level, be organic wholes. The sub-molecular parts may contribute value, in the form of simple feelings, to the molecules, and the molecules may contribute value to the cosmos.

Organic monism, in the sense just indicated, includes within itself a limited or relative dualism. The assertion is not that all wholes are purposive or organic; but that, first, all well-unified wholes are organic, and second, that all wholes whatever both involve and are involved in organic wholes. But what wholes are well-unified? My suggestion is that any whole which has less unity than its most unified parts is not an organism in the pregnant sense here in question;[2] though, according to organic monism, its most unified parts, and some unified whole of which it is itself a part, must in all cases be organisms.

For example, botanists incline to regard the plant cell, rather

[2] The reasons for this principle are given in my essay on "The Group Mind" in *Social Research*, IX (May, 1942), 248–265.

than the entire plant, as the primary unit of vegetable activity. A plant is a *quasi*-organic colony of true organisms, the cells, and not, like the vertebrate animal, itself an organism. Again, a termite colony exhibits definite analogies to a single animal organism, but to an organism with less unity than termites, say a flat-worm. The colony in relation to its members is not a super-organism but an epi- or quasi-organism. There is little reason to suppose that the colony feels, though good reason to think termites feel. Or again, a mountain has inferior dynamic unity to its own atoms. Remove a part from an atom, and the whole responds with a systematic readjustment of its parts, a response to which the activity of the mountain as a whole offers only a feeble analogy, even if the mountain be a volcano. Thus it is reasonable to deny that mountains, trees, or termite colonies enjoy feelings, but not so reasonable to deny that atoms, tree-cells, and termites enjoy them.

Similarly, with all the talk about the "group-mind," there are no good indications that human groups are organisms which could think and feel as individuals. All that one can show is that human beings, like termites and atoms, act differently according to the social environment, the neighbors, which they have. Yet there may be a hidden truth in the group-mind concept. As we shall see, there is reason to think that the cosmic community, the universe, does have a group mind.

The vertebrate organism, as we know it in ourselves, has a group mind, our mind, and this suggests that quantum mechanics is not the whole account of dynamic action. For this mechanics assumes that nothing influences what electrons, protons, atoms, and the like are doing in an organic body except what other electrons and the like are doing. What then of what the man, say, is doing, for instance, thinking? This thinking is not just an arrangement of particles and/or waves; and either the thinking is an effect which produces no effects, a detached miracle in nature, or electrons in the human brain must move as they do partly because the human being thinks as he does.

However, when one is in deep sleep, what goes on in the body may indeed be little more than mere group action — not, to be sure, of particles, but of cells. And if a cell dies, then what happens in its remains will be no longer what it is doing, but what its molecules or atoms are doing. Experiments to show the merely mechanical character of the organism may, in fact, only show that the organism can at times be reduced to an approximately inorganic state.

Let us return to our main thesis, organic monism. Part of the justification of this monism is that the organic principle is sufficiently flexible to explain the relative lack of organic wholeness found in certain parts of nature, whereas the notion of absolutely non-purposive or inorganic wholes throws no light whatever on the existence or nature of purpose. If there are wholes which are directly valuable in and for themselves, there can be groups of these wholes which are valuable not directly, but for the sake of their members, or of some larger whole. Given the concept of purpose as ultimate, we can restrict its application by employing the distinction which purpose involves between end and means, or the distinction between simple and complex purposes, or purposes merely felt and those consciously surveyed. But given mere purposeless stuff or "matter," we have not, in so far, any notion of purpose.

The idea of a means or instrument does not require the notion of mere or dead matter; for an organism can function as a tool for another organism, and this assumes only that organisms influence each other, which in turn follows from the notion, to be considered presently, that all lesser organisms are parts of one inclusive organism, the universe. All that dead matter could add to this is the purely negative and empty notion of something that is absolutely nothing but means. Such an absolute negation seems devoid of philosophical or scientific utility.

There are, however, some apparent difficulties in the organismic doctrine. For example, the definition of organism calls for a whole with parts, and an electron, for instance, is not known to have parts. Even if it has parts, or if one denies the reality of electrons, must there not be something simple, the ultimate unit of being, which being without parts is not an organism? We must here reconsider the meaning of the term "part" as occurring in our definition of the organic. This meaning implies that an organism involves a plurality of entities contributing directly to the value of a single entity, the "whole." But the contributing entities need not be internal to the whole in the sense of spatially smaller and included parts, as electrons are smaller than and within an atom, or atoms within a molecule, and as nothing known is smaller than and within the electron. To render an electron or other particle an organism it is only necessary that neighboring electrons or other particles should contribute directly to each other's values, that is, should directly feel each other. Physics does not assert that particles are in every sense external to each other. On the contrary, a particle, as inseparable from its wave-field, overlaps other particles. This seems to be all the internality that is required by the general idea of organism. With the simplest organisms it is the community of neighboring entities that constitutes the plurality contributing to each entity — in a different perspective, in each case, since no two electrons, say, will have the same nearest neighbors. Where there are no smaller entities as parts, there will be no sharp distinction between internal and external. An ax seems external to a man because the man's immediate intimate relations are with the parts of his own body, so that by contrast the ax is something that contributes to his being and value only indirectly, only by first contributing, through several intermediaries usually, to the parts of his body and thence to his mind. But perhaps a particle, like a disembodied spirit, has no bodily parts. Its intimates, if any, will be its equals, the neighboring particles, or the larger wholes which they and it constitute. It will be an organic democrat and proletarian, but not an organic aristocrat.

One may well ascribe intimates, even though "external" intimates, to particles; for such entities respond immediately to neighboring particles. If an electron feels anything, it must feel its neighbors, for what else could it feel? We, on the contrary, feel chiefly our bodies, and through these, other things. Just this indirectness of feeling, mediated by entities of lesser power and complexity than oneself, is what is meant by having a body. To have no body is to have no inferior servants immediately bound to one's own purposes and feelings. Hence it is the particle, the lowest, not the highest, organism — in spite of what has often been said about God — that best fits the idea of an unembodied spirit. The particle, one might say, is embodied only in its environment, not in itself.

The mention of God brings us to the question at the opposite extreme from that about particles. If the simplest of beings can yet have complexity in the sense required for organic wholeness, can the most complex of beings, the universe, have sufficient simplicity in the sense of unity to be an organism, no doubt the supreme organism? If lack of internal parts does not prevent organicity, what about lack of an external environment? The same principle, though in opposite application, solves both problems. All that an organism requires is "an immediately contributory complexity." An organic whole must deal with or "respond" to some field of entities or environment, but the term "internal environment" is not a quibble. An organism can respond to its parts, if it has them, or its neighbors, if it has them, or to both, if it has both. An electron has only neighbors, the universe, only parts, to respond to; but both may be responsive, and in so far, organic, entities.

It may indeed be urged that the only purpose of internal adjustments, or responses to parts, is to serve as basis for desirable external adjustments, responses to neighbors. But it can, with more truth, be retorted that external adjustments are desirable only as means for the attainment of the internal organic state known as happiness. The only error in this second position is that with organisms other than the cosmos the internal field of response fails to include more than a fraction of the low and high-grade life in existence. Thus it is not a case of external relations for their own sake, but of such relations for the sake of dealing with what would otherwise be missed entirely. The cosmos, which deals with everything through its internal relations, can perfectly well dispense with external ones (except toward the future, which is never in its concreteness intrinsic to the present). To view this privilege of unique inclusiveness of organic unity as a lack of such unity is simply to lose our way among our own abstractions.

But if the universe has organic unity, where, some have asked, is the world-brain? Fechner long ago, following a trail blazed in the *Timaeus*, pointed out how unscientific the question is. On each great level of life the basic functions are performed by organs that have only a remote analogy from one level to another. We smile at the lack of generalizing power shown by those men of earlier times who supposed that microscopic animals must have, in miniature, all the organs of macroscopic ones. Is it any less naive to think that the world, if organic, must have a magnified brain? If any organic level must be a special case, it is the universe, at the opposite end of the scale from that other special case, the particle.

As we have seen, the particle has no special internal organs, because its neighbors serve it as organs. The universe, conversely, has no neighbors as organs, because everything is its internal organ. Everything contributes equally directly to the cosmic value. This means that the world-mind will have no special brain, but that rather every individual is to that mind as a sort of brain-cell. The brain is only that part of the body which most immediately and powerfully affects and is affected by the mind, the value-unity of the whole. The rest of the body is by comparison a house for the nervous system, a quasi-external environment. As the cosmos has no external environment, so it has no gradations of externality, and not even a quasi-external environment, and thus the cosmic analogue of a brain will be simply the entire system of things as wholly internal and immediate to the cosmic mind. A special world-brain, so far from confirming the supposition of a truly cosmic mind, would negate it.

You may object that if the cosmos has no external environment to deal with it does have an internal one, and that the coordination of internal actions requires a brain. But remember that the brain is only a very rough and partial coordinator of internal actions. It has almost no direct control over myriads of actions that go on in the body, even in the brain cavity itself, and this not because of any deficiency of the vertebrate brain in particular, but as a consequence of there being a brain at all as a special organ. What is needed for supreme control is obviously that every organ should be directly, and not via some other organ, such as a nervous system, responsive to the whole. The idea of a perfect yet special brain-organ is a contradiction in terms, but the idea of a perfect mind, a mind co-extensive with existence and thus omniscient, is not for all that a contradiction. For such a mind must have, not a world-part as brain, but the whole world serving as higher equivalent of a brain; so that just as between a brain cell and the human mind there is no further mechanism, so between every individual in existence and the world-mind there is no chain of intermediaries, not even a nervous system, but each and every one is in the direct grip of the world-value. The higher the organism, the larger the part directly responsive to the whole; the highest organism must be the largest organism as all brain, so to speak.

But what, you ask, would the cosmic organism be doing? To what end is the coordination of internal activities, where no external action is possible? The answer is that the end is the prosperity of the parts and of the whole as the integration of the parts. As our enjoyment of health is our participation in the health of the numerous cells, so the happiness of the cosmos is the integration of the lesser happinesses of the parts. The benevolence of God is the only way the psycho-physics of the cosmic organism can be conceived, as Fechner, one of the first great experimental psycho-physicists, was at pains to point out. Theologians have generally missed this valuable argument, for reasons which I believe to be specious.[3]

It has been argued for instance that if the cosmos were one divine organism there could be no conflict or suffering. All would be perfect peace, flawless interadjustment. This, I think, is an error.

To show this we must correct the vagueness of our concept of organism, as so far employed. An organism is not a "whole which determines its parts," but something more complex and less dialectical. Strictly speaking, in so far as an organism is a whole, in the logical sense, it does not even influence its parts. A collection of agents is not itself an agent; and if the whole is more than a collection, a genuine dynamic unity, and yet acts on its parts, then since parts obviously constitute and by their changes alter the whole in certain of its aspects, we should have each part in a relation of mutual determination with the whole, and hence with every other part. How then could we distinguish one part from another or from the whole? Would not every part be the whole? Only if each part is something in abstraction from the whole can we analyze the whole as a collection of parts or members. We can think of a collection distinctly only by adding its members in thought, and this is impossible if the members presuppose the whole.

But surely, you say, an organism is more than a collection, even an organized collection. Yes, but how? Only a creative synthesis of the parts can have its own unity, not identical with the parts and their interrelationships. But the very meaning of such a "synthesis" (see Chapter Eight) presupposes the parts as

[3] See my *Man's Vision of God*, especially Ch. V.

given, prior to the synthesis, and constituting its materials or data, not its products. Thus any actual whole-synthesis has no influence upon the elements entering into it.

Consider a momentary human experience as a synthesis of events which have just occurred in various parts of the organism, especially the cortical parts of it. This experience does not alter the events which it synthesizes. It may, however, influence subsequent events in the brain and hence in the muscles, etc. Only by neglecting the time structure of the situation, as philosophies of being may be expected to do (and they seldom upset our expectations in this regard), have "holistic" philosophies fallen into the confusion of a whole determining its individual parts. The symmetrical idea of "interaction" between whole and parts is due to treating a complex of one-way relations en bloc. What happens in my brain or nerves influences what I feel immediately afterward, and what I thus feel influences what happens in my brain at a slightly later time.

My feeling at a given moment is one, that of my cells is many. The diverse cellular feelings become data for the unitary human feeling, and this feeling is the momentary "whole" summing up the antecedent states of "the parts" and subsequently reacting upon later states of these parts. Thus the many-one action is turned into a one-many action. Not the whole as collection of parts acts upon those very parts, but the one actuality which is my feeling now, and which reflects the actualities previously constituting my body, acts upon the many actualities which subsequently compose that body.

An organism may be viewed as a society — of cells, molecules, or the like. There are two types of such societies. (The distinction goes back to Leibniz.) One type is what might, broadly speaking, be termed a "democracy." It has no supreme, radically dominant member. Certain cell colonies, and probably many-celled plants in general, and some lower forms of many-celled animals, are examples. But a unitary organism in the narrower or more emphatic sense is one with a dominant member, which is the synthetic act, or rather act-sequence, in the vertebrate case corresponding roughly to, or deriving its data from, the nervous system. My "stream of consciousness," an old metaphor which (with reasonable caution) is still usable, is the dominant member in the very complex society of sequences forming my human reality. When I am deeply asleep, there may be no dominant member then actualized. The real agent is always momentary, the stream or sequence of acts being realized only in its members. The abiding ever-identical agent is an abstraction.

In this way we avoid the mysticism of wholes acting on their very own parts, a notion which would imply unrestricted and symmetrical internal relatedness between every part and every other, dissolving all definite structures into ineffable unity, a consequence which has caused clear thinkers to turn away from "holistic" or "organicist" doctrines. To the physiological commonplace which says, the body is a society of cells, we add, not something unknown or speculative, but the given reality of human feelings or experiences, unitary at a given moment (say, during about a tenth of a second), but multiple through time. (They are given not intro- but retro-spectively, in long- or short-range memories.) The cellular processes are not the whole of a man, there is also the process of his experiences. This is not a "ghost in the machine," *pace* Gilbert Ryle. In the first place, there is no machine, but a society of living creatures, each a sequence of actual events. To this we add, as an empirical fact, the sequence of human experiences. These too are events, influencing other events.

The Cartesian division of events into extended and material, and inextended and psychic, is based on no clear evidence on either side of the division. Nothing shows that the psychical events, the experiences, are point-like, or that they are nowhere; and nothing shows that the extended events are simply without feeling, or are merely material (spatio-temporal). And both obviously have causal conditions and consequences. Ryle's apparent assumption that anyone who believes in psychical events must regard them as non-causal seems wonderfully arbitrary. Experiences must have data and, as I have argued elsewhere, this is the same as to say that they have causes.[4] And since, at least in memory, experiences are data for other experiences, it follows that experiences can be causes as well as effects.

The social view of organic unity is that individuals form organs for other individuals. This proposition is convertible: namely, if individuals are organs, organs are individuals, singly or in groups. Now an individual is self-active; if there are many individuals in the ultimate organism there are many self-active agents in that organism. Being is action, what is really many must act as many. The higher is compounded of the lower, not by suppression but by preservation of the dynamic integrity of the lower. The cosmos could not guarantee that the many individuals within it will act always in concord; for to carry out such a guarantee the cosmos must completely coerce the lesser individuals, that is, must deprive them of all individuality. Existence is essentially social,[5] plural, free, and exposed to risk, and this is required by our conception of organism. For if the action of the parts had no freedom with respect to the whole, there would be no dynamic distinction between whole and parts and the very idea of whole would lose its meaning.

It is true that the many individuals, being organs of the cosmic individual, must, according to our definition, contribute to the value of the one, but this contribution is both negative (in a sense) and positive. It includes suffering as well as joy. The all-inclusiveness of the world-mind means, not that it is exalted above all suffering, but that no pain and no joy is beneath its

[4] "The Logical Structure of Givenness," *The Philosophical Quarterly*, VIII (1958), 307–316.

[5] This essay could have been written as a generalization of "social" instead of "organic." *Cf.* Whitehead, *Adventures of Ideas* (New York: The Macmillan Company, 1933, 1948), Ch. XIII.

notice. All things make immediate contribution to the one, but they contribute what they are and have, their sorrow as well as their joy, their discord with their neighbors as well as their harmonies.

A century ago in his *Zend Avesta* (Ch. 11) Fechner argued that an eminent consciousness must resemble all consciousness in containing a contrast between voluntary and involuntary, active and passive, elements. Even eminent volition cannot act in a vacuum, or merely upon itself. But that upon which it immediately acts must be present within it; for action and its material are inseparable. In Fechner's terms, there must be involuntary impulses even in God, or there can be no divine volition or purposive activity. But these impulses must come from something. Why not from the volitions of the creatures, the lesser individuals? Our deliberate acts set up currents, as it were, in the mind of God, as the activities of our brain cells set up currents in our human minds. Each of us is a "pulse in the eternal mind" (Rupert Brooke). God then controls, checks, encourages, redirects, these pulses or impulses. But He cannot wholly initiate or absolutely control them, not because of any weakness on His part, but because absolute control of impulses, or indeed of anything, is a contradiction in terms. God is not limited in His power to do what He wishes to do, but He is not so confused as to wish to destroy the very nature of being, which is its organic character as many individuals in one, the many being as real as the one.

The lesser individuals, being more or less ignorant of each other, act somewhat blindly with respect to many of the effects of their acts. The divine love is not contradicted by the discords which result from this blindness; for love includes tolerance for the freedom of others. The divine perfection lies, not in the suppression of freedom wherever it involves risk, for at all points freedom involves risk, but in the wise and efficient limitation of the risks to the optimum point beyond which further

203

limitation would diminish the promise of life more than its tragedy. Perfection is not to be defined independently of freedom, for then it would be meaningless. Rather perfection is to be defined as the supreme way of mitigating the risk and maximizing the promise of freedom, the optimum of control, beyond which or short of which more harm and less good would result. Statesmen know that beyond a certain point interference with the lives of citizens does more harm than good, and this not solely because of the weakness or stupidity of statesmen but also because of the meaning of good as self-activity. This is part of the reason for the ideal of democracy, that people need first of all to be themselves, and this self-hood no tyrant, human or superhuman, however benevolent, can impose upon them.

But is the cosmos genuinely and organically one? Let us recall that nothing happens anywhere but its effects are communicated with the speed of light in all directions, that the same basic modes of action, expressed in quantum mechanics and relativity, pervade all parts of space. But the unity lies deeper than any such considerations can make clear. All groups short of the universe can break up, fall to pieces, in various ways and degrees. But from the cosmic community there is no secession. There is nowhere to go from the universe. It is the only aggregate that is its own foundation. This fits to perfection the idea that it is its own reason or purpose and the integration of all purposes.

We confuse ourselves in this matter by supposing that in the cosmos must be summed up all the loose-jointedness we see in various portions of the cosmos. This would be true if the loose-jointedness were, at each point, the whole story. But it is not. A sand pile is loose-jointed so far as the pile taken as a whole is concerned. Its parts serve no imaginable unitary purpose enjoyed by the pile. But it does not follow that they serve no unitary purpose. There is no unity of action *of* the sand-pile, but there is unity of action *in* the sand-pile, a unity pervading the grains of sand but referring to a larger whole than the pile. Physics tells us that the entire universe acts upon each particle to constitute its inertia. This unity of action is cosmic, and it is unbroken and all-pervasive.[6] All looseness and disintegration presuppose and cannot contradict the cosmic integrity. The one cosmos arranges and rearranges itself from time to time in subordinate centers of activity (which it can properly be said to create, in the sense of eliciting as partly self-determining), but this formation and disintegration of the subordinate centers expresses the cosmic integrity somewhat as a man may rearrange his thoughts around different idea-foci, or make different movements of his body, without ceasing to enjoy the unity of his personality while doing so.

To all the foregoing, it may be objected that explanations in terms of purpose, teleological explanations, have been discredited in science, above all through the work of Darwin. This is a contention with grave implications; for if science, or at least if rational knowledge, cannot deal with purpose, then so much the worse for purpose, for knowledge, and for human life. But perhaps it is only certain forms of teleology that have been discredited. One form of teleology that we are, I think, well rid of is the notion of a single absolute world-plan, complete in every detail from all eternity, and executed with inexorable power. The objection is not solely that God would be made responsible for the imperfect adaptations and discords in nature. There is the further objection that the world process would be the idle duplicate of something in eternity. A God who eternally knew all that the fulfillment of his purpose would bring could have no need of that fulfillment or of purpose. Complete knowledge is complete possession: it is just because a man does not know in detail what "knowing his friends better" would be like that

[6] The action is not, according to physics, instantaneous. This is a serious complication, though not, I believe, an insuperable difficulty for our thesis.

he has the purpose to come to know them better. As Bergson and Peirce[7] were among the first to see, even a world-purpose must be indeterminate as to details. For one thing, an absolute and inexorable purpose, supposing this meant anything, would deny individuality, self-activity, hence reality, to the lesser individuals, the creatures.

It follows that ill-adjustments, evils — apart from moral evil, evil deliberately chosen — are not willed but are chance results of free acts. But if evil results partly by chance, so does good. Nevertheless, the idea that adjustments are the result of natural selection among unpurposed or blind variations is not incompatible with that of cosmic purpose. For the maintenance of the general conditions under which chance and competition will produce evolution may itself be purposive. Darwinism derives generally higher forms of interadjusted species from lower; but interadjustment itself and as such is assumed, not explained. Interadjusted atoms or particles involve the same essential problem. Theism can explain order as a general character of existence; can any other doctrine? And an order capable of evolving such a vast variety of mutually compatible creatures seems all that providence could guarantee, granting that freedom is inherent in individual existence as such.

Why should the dinosaurs be any less satisfying to God or to us because they were not specifically predesigned? What after all did the old teleology accomplish, except to swell the problem of evil to impossible proportions, and to make an enigma of the process of human choice? Chance, the non-intentional character of the details of the world, is the only remedy for these two

[7] Peirce seems to hesitate between a classical and a neo-classical idea of God. Compare, in *The Collected Papers of Charles Sanders Peirce*, edited by Charles Hartshorne and Paul Weiss (Cambridge: Harvard University Press, 1934, 1935), pars. 5.119, 588; 6.157, 346, 465 f., 489, 508. As a contrast to Einstein's disbelief in a "dice-throwing God" note 5.588! See also "A Critique of Peirce's Idea of God," *Philosophical Review*, L (1941), 516-523.

difficulties. But, as Darwin repeatedly declared, chance cannot explain the world as an ordered whole of mutually-adapted parts.[8] It was because of this dilemma that Darwin gave up the theistic problem: purpose could not explain details, and nothing else could explain order as a general fact.

Here I think Darwin showed admirable care and honesty. There must be cosmically pervasive limitations upon chance, since unlimited chance is chaos; supreme purpose or providence is the sole positive conception we can form of this chance-limiting factor. And Darwin actually suggests that perhaps the solution is "designed laws" of nature, with all details, good or bad, depending upon "what we call chance."[9] But the great naturalist could not think this thought through, declaring that he was quite unsatisfied with it. Why? The answer may at least be guessed at. (1) Darwin, like so many others, tended to think of science as committed to determinism. "What we call chance," he explains elsewhere, is not properly that at all, but causes unknown to us.[10] Moreover, (2) it was probably not apparent to Darwin why cosmic purpose should leave anything to chance, at least apart from human free will. Only a philosophy of universal creativity can untie this knot. The "metaphysics" of his day, about which, with his wonderful modesty, Darwin sometimes spoke with quaint respect, did not present him with a clearly-conceived creationist philosophy. For this he was scarcely to blame.

Since Darwin was on the whole committed to determinism, he could admit no genuine element of chance for providence to limit. God must then do everything or nothing; but to do everything is to do nothing distinctive! It is also to leave nothing for

[8] See F. Darwin, *The Life and Letters of Charles Darwin* (New York: Appleton, 1898), II, 146; I, p. 276. I first came upon this quotation in that fine book, *Charles Darwin and the Golden Rule*, by W. E. Ritter (Washington: Science Service, 1954), p. 75.

[9] F. Darwin, II, 105.

[10] See the 2nd and last sentences of Ch. V of the *Origin*, 6th Ed.

the creatures to do. (The long debate about the efficacy of "second causes" remained on an essentially verbal level, since no party to the dispute would make the one concession which alone would give it content.) The "mud" in which Darwin said he was immersed was the opacity which always characterizes a deterministic world-view.

Darwin also illustrated, though this time less consciously, the absurd consequences of overlooking the truth, so much stressed in this book, that divine perfection cannot exist as a contingent fact only. Thus he worries about the question, what could have been the origin and genesis of the first cause, if we postulate one—as though its existence would be a "fact" among facts, something made whose manner of making we should inquire into.[11] Or, when asked by Gray what would convince him of cosmic Design, he says that this is a "poser," and tries to imagine experiences which would be convincing. Then he gives up the effort as "childish."[12] I suggest that it is indeed childish, because it implies that "God" stands for some great special fact, to which lesser special facts might witness, and thus it fails to grasp, as adult thinking about this matter should, the impossibility that the "creator of all things, visible and invisible," the ground of all possibility, should itself be among the things created, or actualized out of some possibility. Or, if not created, actualized out of possibility, in what intelligible sense could it be contingent, or what could its factuality have in common with that of any facts which we know to be such? I labor this point once more, for it seems to me that the learned world, with almost insignificant exceptions, has been missing it "as if by magic," and I know not how to startle, coax, or lead it gently to take a candid look, at last, at the logic of the concepts involved. (This is also my excuse for certain other cases of repetition in this book: I repeat not what nearly everyone in the intellectual world is saying, but what they are ignoring or denying without careful consideration.

[11] F. Darwin, I, 276.
[12] *Op. cit.*, II, 169.

The same excuse must serve for the polemical tone of much of this book. The theories I attack have so many friends that no one, it seems, need feel badly because of my rather isolated onslaughts.)

The reader may still not quite see why, if teleology, as conceived all along, was a "hopeless muddle," Darwin's contributions made such a difference. Darwin seemed to show that creative potentialities were inherent in the general features of living things. Since teleology had been thought of as unilateral creativity on the part of deity, unshared in any appreciable degree with the creatures, indications that the world had far-reaching potentialities for self-creation were naturally startling. But only because creativity had not been grasped in its proper universality, as the principle of existence itself.

Darwin saw all this, but as through a glass darkly. And he was misled, like many another, by the apparently factual character of the problem. The facts of evil, which he repeatedly mentions as conflicting with the belief in Design,[13] and the at least alleged fact of human freedom (it is not easy to say in what sense Darwin accepted this as a fact) were the obstacles to teleology, plus only the one new difficulty that in fact variations seem not designed but rather random, in all directions, good, bad, or indifferent. However, freedom, chance, and evil in general are inherent a priori in the mere idea of existence, construed as a multiplicity of creative processes; and it is arguable that no other construction makes sense (see the previous and the following chapters). As for the randomness effect, neither monolithic design nor rigorous law throws any light upon it. Analysis shows, as Peirce and others have argued, that without chance, its opposing term necessity is unintelligible, and indeed everything is unintelligible. Even in mathematics, one must at some point accept arbitrary decisions, if there is to be any rational necessity. If chance is merely a word for our ignorance, then we are ignorant indeed!

[13] II, 105; I, 276, 284.

It is true that chance is not something positive, or a cause of anything. It is but the negative aspect inherent in creative spontaneity (to use a phrase whose redundancy is excused by the supposition of many that it is not redundant). Chance is an aspect of the production of additional determinateness, or more simply, of determination as an act: not merely being, but becoming, definite. Determinists want things just to be definite without ever becoming so. This is in effect the denial of becoming itself, or at least its trivialization. Moreover, and this, too, Darwin dimly saw, if the universe is taken as one absolute causal system, while theism is rejected, then it follows that the system as a whole exists only by true and mere chance, that is, neither by intention nor (on pain of an endless regress) thanks to any further cause. So chance is not escaped.

What integrity there was in the honest facing of this impasse, without favoring either of the cheap and easy pretended escapes, by a man who liked to please and console, more than to upset or startle!

Another respect in which Darwin showed wisdom was in his refusal to claim that he had found the solution to the problem of the origin of life on earth. As mere chance cannot explain order, so mere matter cannot explain life and mind. The reason is the same in both cases: chance and matter are essentially negative conceptions which imply but do not explicate something positive. This is overlooked in the case of matter because "extension," spatio-temporality, is positive; but since analysis shows that mind must have this positive character, what distinguishes matter from mind remains merely negative, and therefore the first concept cannot in good logic explain the second. There must be something positive limiting chance, and something more than mere matter in matter, or Darwinism fails to explain life.

Today, some eminent contributors to evolutionary theory — Wright, Huxley, Teilhard de Chardin, and others — meet the second requirement by denying the self-sufficiency of the concept of matter, which they hold is "mere" only as observed from without, and known only in its bare spatio-temporal relationships, while in its intrinsic qualities it is mind or experience on various levels and scales of magnitude and temporal rhythm, vastly different mostly from our own. Darwin lacked this explanation of matter, hence he could only confess his ignorance by referring to the "creator" (in the famous closing passage of the *Origin of Species*).

By admitting that mind is primordial and only its species emerge, we surmount various difficulties in a more materialistic Darwinism. We then do not have to explain how from a world without any positive principle of organization (would this be a world or anything conceivable?) organic forms are derived. We have only to explain how some forms of integration come from others, or how such forms alter gradually through long ages. Mind is intrinsically and by its essential core of meaning a principle of integration. Any mind is at least a felt unity, in which various data are responded to in such a way as to attain enjoyment or satisfaction, in some degree, through unity in contrast. The orderliness of the entire world can then be interpreted through this same principle of responsiveness operating on many levels at once, as will be discussed somewhat further in the next chapter. Moreover, if the materialist wants to say that his matter has tendencies toward integration, and so mind is not needed for this, then he can be led to face the other horn of the dilemma of materialism: how to distinguish those forms of integration which show the presence of mind somewhere in a system from those which do not. Any criterion, I affirm, will either be arbitrary or will fail to divide nature into an older portion without mind and a newer with mind. Since Darwin (like most of his critics) knew little about such possibilities for reducing matter to mind (a topic regarding which much progress has been made during the last hundred years), and almost nothing about the microstructure of physical reality which has since been so extensively explored, he was well justified in refusing to deal with the origin of life, save by vaguely attributing it to the power responsible for the world-order generally.

The Vitalists of several decades ago have in a way gained their cause, though in other ways they have been proved mistaken. They have gained their cause in that a living thing is now seen not to be mechanical, if that means anything like, consisting of parts which touch and push or pull each other, and in this manner constitute the actions of the whole. Digestion, metabolism, growth, and nerve action are not essentially mechanical. But then neither are chemical processes generally. The gratuitous denial of organismic characters to the "inanimate" was the first basic error of vitalism. The inanimate is that part of nature in which organic wholeness is confined to the ultra-microscopic level, where it eludes the competence of the human senses. The second mistake was to see in life a third "force," distinct from matter, on the one hand, and mind on the other. But a process either involves sentience (sensation, feeling, memory, and the like) or does not involve it, there is no third possibility; and apart from spatio-temporal structure or behavior, and modes of experience or feeling, there is nothing positive with which we can be acquainted whereby phenomena may be explained. The third mistake was the converse of the first, for just as primitive, minute organisms may be loosely associated to form an apparently quite inorganic assembly or whole, so on a higher level they may also be associated in a somewhat more integrated way which simulates but does not quite constitute an individual organism. Thus a nation may be viewed as an organic individual, but this is generally regarded as a metaphor or illusion. Similarly an embryo in Driesch's experiments seemed to be doing remarkable things, as though inspired with a plan of its growth-aim, when really it was the cells which were doing whatever was done, and any "entelechy" should have been sought on the cellular level.

While there is no third force, there is a third level, or group of levels, of organization, between ordinary atoms or molecules and ordinary perceptible animals and plants: the level of cells, nuclei, and those giant molecules whose chemistry and arrangements constitute the gene-characters by which life is guided. Here things are even more wonderful than anything Driesch observed. Myriads of activities, simultaneous or overlapping in time, effectively coordinated and controlled! It is cells, genes, and things of that order of magnitude which, as it were, "know" (feel) something of what they are up to, not embryos (except when and as they turn into animals with functioning nervous systems). The problem is one of cellular psychology, sociology, or ecology, and then of molecular psychology and ecology. Finally, everything is a matter of individual and social psychology, on we know not how many levels. But this picture cannot be made clear unless it is firmly grasped that the cells of a tree, for instance (or the atoms or molecules of a solid), may be the highest form of dynamic individual in the tree (or solid). Thus the "vegetable soul" (or growth factor) of Aristotle may be like the "soul of the state," a metaphor or illusion. Cellular souls are another matter, for cells really do the growing, while the "growing tree" is merely the overall view of the process. But the cellular souls are almost rather "animal" than vegetable, in Aristotle's sense, for they respond to internal and external stimuli, and control their activities accordingly. They should therefore probably be viewed as sentient, as sequences of feelings, in addition to their molecular constitutions.

The problem of mind and matter is a problem not of two kinds of stuff or force but of the one and the many, and of numerous levels or kinds of one-ness and many-ness. Leibniz, with a flash of the highest genius, discovered this, two and one half centuries ago, after all mankind, so far as I can find out, in East and West, had missed it from the beginning. Many, however, are still pre-Leibnizian in their thinking. This is the sad aspect of the story. Here truly is a "cultural lag," and one affecting the scholar almost as much as the plain man.

The great mistake of "teleology" consisted in never seeing

clearly the one-many problem in relation to purpose. (At this point Leibniz was not a Leibnizian.) An absolutely controlling purpose would be the sole purpose, and could not have as its aim the creation of other purposes. If there be even two purposes, two decisions, then the conjunction of these two into a total reality must in some aspect be undecided, unintended, a matter of chance. Since a "solitary purpose" is meaningless or pointless, chance is inevitable, granted purpose.[14]

Without the recognition of chance, no teleology! Paradoxical as it may sound, only good things which in details come about by chance may concretely fulfill purpose. A man who goes to the theater to be amused can say that he has accomplished his purpose without implying that he knew in advance just what jokes he wished to hear! And so can a parent whose children think and feel in a spontaneous and unforeseen fashion, just as the parent wished they should do. Must God be without analogy to us in this? And if without analogy, could he be God?

The conception of the ultimate or cosmic organism is the remedy for two great errors of political thought, abstract individualism and abstract or mythical collectivism. Neither the human individual nor any human class or race is an absolute end, but only that whole in which men and nations and all existences have their place and value. We are members one of another because we are members of one ultimate body-mind, one inclusive, unborn, and imperishable organism.

But is the cosmos imperishable? What about the "heat death"? The present world-order, as an arbitrary choice out of the infinity of possible orders, is doubtless perishable. For as Goethe put it,

[14] I find it very odd that Pollard, in the book already referred to (footnote 12, Ch. 6), after giving a brilliant exposition of the irreducible role of chance in science, should relapse into precisely the old "muddle" of attributing details (or have I misunderstood him?) to providence. At least he wants to attribute some details. And so it is to be expected that he should ignore the problem of evil and pass off the question of freedom by the old denial that we could hope to understand such things.

in the mouth of Mephistopheles, "Whatever comes to be, deserves to be destroyed" (except in one sense — see Chapter Nine). All definite patterns lose their appeal after sufficient reiteration. The history of art and all aesthetic experience show this. It is absurd to suppose that God would be satisfied with less variety than we ourselves require, when we stretch our imaginations sufficiently to see what is involved. So (in spite of astronomers Hoyle and Bondi) I do not doubt that the present quantitative system of the cosmos is doomed. But this is compatible with there being a deeper qualitative identity through change whereby the universe as the "living garment of deity" retains this status forever.

CHAPTER EIGHT

Mind, Matter, and Freedom

"The 'matter' of materialists and the 'spirit' of idealists is a creature similar to the constitution of the United States in the minds of unimaginative persons. Obviously the real constitution is certain basic relationships among the activities of the citizens. . . . Similarly what we call matter is that character of natural events which is so tied up with changes that are sufficiently rapid to be perceptible as to give the latter a characteristic rhythmic order, the causal sequence. . . . It is no . . . principle of explanation; no substance behind or underlying changes. . . . The name designates a character in operation, not an entity. . . ."

> JOHN DEWEY, in *Experience and Nature*, p. 73.

"The intellectual destiny of the West has been to interpret the inert and material as pure dynamism, and in place of what appears as immovable, fixed, underlying 'thing,' to put forces, movements, functions."

> JOSE ORTEGA Y GASSET, in *Obras Completas* (Revista de Occidente, Madrid, 1950–52), Tomo iv.

PHILOSOPHERS AND natural scientists are, in our universities, two rather distinct sorts of human creatures. They occupy, during working hours, quite different buildings, often consult different libraries, and meet only casually, perhaps at faculty meetings or at lunchtime. Members of one group are likely to be either afraid or aggressively disinclined to communicate intellectually with those of the other. This mutual isolation (intensified, though not created, by "security" measures) has its disadvantages. Certain recent developments in science, especially in microphysics and biology, are strikingly paralleled by some tendencies in philosophy — having in part different origins and motives — and the full intellectual and practical meaning of the scientific changes can, I believe, be appreciated only when their philosophic counterparts (not merely echoes!) are also attended to.

That there is less agreement in philosophy than in science must be admitted. Consequently, I can at best speak only for certain philosophers, at worst for myself alone. Fortunately, some scientists inclined to indulge in reflections of the philosophic degree of generality offer a certain amount of support to my contentions. I shall now try to indicate in advance something of the nature of these contentions. I shall hold that "mind" and "matter" are not two ultimately different sorts of entity but, rather, two ways of describing a reality that has many levels of organization. The "mind" way I take to be more final and inclusive, so that my position is the opposite of materialism. However, I recognize that the material mode of description is that part of the complete mode which is capable of scientific precision and that, accordingly, "methodological materialism," or the restriction of attention to this mode, is a natural bias among scientists. Much depends on seeing that what I have called the complete mode — that is, an ultimate idealism or psychicalism — does not exclude any scientific procedure, but merely opens our eyes to the beyond that tends to escape any save a vague, intuitive apprehension. No exact analysis or observation in physical or spatio-temporal terms is forbidden, but rather we are enabled consciously to experience the world both with all possible accuracy and with the dim background (which, consciously or not, is always there anyway) of invincibly indefinite feeling for the "life of things" (Wordsworth). In the end, this consciousness may actually increase the extent of our accurate knowledge, and it is sure to increase our enjoyment of the world, peace of mind, and understanding of ourselves.

Preliminary to discussing mind and matter, we must consider two notions common to both, those of individual and of event. We tend to conceive the latter as a function of the former; events are the adventures of "things" or "persons." However, science now considers nature as most fundamentally a complex of events related together in a spacetime system. The everyday notion that happenings must happen *to* something which (or to someone who) moves about seems for current physics at best only a convenient way of talking. Atomic events do not literally occur to a moving entity called an atom; rather, by an atom we simply mean a sequence of events having a certain persistent atomic character, the same atomic number, say, and a certain continuity, or near continuity, through space-time. On the lowest or simplest level, that of electronic or protonic events, it is, according to some authorities, impossible and in violation of well-attested laws to interpret such elementary events as the motions of self-identical entities. The laws allow no possible paths for such movements and no meaning for such self-identity. There are, then, if this interpretation is correct (and not all scientists accept it), no such things as particles; there are only particle-like events. Each successive observation discloses a new entity, not the same entity in a new location. A simple account of this revolutionary conclusion is found in Schroedinger's little book, *Science and Humanism.*

Many philosophic systems cannot readily accept the notion of happenings that are not happenings *to* concrete things, but are themselves the concrete things in the case. But, even before quantum mechanics, certain philosophers had proposed to dispense with the notion of enduring individuals or substances to which events occur and to take the events themselves as the concrete units of reality. I am thinking, for example, of Mahayana Buddhists, and then, in the West, Hume, Peirce, and James. Simultaneously with the rise of quantum mechanics, Whitehead developed an elaborate metaphysical system completely free from substance, in any sense that could conflict with the theory of electronic events.

By metaphysical system, I mean one in which the attempt is made to generalize all ideas to the fullest possible extent. Whereas, in science, ideas are generalized only so far as the predictive control of some class of currently known facts requires, the metaphysician, as I conceive him, is trying to provide for all possible classes of facts rather than to predict which will be actualized. He wants to forbid no scientific hypotheses except those which, unaware, cross the line between the use and the misuse of categories — that is, terms of most basic or ultimate meaning, such as the meaning of fact itself. According to Whitehead, any possible fact must represent an aspect of events or happenings, actual or potential. Things or persons can then be only certain stabilities or coherences in the flux of events. The stabilities are in the events, not the events in the stabilities. You, for example (as something always the same through the years), are in your experiences, but there is no ever-identical you which, from the time you were born onward, has contained all your experiences. The very idea seems dubious, for with each new experience must there not be a slightly different or new self? Each new experience possesses relationships to the old experiences, in the form of memory, conscious or unconscious; hence, if the self is what includes or really "has" experiences, there is at each moment a new self, partly inclusive of old experiences, not an old self with partly new experiences. The latter may also be said, provided that one means by the "old" self a certain kernel of personality traits and bundle of memories, and provided also that one admits that this kernel is contained in each new experience, not each new experience in the kernel. For whatever has both old and new constituents is itself necessarily new, since the old, say X, and the new, say Y, make up a new totality, XY, which cannot be real until Y is real. Furthermore, there is nothing in the mere idea of an event, or even of an experience, that requires it to belong to a sequence repeating the same personality or character in successive members. Accordingly, the physicist's denial of persistent self-identity to electrons need be no puzzle for philosophy. To be sure, electronic events cannot enjoy certain privileges that personal memory, anticipation, and the sense of harmony between previous purpose and present fulfillment alone can furnish. Personal identity does enable events to enrich later events in a manner otherwise impossible. (Really, it is this enrichment.) But events lacking such persistent identity may nevertheless occur.

The absence of continuity in electronic events — that is, the spatial gaps between their successive occurrences — is also not especially paradoxical. We seem to have a partial analogy for it in everyday life. Consider a man in deepest sleep being carried through space. The man's body is moving along, apparently continuously. But let us set this aside for the moment and think about what is sometimes called the man's soul or the man as a conscious individual. Between the time when he falls into dreamless sleep and the time he awakes — or, at least, begins to dream — no conscious individual is there. Of course, we may say, yes, such an individual is there but is sleeping, meaning that a certain potentially conscious individual is without actual consciousness. But so far as by a soul we mean an actually conscious individual or "stream of consciousness," a sequence of experiences related by memory and personality traits in the manner described, should we not say, "No soul is there but only a sleeping body"? An observer would behold nothing else, and the man's memory, when he awakes, refers to an earlier time, before he fell into dreamless sleep.

It may be said that sleep is never for a moment without dreams; but is not this assertion rather arbitrary? If souls can be born in all embryos, they can be reborn every morning. The difficulty, if any, is no greater. What now, I ask, is the difference between a body whence, as we say, "the soul has fled," and a body "whose soul is in dreamless sleep"? Only this: the soulless body lacks certain physical activities, such as breathing and heartbeats, and can never awaken, while the still-besouled body has these activities and can and probably will awaken. If you say, "At least God might observe the soul as something present in the sleeping man," one must ask, what is the sense of this, if we have no idea what sort of thing God would be observing. I find in my own mind no such notion, if "soul" means anything more than the probability or potentiality of certain modes of action and experience, embodying the man's personality traits and memories. However, a probability is not a concrete thing, all by itself. The actual thing "moving" along is, then, the sleeping body, which not merely can produce certain events but consists, at each moment, of events actually taking place. If, now, we learn from physics that the body itself is only relatively continuous through space-time, so far as it consists of discrete particle-like events separated by minute space-time intervals, why should we be astonished? The soul, too — or at any rate the sequence of experiences — goes into and out of actuality, and the only reason we can speak of a self-identical person is that, with each awakening, certain modes of action, experience, memory, reappear. However, in very abnormal cases of multiple personality or psychic degeneration, this is much less true. The persistence of individual traits through a single linear sequence of events being thus a matter of degree, why may there not be events that do not belong to any such sequence, that is, do not constitute any individual history, even a discontinuous one?

Our analogy between soul-discontinuity and electronic discontinuity might be questioned on the ground that, taken as a "potentiality for certain types of action" the soul in a man's moving body does follow a continuous (or virtually continuous) path through space, the path of positions at which he could wake up, while there is, perhaps, not even for the potentiality of electronic events any such continuous track of points. However, since the path of positions of the sleeping soul is derivative from the positions of successive clusters of particle events composing a human body at different times and places, its continuity is in any case a construct, not a primary datum for our thought about this problem.

It is interesting to consider the ancient Aristotelian doctrine of "substance" as owing its self-identity through time and space to its being made up of the same "matter" with the same "essential" form, though with inessential differences from moment to moment. Since the sameness of form (for example, the gene structure of a human individual) is admitted by our doctrine, the difference lies in the notion of "matter." Here we point to the scientific facts showing that the matter of a macroscopically perceptible substance owes its identity through time to the persistence of certain forms (statistically, rather than absolutely, persistent) exhibited by microscopic events. Anything beyond this formal identity seems absolutely unknowable and unimaginable when we get to the ultramicroscopic or particle level, which contains the whole of the material of the physical world. Thus, events and their forms and relationships (such as similarity, causal influence, or memory), are all the "substance" we can give any positive meaning to. The explanation of sameness as both formal and material was in reality an explanation in terms of many levels of event-forms, including relational forms. The "same matter" meant the same microscopic forms! Unless there be an endless regress, there is a bottom level where it no longer has a meaning to contrast persistence of form with that of matter, and where there are merely interrelated events with a certain partial repetitiveness of form. The only "stuff" of change is finally just process itself and its unit is an event, not a bit of persisting substance. (In what sense there are least quanta of process, unit-processes, we shall not here attempt to discuss.)

Let us now turn to the question of freedom. I give this term a common-sense meaning. A man, in a given situation and with a given past history, can, really can, do *either* this *or* that. But many older systems of metaphysics, and also Newtonian science (at least in its most obvious interpretation), viewed causal laws as uniquely determining the outcome of every situation. Given adequate understanding of the conditions, the result would be wholly a foregone conclusion — for those with adequate understanding of the laws and the situation. Both science and speculative philosophy (I am not speaking of all that is sometimes called philosophy) have grown increasingly critical of this assumption during the past 75 years. Today quantum mechanics strongly suggests, if it does not actually prove, that on the basic level causality is something essentially different from this classical conception. Individual events are at least *as if* genuinely random or fortuitous, within certain limits, and causality consists in the limits to the randomness. Only when large numbers of similar events are dealt with can we have highly exact predictability.

Does this new concept of causality suffice to explain human freedom? The view we take of this question depends upon our answer to another: do particles (shorthand for electronic-protonic events) in inorganic systems, where there is nothing at all closely comparable to human thoughts and feelings, act according to the same laws, precisely, as particles in systems that do involve human experiences? Or again, do we define a "human body" as simply a very special, complex system of particles, or as such a system somehow woven together with human thoughts and feelings? Only the latter view corresponds to the known facts. We do not know ourselves as just a set of interacting particles; we do know ourselves as consisting, in part at least, of a stream of experiences—broken, to be sure, by sleep. What right then has anyone to assume that there are events in nature that make *no* difference to certain events intimately associated with them? Only by making this assumption (as Schroedinger, for example, apparently does) can one infer that our human freedom is no more than that which the laws of quantum me-

chanics allow. Particles under the influence of human consciousness are not necessarily just ordinary particles. Seemingly there
must be a difference, although it may be slight; and in this
difference lies our freedom, so far as it is expressible in bodily
behavior. Moreover, as Nils Bohr suggests, one may reason by
analogy: if individual events on the particle level are not rigidly
determined by causal laws, then we should expect that on higher
levels, where there is greater depth of individuality and conscious
alternatives of action, individual events will be less fully determined by their causal antecedents. A human experience is a unitary individual event, not a mere mosaic of events on the
electronic level. Indeed, if our experiences did not have unity,
should we know what "unity" meant? Thus the physics of
inorganic particles and their statistical regularities cannot be the
whole truth about human behavior. True, we should assume
that quantum physics has approximate validity in application to
higher organisms, for only in this way will be be likely to find
out the limits of this validity. But absolute validity is not lightly
to be assumed in science. The ultimate laws, if we can ever find
them, must allow for the difference which the presence of human
experiences makes in certain bodies in nature, and this no physical law as now stated even attempts to do.[1]

But how, you may ask, could a physical law allow for the
influence of thought upon mere material bodies or events? Can
mind be conceived to act upon matter? When (for better or for
worse) the whole face of the earth is being modified as the result
of human thought, it is strange to deny that mind acts upon
matter. But we must be careful in using highly abstract words.

[1] See W. Heisenberg, *Philosophic Problems of Nuclear Science* (New
York: Pantheon, 1952), last two pages. Heisenberg speaks of the "limited
applicability" of the mathematical laws of atomic physics, which will have
to be "broadened" if they are to apply to living processes and to thought,
and which we may have to "limit in range by attaching specific new conditions to them." See also Heisenberg, *Physics and Philosophy* (New
York: Harper & Brothers, 1958), p. 199.

Science does not reveal two things in nature, "mind" and "body." It reveals rather many levels of process, from nuclear particles to man. Each type can be described with respect to physical properties — size, shape, motion, vibration rate, and the like. (On the lowest levels there are certain difficulties, or qualifications.)

But the higher levels, at least, can also be described in terms of psychical aspects — emotion, perception, memory, desire, as known to us in ourselves through more or less "immediate" memory. It has been said that if ordinary people had watched one-celled animals in action as often as they have dogs and horses, it would be as good common sense to attribute feeling and sensation to microscopic creatures as to the higher animals. Thus, far below the limits of direct vision we find the apparent scale of "mind" extending downward as our knowledge increases. Who can set a limit to this extension? And if "feelings of an electron" seems odd, remember that "size, shape, motion" also assume odd forms on the particle level! I think we have good reason to take seriously those philosophers and scientists who believe that there is no such thing as "mere matter," upon which mind must act, or be unable to act. The ultimate understanding of nature, such thinkers hold, would be a generalized comparative psychology that would absorb all physics. Physics would be the behavioristic psychology of particle-events, atoms, and molecules, showing how they "respond" to their neighbors as "stimuli." Psychology, as more than merely behavioristic (if such a thing be possible), would tell us how things feel as they thus respond, what their (perhaps rudimentary) memories, perceptions, desires, and so on, are like.

This may very well be far beyond our human powers. But if the idea makes any sense at all — and to me and to others[2] it does make sense — then all talk about how human thoughts

[2] See Sewall Wright, "Gene and Organism," *The American Naturalist,* LXXXVII, 5 (1953); or R. W. Gerard, "The Scope of Science," *The Scientific Monthly,* LXIV (1947), 500; and W. K. Clifford, *Lectures and Essays,* II (London: Macmillan and Co., 1886), 321.

might influence, or be unable to influence, mere bits of insentient matter is beside the point. And then the question, what difference it could make to an atom that it is in the presence of human thought or emotion is really the question, how the presence of high-level experiences can make a difference to low-level experiences. Now it is, if I may so speak, an upside-down world if the trivial and low types of reality are simply immune to guidance by higher-level types. It would be as if stupid people never paid attention to the suggestions of brighter minds, and children none to those of their more experienced parents. There would be nothing at all like hero worship. Superiority would have no fascination or charm whatsoever. The religious idea that the world as a whole is swayed by a supreme level of consciousness simply would be wrong in principle. And, on a humbler level, the fact that everything is *as if* the cells of my brain and, hence, those of my muscles were constantly being influenced by my human thought and feeling would be a sheer illusion. I suggest that the contrary supposition makes better sense, that superiority in principle tends to have influence, to exert guidance. Even rascally tyrants have something, a certain intensity, or boldness; not everything about them is inferior! And besides, the direct power of the tyrant need not be very great. If a few subordinates obey him, and these have considerable power, owing to historical accidents of social development, then he may for a time sway a great society. But the basic power relationships in nature, like the power of vertebrate minds (that is, their thoughts and feelings) over their bodies, cannot rest upon such accidental and artificial arrangements.

You may be asking: how is influence transmitted from one level of experience to another? When parental ideas act on child-minds, there is a mechanism of this action: speech, sound waves, gestures, hearing, and sight. But what mechanism operates between my thoughts or decisions and my brain cells? No mechanism. Not all action can be indirect. This does not mean that explanation is impossible in this case, for not all explanation needs to be mechanical.

We have only to consider what experience is in order to find a clue to the mutual influence between the body and experience. Experience has to have a content; it is experience *of* something. Philosophers have argued about the proposition, "Perhaps all we directly experience is our own mental state at the time." But mental states are just experiences over again, so that the proposition means, "Perhaps our experiences are of nothing except themselves." We must reject the absurd idea that any experience can thus furnish its own sole datum. A mere awareness of that same awareness is nonsense. Discarding this nonsense, let us see what the data of experience can be. In memory, the datum of present experience seems to be furnished, in part at least, by some past experience. Now this amounts to saying that past experience influences present experience. To be aware of something is *ipso facto* to be influenced by it. For example, remembering past pleasure is a different sort of experience from remembering past pain; remembering a past subtle thought is still to possess its subtlety. Thus, to explain how something influences an experience, we have only to explain how this something comes to be an object or content of the experience. The answer is simple: the objects come to be experienced just by being there, by being actual, and by having a character suitable for objects of the given sort of experience; the experience takes advantage of this suitability and actuality, and that is all there is to it. No mechanism is required for experience to be enabled to lay hold of its appropriate objects (not too complex or disordered). It simply *is* the experience of these objects, by virtue of their natures and its nature, and nothing else whatever. Thus, in memory, past experiences, since they have actually occurred, are available for experiencing, and present experience enjoys them as its objects.

But, you ask, does not the brain somehow preserve the past experiences and make memory of them possible? The brain has an essential influence upon human memory, this I grant, but how? Is there any way for a thing to influence an experience save by becoming one of its objects or contents? But suppose that the situation is this: past human experiences are not sufficient contents for present human experience; they must be supplemented by something new. Suppose, also, that the function of the brain is to furnish at each moment the required additional content. This new content must be harmonious with the experiences that are to be remembered from the past. If, for example, I am seeing green grass, this will inhibit some memories and favor others, partly for reasons of esthetic harmony and discord. But where is the greenness coming from? There is no scientific evidence that it is coming directly from the grass. I might have on green glasses and be looking at straw-colored grass. It is even possible to have vivid sensations of color with closed eyes in darkness. It seems then that color comes to us directly from brain or nerve cells. Moreover, connections have been formed between these and other cells, so that the latter are also at least slightly activated, and only such past experiences as can fit with all this new material coming to me as data from the brain can be remembered consciously. (*Fit* means, roughly, to help form a tolerably coherent pattern.)

We have said that qualities, such as colors, come into experience from cells. How can cells cause me to experience a certain quality, save by themselves having this quality, which becomes mine as they become immediate content of my experience? (If anyone asks, why then do we need science to tell us about cells, I remind him that grass too consists of cells, so that, if *it* is said to be the direct object of experience, we have the same problem; the solution is that experience may be direct without being distinct regarding details.)

Consider the case of pain. The usual view seems to be that the object of the experience is just the pain itself. One feels simply one's own feeling or sensation. But this is the view we have rejected, that a state of awareness can have itself as sole datum. True, our direct experience seems in certain cases to disclose only an ache or pain as object; but is this pain simply *our* feeling of suffering? If, as we have argued, it cannot be just our feeling, then what could it be but certain aching bodily cells? And why not? Cells are living, individual organisms; and if living, why not sentient? When intense heat reaches them they undergo injury. They can hardly enjoy this. If they suffer, then our sense of physical pain is our experience of their experience of injury. They are feeling the heat as unduly agitating their molecules and, thus, disrupting them. We are feeling their feeling of disruption. (I cannot stop to discuss the possible role of pain nerves in this connection.)

The point we have reached is that cells can influence our human experiences because they have feelings that we can feel. To deal with the influences of human experiences upon cells, one turns this around. *We* have feelings that *cells* can feel. Since a human experience is vastly more important and complex than any we can sensibly attribute to a cell, its feeling of our human feeling must be very inadequate indeed, a faint, almost infinitely simplified echo. But no more is required. For since the body thrives during deep sleep, it is plain that the cells are largely independent of us, receiving only slight influences from our thoughts and feelings. It is like the touch of a button that alters the operation of heavy machinery. The nervous system is that kind of trigger mechanism.

The foregoing theory, largely due to Whitehead,[3] in principle solves the mind-body problem that Du Bois-Reymond thought insoluble. The rest is detail. That a blow on the head may abolish consciousness is just what might be expected from the theory. Consider this: experience cannot go on without suitable data; accordingly, the material that nerve cells furnish for our human

[3] *Modes of Thought* (New York: The Macmillan Company, 1938), p. 29.

experience must be properly coordinated, to the extent that a coherent awareness requires a coherent object of awareness; the healthy waking brain furnishes as datum for experience a coordinated, integrated pattern of activity; the sleeping brain, or the bruised brain, no longer presents the required integration. There is nothing to experience of a humanly manageable sort.

This is a revolutionary theory of power or influence. It says that nothing influences experience except the things that are experienced. There are not two grounds of possibility for an experience, the total datum to be experienced and something else. There is only the datum. The body itself is simply the main thing experienced. But because the sense organs echo the environment, it comes about that, in experiencing the bodily states, we gain knowledge of the world outside the body. So, in watching a television screen, we gain knowledge of what is happening miles away. The experience of the body is the same sort of thing, except that we do not primarily experience the body indirectly, with our eyes, as we do the screen, but rather we directly feel the feelings of bodily cells. Yet, since the spatial and temporal and qualitative patterns tend to duplicate patterns outside the body — as those on the screen do those on the stage where the play is being enacted — in both cases we feel that we are grasping an action not, in the first instance, on the screen, or in the body, but elsewhere. And so, in a sense, we are!

The foregoing theory of experience implies the reality of freedom. For, while experience is certainly influenced by its data (which are its only conditions), it seems evident that it can never be wholly determined by them. A "creative synthesis" is required, without which the experience would merely be the given data over again. It follows that nothing and no power, even God, decides for us exactly how we are to put the data together into our experiential reactions to them. In influencing us, God himself could only be the supreme datum! Hence, freedom in some degree is inevitable, no matter by what rulers, human or superhuman, we may be governed. To rule is to sway all by a common influence; but something must, in each individual case, be freely added to constitute the response to the influence. Ruling or governing is always the imparting of certain common characters or limits to the self-determining of the the ruled or governed. The citizens decide for themselves within the limits set by the ruler. If the latter decided everything, there would be no citizens and no rule. The ideal rule sets those limits outside of which freedom would involve greater risks than opportunities. Risks cannot be banished, for opportunity would go with them, both having the same root in freedom or self-determination. But too much freedom would extend risks more than opportunities, and too little would restrict opportunities more than risks.

Freedom is an indetermination in the potentialities for present action which are constituted by *all* the influences and stimuli, all "heredity and environment," all past experiences, an indetermination removed only by the actuality (event, experience, act) itself, and always in such fashion that other acts of determination would have been possible in view of the given total conditions up to the moment of the act. A free act is the resolution of an uncertainty inherent in the totality of the influences to which the act is subject. The conditions decide what can be done and cannot; but what is done is always more determinate than merely what can be done. The latter is a range of possibilities for action, not a particular act.

It is not only in relation to other "individuals" that there needs to be some self-determination with respect to issues not prejudged by these others. In relation to one's own past, also, present experience must freely achieve its unique synthesis of influences. For the final units of actuality are not, as we have seen, things or persons but "experient-events," new total acts of response to events already actualized. The final "self" having "self-determination" is the present unity of experience. Slavery to one's character as it was in infancy or has been up to now is not freedom. If there is any free acting it is ultimately in and by the present, and the whole past world is the set of conditions or data for the act, with one's own past being included essentially in the same way as other conditions, except for its greater relevance, in most respects and cases.

It is really analytic to say that experience is incompletely determined by its stimuli, its conditions. For an experience has a unity not in the stimuli, and this must be created; it can be only an emergent synthesis, however trivial in its novelty. Thus, nothing can prevent persons, while they exist, from having some degree of freedom. Nevertheless, human laws and actions can either favor or hamper the optimal development of freedom, can influence the extent to which the majority of men may achieve the fullness of their human privilege. Although self-determination, in at least some slight degree, must (if our view is sound) be a property of all events, yet only where there is consciousness of ideas and ideals does such power of decision have the radical importance for good or evil that we feel it to have in our own species.

With respect to this power, underestimation and delusive exaggeration are alike harmful.[4] There is indeed an open horizon, and each of us adds to the world something that no wisdom could have wholly foreseen. This creating, this deciding of the otherwise undecided, this forming of the previously inchoate, is our dignity, by which, as Bergson beautifully says, each of us is an artist whose product is life or experience itself. Yet the causal momentum is great; and to make very much of our freedom calls for skillful strategy and tactics. It is vain to say, "Go to, I will now be a different person, brave where I was cowardly, kind and patient where I was harsh and irritable," or even, "I will now be good or excellent in a new direction, manner, or degree." One

[4] On the abuses of the idea of freedom, see Walter Coutu, *Emergent Human Nature* (New York: A. A. Knopf, 1949). In conversation, Professor Coutu conceded that there is a case for freedom as a "continuous variable," present in varying but, in general, small degree.

must employ every suitable indirect means: writing down a new schedule (not too ambitious at first), beginning to read a new sort of book, seeking out new and better friends, discussing plans with trusted intimates, trying to secure a new and more suitable job, in extreme cases consulting a psychiatrist or other counselor. In the foregoing list, some would include prayer, as not the least item.

Man's very fate depends in part upon his adequate recognition of his lowly status as only a *little* more than an unconscious (although complicated) bit of causal driftwood, but also of the preciousness and glory of that slight surplus. The causal drift itself is merely the mass of data formed by acts of freedom already enacted on various levels, human, subhuman, and perhaps superhuman. Causality is crystallized freedom, freedom is causality in the making. There is always freedom, for there is always novelty. There is always causality, for always freedom has already been exercised, and a decision once made can only be accepted, it cannot be remade. Past decisions made with at least minimal freedom furnish the only content of new acts of emergent synthesis. Reality is sheer creation, but present creation adds only its little mite to the organic totality of data already accumulated.

CHAPTER NINE

Science, Insecurity, and the Abiding Treasure

"God has said, ye shall fail and perish,
But the thrill ye have felt tonight
I shall keep in my heart and cherish
When the worlds have passed in night."
RICHARD HOVEY, in *More Songs from
Vagabondia* (with Bliss Carman).

RELIGION, WE have sometimes been told, originated in man's weakness and fear, his inability to understand and control nature. Through the gods, man acquired an illusory sense of security. But now that we have science and technology, can we not be secure without religion? Still, there are grounds for discounting this possibility.

Let us consider, first, the physical causes of anxiety, the chances of discomfort, injury, disease, hunger, and death. To what extent can we expect material and intellectual progress to eliminate these things? To eliminate death as eventually inevitable, nothing, it seems, can be done. Or shall we take seriously those who talk of science conquering death? For reasons which may be guessed, I trust death will not be conquered. (For one thing, what would we do with our population problems if death should become avoidable?) We may very well increase the proportion of deaths from old age (though then we should have somewhat fewer children) — provided that war be avoided and provided, or in so far as, crime and the careless use of dangerous tools, such as automobiles or atomic piles, are kept within bounds. But each invention adds new risks for carelessness or crime to turn into catastrophe. Risks from diseases are diminishing rapidly. Yet consider a mild but bothersome disease, tooth decay. It seems that people want to run the risk of eating the refined starch and sweet foods that are among the causes of tooth decay. Do not many of us fear boredom almost as much as danger and want soothing tastes as much as freedom from decay? Few of our automobiles are equipped with even that most elementary of safety devices for fast-moving vehicles, seat belts, though the proportion is increasing. Surely these belts are more needed in private cars than in planes! If such is human behavior, how secure are we likely to be, with all our science? (Nevertheless, I hope some of my readers will give this matter serious thought. It may enable them to avoid killing or mutilating one or more human beings, perhaps themselves, whom there was no need to treat in this way.)

It seems plain that a considerable probability of many kinds of physical evil and the certainty of eventual death are things to be faced, not eliminated. The sense of insecurity must have another remedy than the abolition of physical danger.

Let us now turn to non-physical forms of insecurity, to mental hazards. We are afraid of social rejection, of arousing the hostilities, or of meeting with the indifference, of others. We are afraid of failure, in the eyes of others — or, perhaps worse, in our own. We are afraid of being forced to change our beliefs through contrary evidence, without being able to find new beliefs that will give us the same satisfaction. Or we are afraid of being forced to change our habits because of new inventions and new methods in business, industry, education, or scholarship. Finally, the impossibility of foreseeing the future may be a source of fear.

What can be done about these hazards? It is scarcely possible that others should always like us or find us interesting; no training, administered by fallible human beings, can equip us all for unvarying success or, unerringly and without false starts, pick out the occupation for which each of us is fitted. With ever-increasing knowledge, ever new errors are found in previous beliefs and unsuitabilities in previous habits. Hence the ever-recurring painful necessity of changing beliefs and habits. And, finally, the unforeseeability of the future is incurable; nay more, though not everyone appears to have noticed this, it is increasing and must continue to do so. We talk of science as prediction — as though we imagined that, as knowledge grows, future events will more and more appear, first as objects seen distinctly through a telescope and then close at hand with the naked eye. A little reflection shows how erroneous this is. Our future, in its important features, does not depend upon eclipses of the sun or moon, which indeed are predictable. Among natural phenomena, the weather and soil erosion are perhaps those in whose future we are most vitally interested. The future of soil erosion we do to some extent anticipate, in a manner that primitive man did not; but then, primitive man produced far less soil erosion to predict. Indeed, he could predict its comparative absence. The chief comfort we can derive from the rather gloomy prophecies of soil experts is that they are based on the assumption that the present careless practices of man in some areas will continue or will be remedied only at a certain rate. So we may hope that the predictions will not come true to the full extent! Another comfort is that certain experts say we must in any case live on algae grown in water or on synthetic food, if the world-population increase goes on. It thus appears that the reliability and human importance of predictions as to soil are heavily dependent upon what human beings may do, and this, soil science does not suffice to foretell. Again we foresee the weather somewhat better than did primitive man; but a new source of uncertainty is even now entering into meteorological anticipation. Man is beginning to make weather, to some slight extent. In time, the extent will be less slight. Whole cities, perhaps larger regions, will be warmed, chilled, moistened, dried out. Will this make atmospheric conditions foreseeable? Yes, if you can foresee the actions of politicians, voters, administrators in your own and other states or countries, of friends, enemies, strangers, and criminals. But foreseeing such things is not a matter of meteorology. Thus the progress of science is tending to turn important predictions into social predictions. Is this likely to enlarge the area of reliable foresight?

As my former colleague Charner Perry long ago remarked, the future of mankind depends upon inventions: to predict an invention is virtually to make it before it is made. We may add: The future depends upon works of literature and art and upon important political speeches and religious utterances, which sway men's feelings and shape their imaginations: to predict such things is to create the works of art or religion before the artists or men of religion have done so. The future depends upon astute or stupid patterns of statesmanship, to predict which is virtually to be, in advance, the statesmen of the future. Could the future of psychology or sociology itself be said to be predictable by psychologists or sociologists?

I am as much an admirer of science and scientists as of my own subject, philosophy, and of philosophers. But must not the aim of a scientist be something else than that of telling the rest of us what we are going to do? And yet, as technological power increases, to foretell future events more and more requires foretelling human actions. Let us put the conclusion bluntly: science does not mean ever-increasing power to predict human affairs. The scientist who can tell us what we or our children are going to do must be a dictator-scientist who informs us of what he intends to force us to do; and in that case, would we not be ill advised to believe him, for is he not likely to be lying or deceiving himself, as dictators customarily do? Truly man cannot, even approximately, foresee his future, and we are receding from this alleged goal, not approaching it! Primitive man knew roughly how he was going to live, namely, as his fathers and grandfathers had lived during his childhood; what we know is that we are going to live more and more differently, but as to the direction and extent of the differences — we must more and more be content to wait and see. Science tells us, not what men will do, but what they can do, and by what methods. Out of the things they can do — and this becomes a wider assortment of possibilities with each new discovery — the men of the future will decide for themselves which things to do. It would be not science but magic to look into their as yet non-existent motives and see their coming acts. The mediocre cannot clearly imagine the mind of the genius; the cleverest among us are but mediocrities, however much science we may know, outside a few types of activity. And must not the genius of the future make ignorant fools of us all? In the foregoing remarks I am not depreciating social science; indeed, I trust I have been using it.

Perhaps the impossibility of a net increase in foresight is one source of the demand for what is called "social security." And it is indeed possible for a society to spread its risks, through insurance or organized charity, so that the danger of extreme poverty will be limited to the possibility of catastrophe for the society as a whole. This possibility of catastrophe seems to comprise war, international and civil; population growth beyond the immediately available means of production (for, alas, one cannot eat food grown through inventions not yet made); and gross mismanagement of the financial system, or other basic economic arrangements. The last of these dangers we appear to be learning to avoid; the other two remain major threats concerning which we may make guesses, entertain hopes, and try to take preventive measures. But serious prediction on a scientific basis is here out of the question. And think of the vast extent which our uncertainty thus spans. One of the following might occur: much of civilization and its peoples destroyed; *or* vast hordes of human beings barely kept alive; *or*, finally, immense increases in material benefits for that half of it which now enjoys practically nothing of such benefits except some elements of hygiene whose chief effect is the perpetuation of poverty through rapid increase in the number of persons to be cared for. An Indian chief, five centuries ago, was not able to foresee very precisely the near future of his tribe, but his uncertainty was over a much more moderate spread of possibilities than ours. Thus our growth in collective power means greater range in the possible uses of power and hence a greater span of uncertainty. Where, then, is security to be found?

My answer is the old one: security is found more in *principles* than in conditions. It consists, not in the absence of danger or in banishing the unsettled status of the future, but in the ideas and ideals whereby danger and the ambiguities of the future can be faced with courage and with joy. What are these ideas or principles?

First, the principle that life depends as much upon our response to events around us as upon the events. As Rufus Jones once said, it is "the steady swing of the will" which chiefly makes life. If we fear that others will reject us, we can at least resolve that we will not reject them. We can bear in mind that the hostilities, the aggressions, in our own hearts may be more destructive, as they are certainly more within our power to influence, than those around us. The determination to be a friend is part of the cure for the anxiety to have friends. The readiness to cultivate other and now neglected resources is part of the cure for the anxiety lest we lose certain resources. For instance, some persons fear the failing of their eyesight. But at least, music will remain, conversation will remain, listening to lectures, the fragrance of flowers, the touch of those we love, these and much more will remain. In the helpful words of one of the greatest contemporary preachers, who happens to be a Negro, Howard Thurman: "It must be possible to act creatively in any situation."

The second principle is that each moment of life is an end in itself, and not just a means to some future goal. Not only is the evil of the day sufficient thereof, but so is the good. Consider a fawn with its mother, in a spot remote from man. A short time hence the fawn may be struck down by a wolf or mountain lion. But this does not poison the beauty of life for the fawn. The harmony of its impulses and perceptions is not less perfect for all the presence of the deadly menace down wind and out of sight. Now suppose a man alone in the forest, knowing that wolves are somewhere about and are hungry from the privations of a prolonged snowstorm. The man is superior to the fawn by his understanding, but this superiority tends to mean anxiety. Man, it appears, has lost a privilege enjoyed by the humbler creatures, that of not suffering from any but immediately present dangers. Should understanding be thus a source of evil? What is the adequate compensation for this evil? Is the sole virtue of understanding that it enables us better to avoid dangers? Fawns avoid dangers to all the extent that is necessary in order for them to exist in such numbers as the food supply can provide for. Something is wrong if understanding robs us of peace in the present, only so that we may, given luck, prolong our anxious existence into old age. Understanding should mean a higher mode of existence, not just the preservation of a given mode. Bacteria look after themselves quite well, thank you. They may die, but so do we. Surely, understanding must justify itself by enriching the present, as well as by providing for the future. Yet it cannot furnish this enrichment if we insist too much upon foreknowledge of a desirable future course of events. To have understanding without loss of serenity, we must also understand, or have faith, that the meaning of life does not lie solely in what we ordinarily think of as the future. Did the lives of those who, with perhaps their closest relatives and friends, teachers perhaps with pupils, died in an instant at Hiroshima lose all meaning at that instant? Does each moment borrow all its value from what may come after it? On the other hand, after life is over, what becomes of its qualities of happiness or nobility?

We now arrive at a third principle, which is that the meaning of life is its relation to something more ultimate than the future, in the everyday sense. The biblical phrase for this relation to the ultimate is the love of God or, as the Jewish doctors have expressed it, for the Holy One, Blessed be He! So long as we do not consciously relate ourselves to Him, by whatever name, we are in the following situation. We may, at one extreme, try to live merely for the passing moment. But this will be folly so far as our own interest goes, besides being largely selfish; for to help others we must make plans and consider long-range consequences of our acts. And wise men agree that the beauty of life is in self-forgetful interchange, in generous creative response to one another's wishes, needs, and interests. Love is essential to human life. But if we love, do we not thereby compound our anxiety for our own futures with apprehension for the future of others and the race? Utopians may try to find a remedy in the ideal perfecting of civilization taken as a settled future fact. But how can they know this fact or know to what extent their lives will have contributed to the ideal outcome? They may not have at all! Is Robinson Crusoe's sole inspiration to be the hope that he may be rescued or his story become known? Suppose the island should sink into the sea, as sometimes happens. Is there no hidden meaning of life that such an outcome could not obliterate?

It is such a hidden meaning that the religions and the philosophies have sought to explain — never, it seems, with complete success; yet, also, it may be held, never with complete unsuccess. And must not the attempt be made? If we care for our human fellows, we care for perishable beings, whose benefit from our efforts is problematic, partial, and, for all we can possibly know, temporary. Yet care for our perishable fellows we must; there is no choice. The question, however, is, What are the final dimensions of this human reality we cherish? Is there nothing permanent about the quality of the moment of life — nothing beyond this, that we may for a time faintly recall this quality ourselves or give others (also only for a time) an echo of it through words or other means of expression? Or, on the contrary, is the harmony of the moment, in fawn or human being, an imperishable contribution to some ultimate treasure, "Where neither moth nor rust doth corrupt, and where thieves do not break through nor steal"? I sometimes call the affirmative view "contributionism." It does not imply that we are mere means to some end beyond ourselves. The fawn enjoys its harmony, and it is this enjoyed harmony which is its primary or most direct contribution. The fawn contributes itself, its own self-fulfillment, not merely the effects of its acts upon others. Our human privilege consists in this, that we may make our contribution *consciously*. We may partially understand our relation to the hidden treasury. Understand, yet so that it remains a mystery.

The minimal, most noncommittal way to express this is to say that the universe contains our entire past histories, our every moment, and it forevermore *will have* contained them. In the total truth, Crusoe's joys and sorrows are indelibly written — somehow, once and for all, there. Were this not so, it would not even be true that he had lived on the island. If it be true, then reality or whatever makes truth true must contain this feature, Crusoe-having-lived-on-such-and-such-an-island-with-such-and-such-thoughts-and-feelings. Thus the permanence of life's values cannot consist simply in what each of us does for our human posterity. For the book of truth must be more comprehensive and durable than the tablet of human memories and human reception of benefits from the past. The religious view is that this book of truth, in which all value is inscribed, is a divine book, to be understood by a mysterious analogy with human memory. Our abiding value is indeed what we give to posterity, to the life that survives us; but is there not one who survives all deaths and for whose life all life is precious? For the believer, it is the Holy One who is our final posterity.

Some readers may have been asking themselves, Is not the

abiding treasure, to which each moment contributes, simply ourselves, as immortal souls, destined to reap the reward of our good actions everlastingly? This view almost seems to set us human beings up as immortal gods—rivals, to that extent, of the One God. Theologians have traditionally defended the doctrine by arguing that surely God will not destroy those He loves. Let us grant this, let us admit that in some sense we must be imperishable. But wherein does this imperishable reality consist? The question we have been discussing is, How can the passing moment have value, once for all, and, in this sense, security? Our answer has been that the passing moment is cherished forevermore by One who knows how to do justice to all its beauty and value. For God to love the earthly creatures which we are for our own sake is one thing; for Him to love us for our alleged capacity to be transformed into pseudo-angels is another thing. It begs the whole question to identify these two loves, or deduce the second from the first. Even should I be there, in some future state, to look back upon my present state, since I am not divine and my memory is faint and entertains but one thing at a time, I could not give just appreciation to this present moment. Must we not rather wish to contribute every experience, in which, after all, our present actuality consists, to the One who alone is capable of accepting the gift in its fullness—the Holy One, Blessed be He? True, no science can predict, as future facts, either His survival or His cherishing of our gifts. But this is because He is not to be regarded as a mere fact, among other facts, present or future. He is rather the very principle by which facts have meaning. Our faith then is as follows: we live not ultimately for self alone, nor yet even for mankind, or "all sentient creatures," but for that hidden reality which enfolds us all, with all that we can rightly claim to be, the book of truth which some envisage as a divine life. That this life is holy means that it gives to every moment of every life its full due—not in subsequent reward (for who can ask a reward for responding to the beauty of life and the joy of fellowship among men?) but rather in absolute appreciation for the worth of each moment. The present need not, then, be poisoned by cares for the future, since the future of every moment, its essential destiny, is to present itself as a gift to the One from whose possession it can nevermore be cast out.

CHAPTER TEN

Time, Death, and Everlasting Life

"We are such stuff as dreams are made on, and our little life is rounded with a sleep." SHAKESPEARE, in *The Tempest*.

O UR LIVES on earth are finite in space and in time. That we are finite in space perhaps means only that we are not the universe but constituents of it. True, the universe itself may, according to some speculations, be finite, but that is a different sort of finitude. Our finitude is our fragmentariness with respect to what exists; the finitude of the universe, if it be finite, is its limitedness with respect to the possibilities, rather than the actualities, of existence. The fact that we are spatially limited means that we have neighbors around us; but the universe has no neighbors. A conscious individual without neighbors seems conceivable only as deity. God has no environment, unless an internal one. Thus either He is infinite, or He is finite somewhat as the universe perhaps is, but certainly not as we are.

The conclusion so far is that our spatial finitude is the truism that we are neither the total universe nor deity. If we were the total universe or deity, we should not be "we"; and so our spatial limitedness is analytic. There is in principle no alternative.

How is it with temporal finitude? It seems clear that, had we never been born but instead had always existed throughout past time, we should not have been human beings and should not have been "we" ourselves at all. How could any one of us have been the same individual at all times past, down to the present? Either he must have forgotten all but the most recent times or else he must be conscious of a personal continuity through the most radical cultural diversities, changes of beliefs, attitudes, and events. But is it not precisely in our limitations that our personal identity consists? To be simply an individual among many rather than, like God, *the* individual is to leave to others all but a few of the actual attitudes, beliefs, patterns of living. Just as one cannot integrate into the unity of one's consciousness perceptions from multitudes of localities, but only from one locality in space, and not from many but only from one set of sense organs, so one cannot focus into this human personality the ideas and purposes of diverse centuries, let alone all centuries.

It seems, then, that temporal and spatial finitude have in some respects the same truistic meaning. I am not the universe or God, hence of course I am not everywhere, and of course I am not primordial, but rather a being whose existence began at a certain moment of time. However, when we consider temporal limitation with regard to the future rather than the past, there seems to be an additional question at issue. Something that exists in a small corner of the world nevertheless does exist there. It is not everything, but it is certainly something. But what once existed, and now has "ceased to exist," is apparently not only limited in scope, it even appears not to exist at all. Is it something, or is it nothing? If you reply that it *once* was something but that now it is nothing, you have scarcely clarified the matter. For something cannot literally become nothing. The word "nothing" and the word "Washington" clearly do not have the same referent. Surely, even now when I say "Washington," what I refer to is not mere non-entity. And yet, in what sense is the no-longer-existent nevertheless still something?

There are two basically contrasting attitudes toward this question. According to the one view, not only after the death of Washington is he still something, still a reality, since he can be referred to by a term whose reference is not the same as that of the term "nothing," but also in any time prior to the birth of Washington there was already a something which may be described as the Washington who was "going to live" on earth, just as our present Washington is the one who "once lived" on earth. Thus, according to this theory, prior to birth, the individual is there behind the stage entrance ready to come on the stage, and after death he is there beyond the exit through which he has passed off the stage. According to the other view, prior to birth there just is no such individual as Washington. No one refers to any individual whose life lies centuries in the future, as many of us do refer to individuals who lived centuries in the past. Where there is no reference there need be no referent; and thus the argument that "Washington must still be something" cannot be used to prove that thousands of years ago he was already something.

According to either of the views just outlined death is not sheer destruction, the turning of being into not-being. To me at least it is a truism, though one often forgotten, that whatever death may mean it cannot mean that a man is first something real and then something unreal. He may first be something unreal and then something real (the second of the views presented); but this is only an unnecessarily paradoxical way of saying that once there was neither the name "George Washington" (for example) with the meaning which that term now has, nor any such individual person as the one we now call "George Washington." As soon as there was this particular he, there was a real he. Every he or she is real, but there are new he's and she's each moment. But once an individual is there to refer to, he continues to be there even after death, as object of reference, as a life which really has been lived. The only question is: Was it there all along as a life that was going to be lived?

One argument for this latter notion is based on relativity physics. Since there is held to be no unique simultaneous present moment dividing past from future for the cosmos, it is not easy to see how there can be objective validity in the idea of an individual's coming into reality at a certain moment in cosmic history. The correct conclusion, some say, is to regard all happenings as forming a single complex totality, the whole of what happens, whether in what to us now is the past or in what to us now is the future or in the region intermediate between our past and our future. This whole of space-time as a single complex entity is real, not now or then but just eternally. In our ignorance we may know it chiefly in those parts which are past relative to us, but its total reality is not now or then. It does not happen or become; it just is. This view does seem to fit more painlessly into the general theory of relativity than the view that happenings form no final totality since new individual lives or event-sequences are added to reality from moment to moment. For from the standpoint of the cosmos it seems impossible to find any such "moments."

In spite of this difficulty, a means of escape from which I hope to present elsewhere, I agree with Peirce and many others that the contrast between past and future is that between actual and potential individualities. *Being* is intelligible as the abstract fixed aspect in *becoming*, and eternity as the identical element in all temporal diversity. To hold that happenings form a totality which simply is and never becomes is to seek, on the contrary, to put all the reality of becoming into a being. This attempt is as old as Parmenides and Shankara. It does not necessarily lose its artificial and paradoxical character by being given a modern scientific dress.

Apart from relativity problems, there seems to be no paradox in the view that becoming contains being. For if Ey succeeds Ex, E persists as fixed item, although the total, Ey, is new. The novel can contain the non-novel. But if the whole were non-novel, then nothing would be novel. For then we could have only Exy and Exy and Exy. Change would be the shifting of our consciousness from one portion of the whole to another; but does this not repeat the problem? On the other hand, if Ey succeeds Ex, as total state of reality, then the second state is in fact Ey (Ex), where the parenthesis indicates that Ey contains Ex as its predecessor. In this way, if process is conceived as cumulative change, the having-occurred of previous events may become a fixed item in later events, and so the reality of the past as object of reference in the present can be accounted for. And one may argue that in order to house temporal relations it is enough if events contain earlier ones as their referents, for if b follows a and c follows b as following a, and so on, every item is given a place in the chain, even though there is not in a a real reference to b as something which is going to follow, or in b to c as its successor-to-be. Nay, if the reference were to run both ways, then temporal relations would find a home in events only by ceasing to be temporal, ceasing to be relations of becoming, since they must then be viewed as timelessly there in a total reality which is not subject to addition and at no time has been actualized.

If temporal relations are not real as references running either way in time, then it is hard to see what they can be. For then it is not true either that Washington (before he is born) is something with the character of what is going to be or that (after he is dead) he is something with the character of having been. But then there just is no truth about the temporal process at all. Only as something happens could it be referred to. The implication is that there is nothing to refer to, since the passing moment can hardly speak concerning itself.

If we drop this impossible extreme, then we must also break once for all with the idea of death as simple destruction of an individual. Either individuals are eternal realities — items in a complex of events (so called, for on this view they seem to lose their character as happenings) which as a whole never came to be and cannot cease to be but simply is — or else individuals are not eternal, since there are new ones from time to time, but yet, once in the total reality, no individual can pass from this total. An individual becomes, he does not de-become or unbecome; he is created, he is not destroyed or de-created.

And yet death seems correlative to birth. Fragments assemble into a man and then de-assemble into atoms again. But this language is on a different level from that which we have been using. It assumes individuals whose origin is not considered (atoms), and it never really arrives at the human individual in question. Prior to my first experiences, "I" was not "I," the individual which I am. This ego is not identical with a multitude of atomic individuals, however assembled, in spite of the apparent fact that this ego and the assembly are not found apart from each other. According to the view I adopt, there was once no such individual as myself, even as something that was "going to exist." But centuries after my death, there will have been that very individual which I am. This is creation, with no corresponding de-creation. But, again, what then is death?

Death is the last page of the last chapter of the book of one's life, as birth is the first page of the first chapter. Without a first page there is no book. But given the first page there is, in so far, a book. The question of death then is, How rich and how complete is the book to be? It is not a question of reality. The book is already real as soon as the possibility of my death arises; and, as we have argued, reality, whether or not it is created, is indestructible. But truncated books, without suitable extent and proper conclusions, are always possible, until life has continued long enough for the individuals' basic purposes to be carried out. Such truncation can be tragic. But it is not even tragic if the entire book is to be annihilated; for then there will have been nothing, not even something tragically broken off and brief. The evil of death presupposes indestructibility of the individual as such. Washington having died is at least Washington. Not just a certain corpse, for by "Washington" we mean a unique unity of experience and decision and thought, and that is no corpse. So those are right who say to themselves upon the death of the loved one: It cannot be that that beloved human reality is now nothing or is now something not human at all.

We must, however, distinguish between continuing reality, in the form of retained actuality, and reality in the form of further actualization. The realized actuality of the beloved one lay in his or her thoughts, feelings, decisions, perceptions. These are evermore as real as when they occurred. But it does not follow that new thoughts, feelings, decisions, are occurring "in heaven," having the stamp of the same individuality; or that friends who died earlier are now being conversed with in new dialogues, and so on. This would be new reality, not the indestructibility of the old. Perhaps such views of heaven are only mythical ways of trying to grasp the truth that death is not ultimate destruction but simply termination, finitude.

To say that the book of life, be it long or short, is indestructible suggests at least a potential reader of that book for any time in the future. A book which neither is nor could be read is scarcely a book; a chain of events which cannot be known by any possible mind is doubtfully distinguishable from nonentity. Who are the at least potential readers of the book of our lives after they have reached their final chapter in death? The answer nearest to hand is, of course, future human beings, posterity. Immortality as thus constituted has been termed "social immortality." Our children, or the readers of books (in the literal sense) which we have written, or the spectators of the buildings we have erected, or those who recall words we have spoken or the expression of our features — is it these who furnish the actual or at least potential realization of our future reality as an individual with the status we describe as that of "having-existed"? There are two severe limitations to this kind of immortality. No human being will, it seems fairly clear, strictly speaking, "read" even a page in the book we will have written by the act of living, the book of our experiences, thoughts, intentions, decisions, emotions, and the like. Even while we live no one else quite sees the content of our own experience at this or that moment. I see that you smile at me, but I do not see that in the fringe of consciousness you feel a slight discomfort from being too warmly dressed or that you have just recalled that I need sympathy because of some misfortune which you know is to happen to me though I do not yet know it or — any one of a million other complications which your smile cannot distinctly convey to me. If such things are missed even by the closest of our contemporaries, they are even more missed by posterity. For though some hidden facts later come to light, many more are lost forever, since posterity will not have seen my actual gestures, heard the tones of my voice just as they occurred in the context which gave them meaning. And at best one never intuits the exact quality of another's experience. Thus the reality of one's life, as a stream of experiences, sensations, ideas, emotions, recollections, anticipations, decisions, indecisions, is a target at which the perception of others may be aimed but which they never literally reach. The reality of Washington as an individual having-really-lived-thus-and-thus is not a reality by virtue of any experience which we either do or even could now have. The only positive account of this reality which can be imagined, so far as I can see, is that there is an individual who is not subject to the incurable ignorances of human perception, understanding, and memory but who from the time Washington was born has been fully aware of all that he felt, sensed, thought, or dreamed, and of just how he felt, sensed, thought, or dreamed it.

In short, our adequate immortality can only be God's omniscience of us. He to whom all hearts are open remains evermore open to any heart that ever has been apparent to Him. What we once were to Him, less than that we never can be, for otherwise He Himself as knowing us would lose something of His own reality; and this loss of something that has been must be final, since, if deity cannot furnish the abiding reality of events, there is, as we have seen, no other way, intelligible to us at least, in which it can be furnished. Now the meaning of omniscience is a knowledge which is coextensive with reality, which can be taken as the measure of reality. Hence, if we can never be less than we have been to God, we can in reality never be less than we have been. Omniscience and the indestructibility of every reality are correlative aspects of one truth. Death cannot mean the destruction, or even the fading, of the book of one's life; it can mean only the fixing of its concluding page. Death writes "The End" upon the last page, but nothing further happens to the book, by way of either addition or subtraction.

That there can be no subtraction is, in my opinion, more certain than that there can be no addition. For personal survival after death with memory of personal life before death is hardly an absolute absurdity. Perhaps personal existence without a body is indeed impossible, yet the analogy to a butterfly with its succession of bodies, while remote and implausible, is not necessarily strictly inapplicable. But we need to distinguish two meanings of survival. It is one thing to say that death is not the end, in the sense of the closing page, of the book of life, that there will be further chapters; it is another thing to say that there will never be any end, that the chapters will be infinite. This looks to me like a genuine impossibility. For if I am to be I, and not you and not the universe and not God, then I must be limited, a fragment of reality, not the whole. And, as we saw at the beginning of our discussion, temporal limitedness seems to have the same basic meaning as spatial, in that it is an aspect of our individuality as such, as nondivine individuality. If our capacity to assimilate new future content and yet remain ourselves, as much united with our past selves as in contrast to them, is unlimited, then in that respect we are exactly as God is. (For it is one of the divine attributes that no novelty of content can be too much for God's

personal continuity or integrity.) In unlimited future time, unlimited novelty must accrue (unless there is to be ever increasing
monotony or boredom), and yet one is always to be oneself, just
that individual and no other, and not identical with God. (For,
if you say that we are to become God, you merely utter a contradiction.) As for metaphors like being "absorbed into deity,"
they merely evade alternatives that can be stated more directly.
Such crude physical images are surely not the best our spiritual
insight can suggest.

A popular idea of immortality is that after death the artist
will paint new pictures in some finer medium; by the same principle, the statesman will have some finer mode of group leader-
ship opened to him, and so on. I wonder. The chance to paint
pictures or lead groups seems to be here and now, and there
will not, I suspect, be another — for us. Our chance to do right
and not wrong, to love God and in God all creatures, is here and
now. Not only will there be "no marrying and giving in marriage" in the heavenly mansions, there will, I imagine, be no
personal actions of yours and mine other than those we enact
before we die. And there will be no such thing as our feeling
(with a feeling we lacked while on earth) pain or sorrow as
punishment for misdeeds, or bliss as reward for good ones. The
time and place to look for the rewards of virtue are now and
here. If you cannot on earth find good in being good and ill in
being or doing ill, then I doubt whether you will find it in any
heaven or hell. After all, if love is to be the motive, then sche-
ming for reward or avoidance of punishment must not be the
motive; and what should not be motive is irrelevant.

But words are slippery and inadequate. While I have the
notion that the theory of heaven and hell is in good part a
colossal error and one of the most dangerous that ever occurred
to the human mind, I also think that it was closely associated
with certain truths and that it requires intellectual and spiritual
effort to purify these truths from the error.

First, as explained above, I believe it to be true that death is not destruction of an individual's reality but merely the affixing of the quantum of that individual's reality. Death only says to us: "More than you already have been you will not be. For instance, the virtues you have failed to acquire, you will now never acquire. It is too late. You had your chance." This may be thought to be expressed in the notion of the Last Judgment. Our lives will be definitively estimated, the account will be closed, nothing can be added or taken away. But this applies to punishments and rewards also. If you have no objection in advance to having been an ugly soul, lacking in the deeper harmonies of will and love and understanding, then no further punishment will be meted out to you. Sadistic or vengeful men may wish that you should be further punished; but God is not sadistic and he is not vengeful, and the attempt to combine such things with divine mercy should be given up. Each of us has the options: first, of despising himself all his days; second, of avoiding this by achieving a sufficient degree of stupidity and illusion so that he does not know how contemptible he is but also does not know what life at its best really is or what the best lives around him are really like; or, finally, of living a life of loving insight into self and others. The heaven of a life rich in love and understanding, the hell of a life poor in these respects — between these you may choose (of course intermediate states are possible), and you will not escape judgment. But God does not stamp on the bodies or the souls of those who have lived ill; nor does He insult those who found love its own reward with post mortem rewards so out of proportion to all the goods of this life that a reasonable man could think of nothing else if he really took them seriously.

That there are (in my opinion) no post mortem rewards or punishments does not imply that there are no good or bad results to be anticipated from our lives after they have been terminated (not destroyed). It is natural to find inspiration in the thought that another will live more richly because I have lived, and in this thought one may find a reward for courageous and generous actions. But this reward is *now*, while I am performing the actions. I aim at a future result, namely, good to another who survives my death, but this aiming is my present joy. In a sense, the future good to the other will be my reward, but it is one that I never shall enjoy save in anticipation. I shall not be there to share in the future joys that I will have made possible. My participation must be now. Moses must enjoy the promised land through devoted imagination or not at all. But this enjoyment through devoted imagination is not to be despised. The nobler the spirit the more such vicarious participation suffices. Moses perhaps did not especially mind not entering the promised land, so long as he could know it would be entered and that this entering was his doing or, at least, that he had done his part toward it.

Let us take another analogy. There are many men and many women who cannot bear the thought that they are growing too old for the joys of young love. This is no doubt one motive which leads men to divorce their wives, middle-aged like themselves, and marry girls who might be their children. Thus they want to escape, or imagine they escape, growing old. They are in some cases deceived, I really think, by a metaphysical confusion. Seeing that young love is beautiful, they draw the conclusion that it is good that they should have it. The right conclusion is: It is good that young love should be had, by those best able to have it, presumably the young. Much of the art of life, I suggest, lies in being able to distinguish between "this possible beauty of life ought to be actualized," and "it ought to be actualized by and for me." The "by and for me" is irrelevant, in last analysis. "There is a certain good in the life of A" means that there is that certain good. If, instead, the same good is in the life of B, then also there is that certain good. From the standpoint of God it must be the same. We are to love God unreservedly, and this is nonsense unless it means that we are to try to understand that

that is good which is good in the eyes of God. The old man or a young man, but not both, can occupy the central place in a young girl's life. As a rule, it should be the young man. The old men who make exceptions for themselves either have very unusual reasons or imagine that a good is not good unless they enjoy it themselves. I honestly think there is an element of intellectual confusion here in many cases. Such persons do not quite understand and take to heart the truth that the closing of their lives is not the closing of life, the ending of their youth the ending of youth, and that the secret of living consists in the service of life and good as life and as good rather than as essentially my life and my good. The devoted imagination can win such reward as it needs from joys that only others are to possess directly.

For the nontheist, the ultimate future good we aim at must, it seems, be a good for our human posterity. But our promotion of this is always more or less problematic. Perhaps we misjudge or have poor luck. And, also, it is just not possible to live for posterity in every moment of life with every act and breath. How can I know what it will mean to posterity that I now listen to Mozart for an hour? Perhaps nothing of any significance. And this applies to much of my life. But there is One to whom it may mean something. For while God is already familiar with Mozart He is not already familiar with the experience *I* may now have of Mozart, which is bound to be a variation on the theme, human experiences of Mozart — how significant a variation depends on my alertness, sensitivity, and imagination. All of one's life can be a "reasonable, holy, and living sacrifice" to deity, a sacrifice whose value depends on the quality of the life, and this depends on the depth of the devotion to all good things, to all life's possibilities, neither as mine nor as not mine but as belonging to God's creatures and thus to God. A poor, thin, or discordant life, made so by lack of generous openness to others, to the beauty of the world and the divine harmony pervading all sad and seemingly insignificant things, is a poor gift to the divine valuer of all things.

It is difficult to avoid onesidedness when trying to think analytically or clearly. It is onesided to contrast social immortality, the nonreligious form of everlasting life, to immortality in the divine awareness, as though to accept one is to reject the other. This is not so. If I do nothing to posterity, then I have no gift to offer deity except just my own life or those I immediately benefit. But if I can inspire multitudes who will never see me in the flesh, then the incense I send up to God will continue to rise anew for many generations. As a theist, I have all the reason the nontheist can have for devoting myself to such a result, if it is within my power. The nontheist at his best loves his fellows for themselves, for what they are. The theist in no sense lacks this ground for love. But the theist has a positive imagination of what it means to say, "what men are." He envisages no mere neutral "truth" as containing all lives and all values, but an all-perceptive, all-participating living receptacle of reality and value. How can this belief make one love creatures the less — the belief that they are integral to the supreme creation, the divine life as newly enriched each moment by the lives of all?

In this sense we can interpret "heaven" as the conception which God forms of our actual living, a conception which we partly determine by our free decisions but which is more than all our decisions and experiences, since it is the synthesis of God's participating responses to these experiences. It is the book which is never read by any man save in unclear, fragmentary glimpses; but is the clearly given content of the divine appreciation. Hell is, in the same terms, simply whatever of ugliness is inherent in the content because of my perversity, which even the divine synthesis cannot remove but can only make the best of, bringing out of it whatever good is possible. In this hell God Himself participates, in the sense that there is because of it a tinge of tragedy even in the divine experiences. No mere peace is the divine self-realization, but a joy containing somehow an element of sorrow.

Thus we escape the horrible dilemma: either God is lacking in love for sinners in hell or He loses His divinity by participating sympathetically in their sorrow. He does participate in it, but His divinity is not so defined that participation means loss of it. Rather it is the absoluteness of participation that is divine. I wish to repeat that, for myself, there is no sinner in hell, if that means an individual suffering from this location, save for those who already feel themselves in hell while on earth. Afterward, only God or other men will know that one has presented himself as a poor excuse for a human being to the immortal memory of deity. But one will one's self forever have known this while still living, or else will have stupefied one's self so that not knowing it will have been part and parcel with not knowing many among the things most worth knowing.

Lequier said that we "make our fame before God." He also said: "God has made us makers of ourselves," and pointed out that in making ourselves we, in so far, decide what God is to contemplate in us. One might say that we mold the picture which forever will hang in the divine mansion. God will make as much out of the picture in beholding it as can be made; but how much can be made depends partly upon the picture and not merely upon the divine insight in seeing relations and meanings. The true immortality is everlasting fame before God.

It may be felt that the consolations of the old faith are lost in this doctrine. What, no chance to make amends for errors in this life! No chance to grow deeper in insight and devotion beyond the grave! No compensation for bad luck in one's earthly career! My suggestion is that these objections involve the confusion spoken of above, between my good and good or between my life and creaturely life in general. Others will make amends, will develop deeper insight and devotion, will be lucky where I was not. All good cannot be my good; only God is heir to all

259

good. Of course there should be higher modes of life than those which we now achieve on earth. But, if present-day astronomy is right, there are hundreds of thousands of inhabitable planets. Who knows how many of them support wiser or more saintly creatures than the best of us human beings? And who knows what the future of the race or the universe may make possible? But that you or I must be there to say, "This good is mine," seems to me as unnecessary as that it must be I who marries this delightful young girl. Renunciation of the claim to put the stamp of myness on everything, save as through devoted imagination I make it mine, is the principle which either case seems to call for. Without this renunciation the argument is not on a level that deserves much consideration. With it, what is left of the argument?

It is said that while we should not demand personal survival for ourselves, it is all right to ask it for others. But yet I do not demand that the other middle-aged man have a young wife any more than I demand that I should have. Similarly there is no essential difference between saying that I ought to have another chance to avoid my mistakes, to grow wiser and nobler than I do in this life, and saying that my neighbor ought to have this chance. The essential question is whether the human personality, or any nondivine personality, is not, just in being nondivine, limited in a sense that is contradicted by the notion that there will always be another chapter to the book of life as lived by that individual.

It is said that if God loves us He will not suffer us to be destroyed. But death, we have seen, is not destruction. It is the setting of a definite limit, not the obliteration of what is limited. If God cannot suffer us to be limited, then He cannot suffer us to be at all, as limited creatures or as other than Himself. Moreover, does God love us as we are on earth merely for the sake of ourselves as we will be in some future life, or does He love us as we are on earth for the sake of ourselves as we are on earth, that is, as we really are? For we really do live on earth and have just certain qualities of experience and thought and intention and decision in this life. I believe that God loves us in our present reality for the sake of that reality. And this reality will never be destroyed. Postponing death indefinitely would only add new realities, not preserve this one.

The best argument for personal survival in the conventional sense is perhaps this: life is cumulative, and many potentialities are lost when a man dies, so that it is wasteful for life always to begin over again with a new individual as a child. Yet children continue to be born! And the argument seems weak. Potentialities were lost when men ceased to write Shakesperian dramas; no art form is fully exhausted when abandoned for new forms. But the further variations would have been less significant than those already actual; it is better to turn to a new art form than to exhaust possible variations on the old. Each of us is a theme with variations. No theme other than that of the divine nature can admit an infinity of variations all significant enough to be worth making a place for in reality. Life is cumulative; but it is just as true that it is self-exhaustive. "In the prime of life" is no mere expression or false theory; it is truth. Those who deny it will, if they live long enough, only illustrate it with unnecessary obviousness. We must accept as our destiny the probability that one's personality will be less rather than more in the closing years of life, if one lives exceptionally long. Miraculous rejuvenations or resurrections might change matters somewhat; but if they are to keep us the same individuals, and yet to enable us to avoid the monotony of insignificant variations on the theme of our personality, they cannot go on forever, so far at least as I can grasp the problem. And I see no reason why we should quarrel with this or think it unjust or sad. Living without zest is sad, and to do so forever —

On the other hand, if "resurrection" means the synthesis of one's life in God, the divine act of envisagement that keeps adding up the story of one's terrestrial existence, producing a total reality that is invisible to us on earth, which moth and rust cannot corrupt and from which naught may ever be stolen, then in such resurrection one may believe without falling into any confusion between my good and good, or between ourselves and deity, and without denying the fact that our life is a balance between cumulative and self-exhaustive tendencies. For the divine theme is the one theme which need not be self-exhaustive, since it is an unrestricted theme, universally relevant, absolute in flexibility. We are individuated by our localization in the world; but God is individuated by containing the world in Himself. Only He does that, and so long as He does it He is distinguished from all other individuals. Were He to exhaust His personality, He would thereby prove that He never was the divine, the strictly cosmic individual; just as, if we were to become inexhaustible, we would prove we never were less than divine or cosmic, never were other than God.

God acquires novelty by acquiring us as novel individuals. Our function is then to be novel, not to be ever-persistent in the sense of ourselves enjoying ever additional novelties. Such persistence is fully supplied by the divine inexhaustibility. We, as themes, are essentially variations on *the* theme. True, inasmuch as the divine awareness is concretely new each moment, God must reform His awareness of us forever, so that we function as a theme for literally endless variations in the use God makes of us as objects of His awareness to be synthesized with ever additional objects. But these endless variations are nothing we shall experience, save in principle and in advance through our devoted imagination, our love of God. Devoted imagination is the better alternative to unlimited claims for one's self or for such as we are. To live everlastingly, as God does, can scarcely be our privilege; but we may earn everlasting places as lives well lived within the one life that not only evermore will have been lived, but evermore and inexhaustibly will be lived in ever new ways.

CHAPTER ELEVEN

Total Unity in Russian Metaphysics: Some Reactions to Zenkovsky's and Lossky's Histories

"The static conception of God as *actus purus* having no potentiality and completely self-sufficient is a philosophical, Aristotelian, and not a Biblical conception." NICOLAS BERDYAEV, in *Man's Destiny* (trans. Natalie Duddington, 1937), p. 37.

P ROFESSOR ZENKOVSKY, the leading historian of Russian philosophy, expresses the belief that "the genuinely vital creative problems of philosophic reflection derive from the Christian gospel and hence cannot be resolved apart from it." [1] In the West, however, it has, he thinks, been difficult to see this because freedom of investigation has there become identified with opposition to the Church, while in Russia it has been possible to defend such freedom "from the religious point of view, taking the ecclesiastical tradition as point of departure, and giving oneself up fully

[1] V. V. Zenkovsky, *A History of Russian Philosophy*, translated by George L. Kline (New York: Columbia University Press; London: Routledge and Kegan Paul, 1953). We are much indebted to Dr. Kline for his lucid translation. One who knows his methods of work will not doubt that it is also highly accurate.

to the 'free spontaneous force of theological investigation,' in Karsavin's familiar expression." The Russian view of the Church, as set forth by Khomyakov and Kireyevski, a hundred years ago, is not that of an "authority" wielded by officials or even councils, but of a community of members forming a spiritual organism in which they reach a level of life involving integral experience of the nature of reality. Ecclesiastical coercion, as in the West, is viewed as heresy. Faith calls us to a life of freedom, rather than of "obedience." Zenkovsky regards as "romantic" the notion of a generally diffused spiritual insight which would make all important truths perfectly evident, but he seems to agree with the rejection of coercion.

Shestov, much later than Khomyakov, goes so far as to declare that it is only secular "reason," with its claims to "universal and necessary" truths, that tries (all too often successfully) to render us docile; and his contention seems not wholly without justification — recalling Hegel, for example, and his most influential followers, the Marxists! Here we may add also that in the Anglo-Saxon world the fashion has recently changed once more. We are not now so often intimidated by claims to prove this or that, but more subtly, by insinuations that beliefs going beyond the commonplace arise from linguistic confusions. The insinuations are subtle enough so that one cannot easily refute them — for just what is to be refuted? — but so insistent that it is difficult to resist. The result tends to be the substitution of the banalities of Philistine existence, elegantly restated in metalinguistic terms, for inquiry into the deeper, more comprehensive, and subtler questions which lie beneath the surface of everyday life and language themselves, and which the older philosophers dared to discuss. I do not mean that no good can come of this new Analysis: I do mean that no great good can come of it until its exclusive claims are broken and it has taken its place as another incomplete and — as now practiced, misleading — approach to the philosophic task.

Although I think that Zenkovsky's characterization of the West is less true of England and the United States than of Continental Europe, his account does seem to me to exhibit certain special values in the Russian tradition.

The Russian thinkers, it seems, seldom lost sight of the basic aim of philosophy — integral wisdom, a reflective sense for the whole man in the whole society in the whole reality. They always took philosophy to be dealing, as Dewey has said it should, with the problems of men, not just with the problems of philosophers. The line between philosophy and literature was therefore less sharp. The excellent account of Dostoyevsky is a fine example of this in the present work. But also the line between ecclesiastics and creative explorers of concepts is less sharp, or at times seems scarcely to exist, not only because the explorers were so often sympathetic to ecclesiastical ideas but also because the ecclesiastics had so much speculative daring and honesty. It was apparently seldom forgotten in Russia that modern science and philosophy must either provide new valuations going as deep as ecclesiastically enshrined ones, or endow the old valuations with renewed effectiveness, if mankind is not to go into a catastrophic decline as science gives us more and more power, for evil as well as for good. This is still the question we all face, and it is certainly not obvious that we know what to do with it.

An astonishing feature of some Russian thinkers is their extreme exaltation of man. Not only for us is man the important reality, but for the cosmos. The world is made for us, the whole universe is out of joint because of the Fall, and it is for man to set it right. Is this idea of Solovyov and others a case of *hubris*? One hesitates, indeed, to set limits to the eventual power of man in the cosmos — more realistically, in the solar system, a very different thing! It is astronomy, our oldest exact science, which teaches us man's extreme insignificance, even with all the space ships you please. And so I dare say that Fyodorov, that weird dreamer of superman, was on the wrong track when he said

THE LOGIC OF PERFECTION

that our basic obligation is to put an end to death itself, and even to bring our deceased ancestors back to life (that some of them would be a great nuisance he seemed not unaware), and to make this achievement (God forbid) a substitute for the having of children! This is far from being the only startling idea reported upon in this book. The author, a most sober person, tends to share in the astonishment.

Another still more characteristic notion of Russian philosophy is that of ontological unity, solidarity, "consubstantiality." This applies on several levels. There is the unity of the human race, perhaps in the Church as the Body of Christ. Even those Russian thinkers who follow Leibniz most closely — Kozlow, Askoldov, Lopatin, Lossky — all abandon the radical pluralism of that philosopher, all admit "windows" in the monads; and while this has been a common trait of most neo-Leibnizians, some of the Russians carry it exceptionally far. The consubstantiality of persons in the Trinity is taken by Florenski to imply consubstantiality in general. (This idea has also been suggested by Whitehead.[2]) Another source of similar ideas is in Plato's notion of the World Soul. This is joined in various combinations with some Patristic conceptions, like that of the "Created Sophia." The creation is not just a set of creatures, it is somehow one creature, and its unity is, in some fashion, ideal or spiritual. (Ironically, or tragically, in a country now officially "materialistic," the notion of mere matter has had exceptionally little vogue, in so far as speculation has been spontaneous or sincere.)

Russian thinkers have not been content to speak only of a unity of that which God creates. Zenkovsky, indeed, as well as the only other historian of Russian philosophy who is available in English, Lossky,[3] wish to leave it at that, and they criticize those who go further. Here I cannot refrain from applauding Solovyov, Karsavin, Bulgakof, and S. L. Frank, among others, for

[2] *Adventures of Ideas,* pp. 216f., 241.

[3] N. O. Lossky, *History of Russian Philosophy* (New York: International Universities Press, 1951), pp. 286–312.

their courage and (in my view) penetration in seeing that one cannot simply say, as Lossky does, that reality consists of the created universe "together with" (a phrase occurring twice in one paragraph) the creator. This togetherness must be something, a real property of the creation, or of God, or a third something on its own. The togetherness of *A* and *B* includes both, yet it must be one entity, for if more than one, there must be a further togetherness of these, and so on. Hence I hold that the thinkers mentioned are somehow right, against their historians. In some sense, "pan-unity" or "total-unity" is an inevitable doctrine. (The point is not that only one entity is "real," but that one entity must really include all the others. A relation being only as real as its terms, a really all-inclusive entity must have real entities to include.)

But now the question is, how do we conceive the entity which is inclusive of God and His creation? There are but three possibilities: God has the world as a constituent of His own total reality; the world has God, in His total reality, as its constituent, or a third nameless entity has both. Accordingly, God in His total reality must either *be* a constituent, or have constituents. If the former, then it seems there is a greater than God; if the latter, then God in His total reality is the most complex of beings, not the most "simple," as tradition has it.

The various expositors of "total-unity" tried various modes of speech here. All are rather baffling, not only to me but to Zenkovsky (also to Lossky), whose explanation is that "total-unity," if taken as including God, is in principle unintelligible, a blunder. There is another explanation. The historian, and nearly all his subjects, tend uniformly and monotonously to assume that "The Absolute" (or "The Unconditioned") are terms interchangeable with "God." In a few cases qualification is suggested, e.g., by Lossky, but it is not made really effective. The possibility that this identification is idolatrous, a philosophical version of the failure to see the vast difference between the supreme or eminent Thou and a mere It, seems to occur to only Berdyaev and Shestov. Doubtless the influence of German Idealism is in part responsible for this. But the main weight of the entire European tradition is on this side. Whatever is relative, conditioned, contingent, and in process of becoming has been regarded as inferior. Becoming is being, diluted, as it were, with non-being. Thus the eminent Being must be free from such dilution. God then is simply The Absolute.

This is no mere verbal convention that in a philosophical context certain expressions are to be used interchangeably with "God." For consider what happens, taking one example out of many. Zenkovsky expounds the view of Solovyov concerning a "Second Absolute which becomes," or is the upshot of the creative process, and then he trimphantly asks, "If it becomes, how is it absolute?" [4] How indeed! But the answer might well be, it is not The Absolute that becomes, but rather God. Is the equating of "non-relative" with "divine" an infallible revelation or an incontrovertible philosophical result? For unless it is at least one of these, to adopt it is to prejudge the religious question by a most tendentious definition. "God," in normal use, refers to the One who is worshipped; but does anyone worship The Absolute or The Unconditioned? Some appear to think they do; I am not persuaded. And I hold that the sound philosophical motives for speaking of a supreme, eminent, or divine reality neither entail, nor even permit, the simple identification of these adjectives with "absolute," or "eternal." As for the word "perfect," which seems less common in the Russian literature, either it is a synonym for "absolute" and open to the same objections, or it is capable of being so construed that it involves relativity as well as absoluteness; and only in this construction, as I have argued many times, does the attitude of worship connote or even permit the ascription of perfection to the object of worship.

Since "God is love" is standard religious doctrine, and since love is interpersonal relationship, it seems on the face of it reason-

[4] Zenkovsky, op. cit., p. 496.

able to identify "divine" with some eminent meaning of "relative," rather than with *any* meaning of "absolute." Time after time the total-unitarians and their historians walk all around this issue, but always with their faces turned away from it. Berdyaev is perhaps an exception. He does protest the identification of God with the Absolute, and insists that it is not enough to admit relationships between the Persons of the Trinity, there must be relationships to the creatures by which God is genuinely qualified.[5] But he is so impressed by the philosophical tradition that he thinks this religious truth is essentially trans-rational or mystical. Yet in a philosophy like Fechner's or Whitehead's it is almost truistic. For, in these philosophies, relativity and process are the inclusive conceptions, and any pure "being," independent of all contingent relations, can only be an abstract aspect of the more concrete reality. So far from resting on any transcendental insight, this doctrine seems merely a taking to heart of a logical truism. The togetherness of Being and Process can itself only be a process; for if *anything* becomes, the total reality becomes, inasmuch as a single new constituent always gives a new totality. Similarly, what includes the absolute and relative, or the necessary and the contingent, can only be contingent and relative. (If X in XY depends on some condition, then so does XY; and if X could fail to be, then so could XY.)

It follows that the togetherness of creator and creature is itself the inclusive creature, and is also the inclusive reality; hence either it is God or super-God. Surely not the latter, hence the former. God, in creating the world, creates a new total reality which is Himself as "enriched" by the world (Berdyaev's term). As one of the total-unitarians says, the whole is self-created. But he leaves this as a mere paradox, because he has never clearly distinguished "non-relative" from "divine." Part of the trouble is due to a confusion between "absolute," as meaning simply non-relative, and "absolutely all-inclusive." These are not only

[5] Nicolas Berdyaev, *The Destiny of Man*, pp. 33–40.

not identical, they are opposed meanings; for what has all things and their relations is made what it is by relations, and in this sense is relative, if anything is, and more than anything else can be. It is the most completely or absolutely relative entity. This is no more contradictory than is "constantly changing." There is a difference of logical type to consider.

Solovyov tells us of the absolute which needs its own other, and therefore "divides itself" and thus realizes itself. But the absolute, by definition, necessarily and eternally is what it is without having to be realized, and regardless of what else there is. If Solovyov had said that the *eminent* or *uniquely excellent* reality needed its own other there would have been no contradiction; for it is a bad theory of value which defines value in terms of independence. That things contribute to my value does not detract one iota from the value which I thus do have. And the unique excellence of God, in one aspect, may very well consist in this, that to Him, and uniquely to Him, do all things contribute, without fail, all the value which they have. It follows that He is bound to have all the value of whatever else exists and incomparably more besides, since there is also the value of His own unity or synthesis of the other values. Thus He cannot be rivalled or surpassed, and hence is worthy of worship by all.

We hear also of the "suffering of the Father," but this "patripassionism" (found in Bulgakof, Karsavin, Frank) is certainly no possible qualification of the absolute. It may for all that be a qualification of God. If indeed one means by the Father (nearly the opposite of what the terms says) the creator merely *in potentia*, just as He would be were no actual creatures created, then this is indeed to conceive the divine simply as absolute. But is this Father the One who is worshipped? A worshipped God certainly has created; He is not merely one *able* to be father but one who is father, really qualified by this relationship. A father qualified by no children is not our God or anyone's God. Lossky, indeed, says that God is "beyond" or "more than" the Absolute, since He must not be made correlative to the relative.[6] Also, both he and Zenkovsky say that God is beyond being.[7] But are there really more than two possibilities here? Either everything that God is, He is without possibility of alternative, or else, in some respect at least, with possibility of alternative. We can put the matter in simple terms from the theory of signs. Either "token-reflexive" expressions, such as "present process" or "reality up to now," are ultimate, or they are in principle dispensable; either there is a final total reality, "world and God," for which this phrase is a label that could always refer to the same totality every time one used it, or there is a new totality every moment. Philosophies of process say the latter; they are correct or not correct. These are the two positions, and if the one is a philosophy of process or becoming, the other can properly be termed one of being. According to philosophies of process, since "the total reality" is never simply the same twice over, and since God must be the inclusive reality, then every time we refer to Him we refer to a new divine totality, even though one embodying the same divine individuality or essence.

It is remarkable how close Frank comes to this position, without being able to state it consistently. He says that "the trans-definite essence of the unfathomable 'never is the same or self-identical, at every moment and in every one of its concrete manifestations it is something absolutely new, unique and unrepeatable.'"[8] But this does not make God, merely on this account, an "alogical" or "antinomic" idea. For a man is a new total reality each moment, too. Frank, to be sure, admits this and holds that all becoming is antinomic. But this is because it has not occurred to him to think of a unit-becoming as the final concrete entity, each unit summing up the achieved reality of its predecessors. Concretely inclusive unity is thus retrospective; and the only unity which is not retrospective is abstract. So

[6] Lossky, *op. cit.*, pp. 128, 230.

[7] Zenkovsky, *op. cit.*, p. 859.

[8] Quoted by Lossky, *op. cit.*, p. 272, from S. L. Frank, *The Unfathomable* (Paris, 1939), (c.) p. 130.

when Frank says that the "deepest levels as primary unity," in the pan-unity of unity and plurality, "must be something absolutely simple, inwardly one," [9] he is confusing by a vague value term ("deepest") the logical points: (1) process can express the same abstract character in each new concrete actuality, (2) it can also express the concrete fullness of previous actualities by adequate retrospection or memory, but (3) only the former or abstract unity can be "simple."

Lacking an explicit doctrine of an eminent relativity, able to contain both The Absolute and all ordinary relative things, our valiant and brilliant Russians have tried every other way to make sense out of the relations of creator and creature. They think of the absolute, or being, as mixing itself with non-being, incarnating itself, and so on. They wish to have a total-unity which is somehow *both* the original power creating all things *and* the final achievement of the creative process. Even Schelling said (against Baader) that God qua Alpha and God qua Omega cannot be simply identical. And it is the second which can include the first, not vice versa. Any other view is indeed "antinomic." It is actuality that includes the potential, not the other way; it is God as having-created, and as possessing the actual results, that includes God considered simply as able to create, as independent absolute.

Of course the charge of "pantheism" keeps cropping up against the pan-unity school, and they themselves keep trying to distinguish their doctrines from pantheistic ones. Thus, for instance, they are at pains to avoid determinism. Some of them, Karsavin, e.g., talk of the "self-creation" or "self-origination" of the creatures (cf. Whitehead's "self-created creature," or Sartre's "causa sui"). Zenkovsky can make nothing of this, objecting that it implies the creature as preceding its own coming to be. But does Schelling's "freedom on the threshold of being" to which he refers really mean this? Only if to "create" here means

[9] See Lossky, *op. cit.*, p. 270.

to be an antecedent cause of. Rather, what is meant seems to be this: the antecedent factors do not wholly determine the becoming, yet when it occurs it is determinate. As Whitehead puts it, it is "internally determined and externally free." If the antecedents were to fully prescribe the process, then the latter must be there before it happens, all except some wholly indeterminate and empty "actuality" to be added to the already established determinations. Decisions would settle nothing not already settled without them. Time would not even so much as "reedit eternity."

Only Solovyov seems to see, with the Buddhists, Lequier, Bergson, and Whitehead, that the total concrete reality in a personal existence is new each moment. Lossky, following Lopatin, scolds him for this and declares that the timeless substantiality of the self is proved by experience, by our ability to know the past and the future. As if either Bergson or Whitehead — or Solovyov — had ever forgotten this ability, or had any special difficulty in describing it in their terms! Or even perhaps the Buddhists long ago, for that matter. (But Whitehead does more justice to the internal retrospective relationships between successive events in a single "society" or sequential system.)

Zenkovsky suggests that total-unity must lead to the denial of divine "creation" of the world, even though its expositors try to save at least the term. He also says that philosophy needs the idea of creation even more than does religion, and in this I suspect he is right. However, the neoclassical distinction between abstract identity, or the absolute, and concrete actuality, which is eminently relative, opens up new possibilities for conceiving creation. The common factor presupposed by all possible world-states is the divine essence (not God, but His essence), the Cause of all things and effect of none, The Absolute. But the total concrete cause of *this* world is not merely the absolute divine essence; rather, it is God as having actually created and now possessing all previous worlds. On this assumption one may in a sense say that God creates us "out of nothing" (an expression which worries some of the pan-unitarians). True, since the present world-state involves memories of past states, to say that the present state is created out of nothing is to say that our memories are memories of nothing. A memory can only be created by a cause which includes that which is to be remembered. Yet God as supremely relative is "the valuation of the world" (Whitehead), wholly containing it as datum of His valuative act. Thus the other-than-ourselves-now which creates us, as of now, is God and in addition to God, nothing. Our past, which, as just pointed out, is required material for our present self-creation, is already included in God's receptive valuation, just as our new present is about to be, or is in process of being, included. God then is the *whole* creative source; but not God as First Cause, or as "absolute" source; rather, God as the ever-new ideal summation of the already created, in which summation the uncreated Essence is also included as abstract factor.

Does the element of "self-creation" in us limit the power of God? The expositors of pan-unity tend, more or less clearly, toward the view that the highest kind of power is precisely supreme power to elicit self-creation in others. Berdyaev (somewhat unperceptively treated by Zenkovsky, granting his point that there is a lot of wilfulness and "hatred of reality" in this writer which mars his work) comes perhaps the closest to doing justice to this question. According to him, "God does not create freedom." For the divine creative action presupposes divine freedom, and it affects others only by influencing, but not determining (a contradiction), their freedom. Berdyaev adds that nevertheless freedom is not ultimately an other to God, since He is all-inclusive. Our freedom is indeed other to God qua creator, God taken merely as acting upon us; but God is more than His action, He is also receptive of the lives of the creatures, which contribute to and thus "enrich the divine life itself." [10] Yet how this can be must baffle rational philosophy, Berdyaev thinks. I

[10] *The Russian Idea* (New York: The Macmillan Company, 1948), p. 243.

wonder. Is it not precisely the rational idea of consciousness that it has data which it does not determine, but accepts as given? Not logic but absolutistic prejudice has compelled philosophers and theologians to try to construe the divine (self-contradictorily) as non-receptive consciousness, or as a supreme good superior to all consciousness. The logical way to conceive an eminent being is to conceive an eminent receptivity, as Fechner and Whitehead have done. How, then, does this give God power over us which yet leaves us free? Power over others consists in this, that one's own reality is rich in value which fits the needs of others and is therefore attractive to them as datum for their awareness. To furnish suitable and valuable content to an awareness is to exert the only kind of influence upon it to which it is subject. Now the divine valuation includes all antecedently actualized value, although it is no mere sum of values but an integrated value incomparably surpassing them all. Thus God is the *whole* of the content offered to our experience, and hence the whole cause in relation to it. But a new awareness is always something besides its data, for it is a new awareness of them, and herein lies its self-creation. Thus one can give a strict meaning both to creation out of nothing and to creaturely self-creation. This is what the Russians tried to do. I submit that they deserve our gratitude for having furnished a new demonstration that it cannot be done without breaking cleanly with absolutism or the philosophy of being which treats becoming as an inferior derivative.

Our author presents a clear and illuminating treatment of Soviet philosophy. I cannot admit that this treatment is unfair because it is severe. The man who cherishes intellectual freedom, and this man clearly does, cannot speak in mild or semiflattering tones of such things, unless indeed he be densely ignorant of their nature and history (as some of our intellectuals have been).

In Zenkovsky's view, S. L. Frank is the greatest of Russian philosophers, his view being carefully worked out in nearly every basic aspect. He has an ingenious view of the Unfathomable as beyond the reach of logical laws, thus paving the way for the presentation of his metaphysical position as "antinomic mono-dualism." But is the unfathomability of God really best viewed as the paradox of the absolute relativizing itself? It may rather lie in our inability to form any but an exceedingly vague notion of the eminently relative actual synthesis of all things in the divine receptivity. We cannot even contradict ourselves here because we cannot so much as formulate an hypothesis. How, concretely, does God evaluate President Kennedy, in relation to all other men, living and dead, and to all other things, present and past? No combination of human sentences could sensibly pretend to answer this question. Here there is silence, surmise, heart-searching, and prayer, not theories, right or wrong. There is not even paradox. There is bottomless ignorance. Concreteness is the mystery; the abstract, essential, and necessary we can grasp, and our theoretical intelligence is thus most at home in pure mathematics, dealing with essences and necessities. Theologians seem slow to learn the lesson of this.

On one question Frank and several of his predecessors are often impressive, namely, on the epistemological question, how do we know the reality of God? We know, they say, by immediate experience, intuition; but the genuineness of this intuition is vouched for by the impossibility of denying it without betraying misunderstanding. "Religious experience is the experience of a reality which we apprehend as the condition of all experience and of all thought," and which it is meaningless or contradictory to deny.[11] Nicolas of Cusa is referred to as showing that "in denying the existence of some particular object we presuppose existence as such from which the object in question is excluded through our negation; hence negation is inapplicable to existence as such." But God is "the essential potentiality or power of all that exists or does not exist and therefore it is self-contra-

[11] S. L. Frank, *God With Us* (New Haven: Yale University Press, 1946), p. 42.

dictory to think of Him as non-existence."[12] This is offered as a version of the ontological argument. And indeed it is not far from Anselm's meaning.

The behavior of the writers of skeptical or positivistic textbooks (they keep coming out every few weeks) in dealing with this argument furnishes an apt illustration of Frank's thesis that the opponents of religious ideas are really talking about something else! Religion in almost any advanced form does mean by "God" One who could neither exist, nor fail to exist, by accident, and this status of being "such that His non-existence cannot even be conceived" is so essential to all that is meant by the perfection of God that nothing is left if it be denied. And if God is conceived as the necessary measure of reality and truth, and just so has religion conceived him, then to deny His reality is, as Cusa says, to deny the presupposition common to both the assertion and the denial of the existence of ordinary things. Any question concerning contingent existence is, in religious terms, a question of what world results from God's creative action, or of what creative decisions God makes, or of what worlds are contents of God's knowledge; He is thus, by the meaning of His "perfection," thinkable only as the common presupposition of all possible worlds, or absence of worlds. Many critics of the argument in effect insist upon taking God as one of the possible worlds! What must rather be done by non-theists is to deny the significance of the theistic idea. Pure positivism is the relevant skeptical reply to Anselm and Descartes. But then there is no longer a question of formal fallacy in the ontological argument, but only of whether some people do or do not know what they mean by certain terms, and also of whether the religious meanings in question are or are not implicit in all our meanings and experiences, so that it is only by self-misunderstanding that some persons seem wholly without them.

But now I comment again on Frank's failure to see that it is

[12] Lossky (p. 274) quotes this from Frank, *The Unfathomable*, pp. 238f.

one thing to hold that our experience, in its "relativity" and dependence, involves an "absolute" or "ground," and in its "fragmentariness" involves something "all-embracing" (he shows with much skill that this is so), and quite another thing to say that these two, ground and all-inclusive summation, are "obviously one and the same." [13] Is there not a rather "obvious" possibility of confusion here? Absolute condition and all-embracing synthesis can, no doubt, only be conceived as together in the One Eminent reality. They constitute the object of worship, *either* in its total reality, *or* in an abstract aspect of itself. But the neglect of this disjunction is scarcely derived from experience! Alas, on the previous page the author had wisely pointed out that we "must beware of confusing the immediate content of our experience with derivative religious 'theories,' i.e., with thoughts and concepts by means of which we attempt — always imperfectly and therefore more or less questionably — to express it." I cannot but see just such a questionable theory in the contrast the author draws between God and "the particular, the derivative, and the relative," as such — as though we were inferior to God simply because we are particular, that is, more determinate than a mere universal or essence, or again, because we are derivative, that is, possessing values that have been derived from data furnished by the free acts of others.[14] Frank himself wants us to contribute, by our free acts, to the all-embracing divine consummation. Why then sabotage this profoundly religious thought by defining God, in defiance of logic, as the sheer oneness of absolute and relative, being and becoming?

A curious writer is Shestov, a sort of Russian Pascal or Kierkegaard, who does not lose perhaps in these comparisons, apart from Pascal's science or Kierkegaard's poetic powers. Shestov almost rails at philosophers, but in a remarkably informed and intellectual way, nonetheless — for he knows what philosophers

[13] Frank, *God With Us*, p. 41.
[14] *Op. cit.*, p. 43.

have been up to — because of their worship of "Reason." According to him, the hallmark of reason, or the cultured alternative to Biblical Faith, is the attempt to see everything in terms of eternity and necessity. Aristotle, Spinoza, Hegel, even Kant, are largely at one here. For Faith, and to God, on the contrary, "all things are possible" (even alteration of the past, it seems!). Faith is freedom, not necessity; and as for eternity, Shestov repeatedly comments on a strange passage in Kierkegaard in which that author imagines God beholding Jesus on the Cross and suffering torture from His inability to come to His Son's rescue because of His own immutability![15] This, suggests Shestov, is not a Biblical dilemma. Immutability is not Biblical but an imputation of Reason. (Of course texts could be quoted to the contrary, but I think he is right.)

What, however, would Shestov say about the new trend in secular metaphysics toward the radical renunciation of necessity and immutability, in Bergson and Dewey, for example? That Aristotle, Spinoza, Hegel, and others tried to reduce all truth, or all important truth, to necessity or to the eternal, is no proof that secular reason must always do this. There are perfectly secular and rational arguments against doing it. A certain wisdom in Biblical faith may in this way receive confirmation, but it remains at least possible that secular reason will catch up with this wisdom, and on other points it may be ahead of it.

[15] See Leon Shestov (Schwarzman), *Kierkegaard et la philosophie existentielle*, trad. du russe par T. Rageot et B. de Schloezer (Paris, Librairie philosophique J. Vrin, 194-), pp. 229 ff.

CHAPTER TWELVE

Some Empty Though Important Truths

"The necessarily existent is the purely existent in which there is not yet anything determinate."   SCHELLING

" SCIENCE," DEFINED as inductive study of facts, can scarcely be coextensive with knowledge; mathematics, for instance, is not inductive.[1] The very principle of induction itself is not obviously a product of induction: at any rate, there is an appearance of circularity in trying to establish it inductively. Speaking vaguely, we may perhaps say that knowledge of the concrete, or of facts, is inductive; while knowledge of the abstract principles of knowledge, or at least, of the most abstract principles, is non-inductive. The prevailing view today seems to be that such non-inductive knowledge is "analytic," "tautologous," or "empty," in that it merely elucidates the import of certain terms occurring in our language. Truths of this empty sort exclude nothing, except nonsense. "Two and two are four" seems to exclude that they are five, or some number other than four, but since, for example, "two and two are five" distorts what we wish to mean by the terms employed, in rejecting it we exclude only a misuse of terms.

[1] This paper was read as the Presidential Address at the sixth annual meeting of the Metaphysical Society of America, Chicago, March 25th, 1955.

By contrast, "there are no more than a million men living" excludes "there are more than a million men living," and the one statement is as significant and consistent as the other. Factual or contingent truth, I believe, is always thus exclusive of significant alternatives. It may seem odd to insert an "I believe" here: for do not all philosophers so believe, except perhaps Spinoza and some "absolute idealists," who deny the contingency of existence altogether?

Yet this widespread agreement conceals an important possibility of disagreement. For there is a common assumption by which the doctrine of exclusiveness is trivialized: the assumption that the excluded alternative can be merely negative. Thus: there are elephants, there might have been no elephants; there is a world, there might have been no world. What the positive fact necessarily excludes, then, is only a privation: in short it may exclude literally *nothing*. But to exclude nothing is not really, I suggest, to exclude. Real transactions are not concerned with non-entity, and exclusion is in some sense a real transaction. If I am just here, I prevent you from being here. If elephants exist, then, in certain portions of the world at a given moment, other large animals cannot exist, for the space they might occupy is otherwise occupied. The non-being of wild elephants in North America is a partly positive fact, for it means (for one thing) that every portion of the land surface of that continent (outside of zoos) is covered either by some solid object different from an elephant, or by empty air.

We have arrived at the oft-debated question of negative facts.[2] The partisans of negative facts soundly argue that every positive fact entails negative ones. If X is round, then X is not square. But is it less true that every negative fact entails positive ones? If X is not square, then it has some other shape or character.

---

[2] See, e.g., Richard Taylor, "Ayer's Analysis of Negation," in *Philosophical Studies*, IV (1953), 49–55, and my comment in *The Philosophical Review*, LXVIII (1954), 488, n. 5.

Negative aspects of fact are one thing, exclusively negative facts would be another.

An example of an allegedly purely negative fact is this, "there was not a sound," or "he heard nothing." But surely we must distinguish between, "he heard nothing," i.e., he observed the fact of silence, and "he did not hear," for example, because he was asleep or unconscious. The perception of silence seems to involve positive characters both in the situation and in the subject's experience. The air particles are arranged otherwise than in the wave patterns which can cause sensations of sound, and the subject's non-auditory experiences have a kind of intensity and coherence which would be somehow disrupted were there the distraction of perceivable sounds. When we detect the absence of food in the ice box, we do not detect the presence of nothing there: the absence of food is implied by positive factors, such as the presence of light waves reflected from the back of the refrigerator at nearly every point. And the absence of food implies that solid objects other than nutrient ones occupy all the space not occupied by air, or by forms of unimpeded radiant energy.

But it seems that the absence of food might be a wholly negative fact if it were included in the great negation, "no world, no positive facts at all." However, what can we really think corresponding to such a pure negation? Obviously no conceivable verification of this or any statement could occur, on the supposition that nothing at all occurred. A "possibility" whose actualization must thus in principle be entirely beyond experience or confirmation is a dubious affair. But perhaps the meaning of "no world at all" is, "God knowing He has not created any world"? This assumes that "God knowing nothing positive other than Himself" represents a significant idea, which I doubt; but in addition, it does not get rid of the contingent positive side inherent in all fact. For God-knowing-that-He-has-not-created is God knowing something which it is not necessary to His nature to know, namely the fact of non-creation. (For the assumption is that He might have created, and then there would have been no fact of non-creation to know.) Thus the non-being of the world is still the being of some positive contingent fact — at least the fact that God has this negative fact to know. If you deny this, you make the possible non-being of the world something in principle beyond all experience or knowledge, and so, I should think, meaningless.

If, then, any possible fact is partly positive, it follows, we shall now see, that there are two sorts of empty truth, only one of which is "merely linguistic," and in that sense empty. "Two apples and two apples are four apples" does not tell us that there are any apples; indeed, it tells us nothing positive, but merely denies that any state of affairs can illustrate two pairs of apples making other than four apples. Modern logic takes universal statements in this negative sense. "All A is B" becomes "There are (or perhaps even, there can be) no A's which are not B," or "$A \sim B = 0$."

To take a step closer, at least, to an a priori truth which is not in this fashion essentially negative, we note that "Two and two are four" not only cannot be falsified in any possible state of fact; but further, unlike "two apples and two apples are four apples," it could not even fail of positive exemplification, except in a very odd world or state of fact indeed, namely one so lacking in distinct items that the number four, or the idea of pairs, would have no application to it. It is perhaps dubious if such a state is conceivable. Still less readily conceivable (if possible) is a "world totally lacking in order," an existing pure chaos. Of course, we can take the impossibility of this as a mere tautology, in that the word "world" connotes an existing order. But it remains to ask what, if anything, we can really think corresponding to the sentence, "No world, no real order, exists." Is this not an absolutely unconfirmable proposition? The possibility of confirmation implies an order of some sort.

What we thus come to is the idea of analytic truths which are positive. Not only can fact not contradict them, but it must illustrate them. If, then, they are called "empty," we should beware of a radical ambiguity in this term. All empty truths are such that nothing can illustrate them negatively (for they exclude only nonsense), but some empty truths (which we may call metaphysical) are such that they are bound to be illustrated positively. How can we recognize truths of this character? By this, that positive illustration of the proposition would exclude nothing positive. If, for example, the idea of a world so fluid or continuous that it totally prevents counting of items is really a positive idea, then "two and two are four" is not metaphysically but only negatively a priori, in the sense in which "two apples and two apples are four apples" is only negatively a priori. But if, on the other hand, there is nothing positive in such complete "fluidity" (I do not here try to decide this), then arithmetical truth is positively and unconditionally a priori. But the difficulty of deciding as to the positive meaning, or lack of it, of pure "fluidity" warns us that the criterion of positive or metaphysical a priori truth, namely, "can be positive without excluding anything positive," may be incapable of clear and certain application by our cognitive powers. Yet metaphysical truth cannot be unknowable in any absolute sense. For what is common to all possible worlds is included in the actual one, and in any significant conception. It is but a matter of abstraction and analysis to find it there.

Ernest Nagel, in his essay, "Logic without Ontology,"[3] tries to prove that there need be nothing common to all possible worlds corresponding to logical laws — for instance, to the law of non-contradiction. Of course, there is no fact common to all possible worlds. But it is a principle, and no mere fact, that any possible world will actualize some possibilities, and thereby exclude the actualization of certain other possibilities. This means,

[3] In *Naturalism and the Human Spirit* (Edited by Y. H. Krikorian, New York: Columbia University Press, 1944), pp. 210–241.

for instance, that in any world choices will have to be made by which some values are achieved and others are renounced. "We cannot eat our cake and have it too" is a maxim with some valid application in no matter what sphere. This is, if you will, an element of tragedy inherent in all existence. As Goethe said, "Entbehren sollst du, sollst entbehren," (renounce, thou shalt renounce). Things (and good things) are possible disjunctively which are not possible conjunctively; there are incompossible possibilities. This is a principle not merely of language or of true belief, but of action also. It expresses the nature of existence itself as a process of exclusive actualization. The principle of factual exclusiveness itself excludes nothing and is not factual.

Metaphysics we may now define as the search for necessary and categorical truth — necessary in that, unlike empirical truths or facts, it excludes no positive possibility, and thus imposes no restriction upon the process of actualization, and categorical in that (unlike mathematics interpreted as deduction from unasserted postulates) it applies positively to any actuality. It will be noticed that the principle of factual exclusiveness is itself nonrestrictive, as well as positive; for, as we have seen, there cannot fail to be positive actualization of some possibility, exclusive of other possibilities.

Metaphysical truths may be described as such that no experience can contradict them, but also such that any experience must illustrate them. Let us take this as an example: "The present is always influenced by the past." Could any experience conflict with this? We cannot know that we are uninfluenced by the past, for to know the past is, in one's state of knowledge, to be influenced by it. By the past, we mean something which influences the present, and one might very well define "fact" as whatever in an exclusive way influences events subsequent to a given date, that upon which it becomes fact. As Whitehead pointed out in his book on Symbolism, the Humian conception of causality fails to understand this point.

What is the use of a metaphysical formula, such as: "Every event is influenced by its predecessor"? It is certainly not a prediction in the normal sense. If an expert predicts that the recent unusual weather is going to make for a small wheat crop, astute farmers, politicians, and bankers will take this into account in their plans. They will act in some respects as they would not act if the prediction were for a large crop. But if the metaphysician "predicts" that the future is going to be influenced by what is now going on, people will say, "Of course, but what of it," and turn to their affairs; while if the metaphysician says that the future will be in no way influenced by what is now going on, they will stare at him to see if he be mad, and again turn to their affairs. No practical consequence (except as to his sanity) will be drawn in either case that would otherwise not be drawn; for no matter what anyone says we always expect the future to be influenced by what is now going on. Every animal qualifies its striving with respect to the future by what it is experiencing now. It needs no metaphysician to tell it to do this. Thus if metaphysics has a function, it must be very different from that of science and technology.

What then is this function? The answer, as I see it, has several aspects.

(1) An affirmation which cannot be falsified, or reasonably denied, and is thus perfectly "truistic" may yet be worth making simply to remind ourselves of something which is satisfying to contemplate, and not less so because it must always be there, and we have only to think about it to enjoy its value. Take the sayings, "Life has a meaning," or "There are real values," or "Some ways of thinking and acting are better than others." In no case can these affirmations rightfully be denied, for if life itself is never worthwhile, then neither is the denial of life's worthwhileness ever worthwhile, since this denial itself is a piece of life, an act of a living being. And to say that no way of thinking is better than any other is to say that the way of thinking thus expressed

is no better than the contradictory way, and such a manner of talking nullifies itself. But yet the saying, "there are real cases of better and worse," may be significant as a reminder that the power to make comparisons of value is a power with a significant use, a power which we share with all men, and in a way with all sentient beings, at least. There is something satisfying in this reminder, something, shall we say, inspiring. Now I hold that all metaphysical truisms have this inspiring character. Here is the argument:

Contemplation, like every life-function, must always achieve some value. But with matters of fact, part of the value may be the realization that what has occurred could, and should, have been prevented. This realization has positive pragmatic value. In matters of fact, there are reasons for being "realistic," for facing things as they are no matter how much we may wish they were otherwise. But in truths that could not have been otherwise, necessary truths, it means nothing to say, "Oh, that they had been otherwise"! Therefore it means nothing to say that they are evil. There is, to be sure, an esthetic value in the recognition of evil; for certain contingent beautiful qualities, such as heroic courage or sacrificial love, include elements of evil. But the esthetic value is achieved only if evil retains its meaning as that which, in each particular case, should have been, and could have been, unrealized. Now it might appear that good must similarly be defined as that which ought to be, or to have been, realized, and this appears to imply that its non-realization was not impossible. Of concrete goods, properly correlative to concrete evils, this is quite correct. Both are contingent in the same sense. But there is this difference between the ideas of good and of evil, that whereas the contemplation of good things is itself a good thing and in so far needs no further justification, the contemplation of evil things is itself, at least in part, an evil, and hence is in need of further justification. With contingent evils, such justification can be given, with necessary evils it could not be. Either, then, they could not be contemplated, which implies that reference to them is nonsensical, or they must be intrinsically rewarding to contemplate, and since contemplation is the only possible act in regard to the necessary, they are then by definition good in whatever sense they could be either good or evil. Necessary goods are not indeed good in the sense that they could be positive goals of practical volition; but the act of thinking about them can nevertheless be voluntary, and its motive must be positive, that of enjoyment of something satisfying to contemplate. Contemplation need not be a wish to alter — indeed, as contemplation it must not be; and clearly the past, as object of contemplation, is beyond alteration. But yet to recognize the past as evil is to view it as that whose avoidance was desirable and has not always been impossible.

The reasoning, then, is: knowledge must have either pragmatic or esthetic value; the necessary is not subject to pragmatic evaluation, and its esthetic evaluation can only be positive. If this is correct, then metaphysics discloses aspects of reality that can be enjoyed but cannot, unless by confusion and selfmisunderstanding, be found ugly or objectionable. Metaphysical truth is in some fashion a *realm of beauty unsullied by any hint of ugliness*. The beauty may be thin, like that of mathematical ideas, wholly lacking in sensuous richness or concreteness, but in its way it is real. All acts of attention must achieve some sort of value, and the only value a necessary entity can provide is that of sheer contemplation of an object which is satisfying simply as object, as something contemplated. This is the most general definition of beauty. Metaphysics seeks "intellectual beauty" in the purest sense of this phrase. Can any inquiry be illegitimate if it discloses such beauty?

Moreover, it seems conceivable that when something like the totality of truistic affirmations has been made explicit, or when all or most aspects of the necessary element in reality have been disclosed, the mildly satisfying or beautiful character of these aspects, taken singly, will be greatly enhanced by the interrelations which will then appear among them. The total truistic picture, as it were, may be much more exciting or beautiful than elements of it isolated by abstraction.

(2) Although the denial of truistic affirmations is not coherently significant, nevertheless, through confusion, people often indulge in such denials. And there is no sharp line to be drawn between destructive emotions of despair and the utterance of absurdities like, "Nothing matters," or "Life is a tale told by an idiot, signifying nothing." Hence it may be worth pointing out that the denials of these cries of despair are truistically true.

(3) To be vividly conscious of the full truistic meaning or value of existence as such is to have a better chance of noting well and steadily the non-truistic or contingent meanings or values. For despair is deadening; lack of hope leads to neglect of opportunities; also, a onesided, deficient consciousness of what all life essentially is tends to induce onesidedness in the observation of the particular values of particular experiences. Thus, if a man takes it as a truism that every creature must, or even can, be actuated by sheer self-interest, then he will tend more or less systematically to inhibit other-regarding motivations (which inevitably will be present in fact, since the correct truism is that every creature is social, "self-interest" being possible merely as a special, sometimes morbidly emphasized, form of sociality, a sympathetic interest in past or future states in the same personal series). Thus a principle which in its literal absoluteness could not possibly be applicable, may become, relatively speaking, only too true by virtue of being supposed absolute. To determine what self-regarding, and what other-regarding, motives are actually present is a factual task; but the task is the better performed by one who realizes that the zero value of either sort of motivation is a mere limit of thought. He will not have to waste his energy on such pseudo-factual statements as that all motivation is entirely selfish (if it were, to argue from an impossibility, we could not

even converse, for all language implies some participation in the interests of others).

(4) An aspect of the foregoing is this: metaphysical truisms, though not factual, may nevertheless include the principle that there must be some contingent facts or other on a level above that of ordinary, imperfect experiences such as ours. I have sought elsewhere to show that a kind of perfection is conceivable which inevitably or infallibly actualizes itself in appropriate contingent states of consciousness.[4] Each particular such state, being contingent, can be known only by empirical intuition, and it must be known as a matter of fact, i.e., as something to which there were significant alternatives. But it does not follow that to the non-emptiness of the class of perfect states of consciousness there was any significant alternative. The principle here is akin to that expressed in the formula, "That accidents happen, some accidents or other, is not itself an accident, but is necessary, inevitable." Similarly, that the Perfect should be embodied in some accidental state or other may be necessary, and this necessity may be metaphysically knowable. Such knowledge will encourage us to consider what light our factual experiences can shed upon the question, Which among possible accidental states of the perfect nature is in fact actual? No doubt we can never know clearly anything remotely like the full answer to this question; for to do so would amount to achieving perfect consciousness ourselves. But some very limited approach in the right direction may yet be possible, and the more so if our metaphysics has told us that there is such a direction to look for.

The full significance of the foregoing four points is realized only when they are considered in connection with religious experience and doctrine. But have we not given a fair answer to

[4] In my *The Divine Relativity* (New Haven: Yale University Press, 1948), pp. 19–22, 41–42, 80–87, 89, 157f; and in *Philosophers Speak of God*, edited by Hartshorne and Reese, pp. 10–11, 404, 504–508; also my *Reality as Social Process* (Glencoe: The Free Press, 1953), pp. 114 fn., 169 f., 204–206.

the charge that metaphysical statements, since they predict nothing specific, are useless or not cognitively significant? To know what is common to all possible experience and existence is still to know something, though not something factual. This knowledge may be valuable; first, because its object is intrinsically satisfying or beautiful, second, because it is sometimes, even if nonsensically, denied, and this denial may be emotionally harmful, and third, because it furnishes a clue or ideal standard relevant to all experiences, regardless of their specific content, and fourth, because it may tell us that there is an exalted kind of factual reality which we can but dimly glimpse in its contingent particular content but can nevertheless have reason to believe is there in its all-surpassing and all-enfolding majesty.

The positivistic objections to metaphysics apparently assume that there is no common factor, at least none worth becoming conscious of, in the alternative possibilities of existence; that we can be aware only of facts, on the one side, and of our language or of arbitrary ideals, on the other. Is it self-evident that no common ideal or meaning or character pervades all possible thought and experience? I suspect that one reason anti-metaphysicians take this stand is that metaphysics has so seldom (especially of late) been clearly stated in its non-factual or non-restrictive character. It has frequently been presented as a superior level of fact. As was suggested above, a superior level of fact may indeed have to be recognized, but metaphysics by itself can know of such superior facts only that there must be such, not what in particular they are. However, something of the higher level of factual truth, which is inaccessible to metaphysics, may be known by particular experiences and in part through science, especially if we realize that there must be something of the sort to know, and are thus led to attend to the profounder aspects of experience in a more conscious and coherent way than we might otherwise do.

The metaphysical as such remains wholly truistic or non-factual; and yet, somewhat as "Two plus two equals four" turns out to be a portion of a beautiful and endlessly useful theory of numbers, so the total truistic consciousness turns out to be the contemplation of something satisfying on its own account, and also inexhaustible in its relevance to possible experiences. People do not ask the theory of numbers to make predictions as to facts, or to tell them how to act. Nevertheless, predictions and consciously directed actions will make use of numerical aspects of things, and the study of number theory is a good in itself. Beauty is its own excuse for being, and purely truistic beauty, the beauty of what could not have been otherwise, needs no particular action to express its relevance; for this relevance is found in a general inspiration for all action, a heightened consciousness of the universal Ideal or Meaning, an improvement in the basic principle of action, a higher level of zest and whole-heartedness, less dependent upon encouraging circumstances, in anything that is done. Nor is this solely an emotive affair, a task only for poets, musicians, psychiatrists, or preachers, for these too face the same problem. They too may need a vision of the eternal ideal, the absolute truistic value, of which all special purposes and goods can be seen as special cases.

Is it wholly foolish for an artist to reflect upon the principle, Unity in Variety, merely because this principle in its full generality is sheer truism, since any experience and any object must be somehow unified and somehow contain variety? It remains possible that, by special means, special degrees or levels of harmony in diversity can be attained, and all the better by one who understands that in a sufficiently dilute sense anything is beautiful. Again, is it necessarily foolish to remind oneself that it is always best to do the best one can in the situation one is in? Yet to deny this is absurd or meaningless.

The mark of a metaphysical truism is its total lack of particularity. The statement, "something exists," for example, is a totally nonparticularized existential statement. Of course, it asserts that there *is* something particular, but it is one thing to say that particularity has an instance, and another to say *what* instance. The allegedly possible contradictory fact, "there are no particulars," would be entirely nonparticular, and being thus unrestrictive or unselective, it could only be a necessary or essential truth. But this is absurd, since it would make existence impossible! The alternative, "something exists," is therefore necessarily true.

There is another existential statement which is wholly nonselective among positive particular possibilities, although there seems to be almost a conspiracy to prevent this from being realized. This is the statement, "There is a being with divine attributes — for example, the attribute of infallible, fully clear, certain, and adequate knowledge." Does this statement exclude any conceivable positive fact? It excludes its verbal contradictory, "There is no infallible and adequately knowing being," or, in other words, "Every being is defective in knowledge," but does this alleged alternative represent a conceivable fact? What positive bearing could this supposed fact have?

No doubt the statement "Every *man* is defective in knowledge," or, "No man (or animal) is omniscient or infallible," does have positive bearings. We test what people say, since, after all, they might be mistaken. But when we refer to an omniscient being we do not mean a man (unless some Christians perhaps actually believe that Jesus, the man of Galilee, was omniscient). We mean a being with other equally unique and nonhuman properties, including that of *not* having a portion of the physical world as one's body. The all-knowing being is at least cosmic, if not supercosmic.

It might seem that if there is one who knows all truth, then success in the effort to hide motives or actions is excluded, since everything is bound to be known. But is this really a positive exclusion? The mere being of God does not prevent men from supposing that they can hide their deeds or their thoughts; they have only to be unaware of the divine existence to entertain this supposition. True, they will be deceiving themselves, but is not the attempt to escape from being known to an all-wise and all-good knower essentially self-deception? It seems equivalent to the self-contradictory effort to dodge the truth itself. One may very well wish to escape the usually impertinent and unwise, often malicious, scrutiny of men, but that is another matter! It may be argued that if there be no deity one may — and this would be a partly positive fact — enjoy immunity from divine punishment. However, the logical connection between divine wisdom and goodness (merely as such) and the here relevant theories of divine punishment is by no means clear, at least to my understanding. I rather think, then, that what is positive in the "escape" in question either concerns special alleged facts concerning "deity" not inherent in the definition of the term or is a flight from self-knowledge, from facing reality, and this flight the existence of deity does not exclude.

Factual existence is always alternative, *this* or *that instead*. But "God or X instead" is not a valid alternative. There is no "instead" in this case. A person may worship an idol instead of God, but the alternative here is in respect to states of mind existing in the person, not in respect to the existence or non-existence of God. There may also be divine acts or decisions which exclude otherwise positive possibilities of fact; but these must be free, factual decisions, not inherent in the mere existence of God.

You can, of course, argue as follows: the existence of God means a divinely-ordered world; the nonexistence of God means either no world or an unordered or poorly-ordered world. Perhaps our world is unordered or poorly ordered. But this line of thought presupposes that there is a particular sort of order which God would impose on the world, and that this follows logically from the bare conception of God. This is plausible, perhaps, if one holds a metaphysics in which the idea of freedom, taken to mean creative choice, is not held to be a basic requirement of creaturely existence. For then it seems reasonable to infer that the world, as divinely created, ought to be a perfect order in which every item is exactly in its place. But on the neoclassical view that any possible world must consist of more or less free individuals, the ordering of these individuals can only consist in setting limits to their exercise of freedom, that is, in the partial restricting of the chaotic aspect inherent in individuality. Accordingly, the divine ordering does not exclude elements of conflict, evil, and disorder; hence no world ordered enough to make knowledge possible could contradict the statement, "There is a divine orderer." And a world which could not be known is irrelevant or meaningless.

I once knew a young man who said, "I want to believe in a man's world, not one coddled by a deity." He was supposing that the divine existence would exclude something positive. But if he meant a world in which much depends on human efforts, and in which we are not told all the answers to our questions but are permitted, and indeed more or less compelled, to think for ourselves, then only an arbitrarily-defined deity excludes this. God might perhaps choose to coddle us, but His mere existence would not require that He do so. And as for the importance of human choices, earlier chapters have shown how deity may be defined in such a way that human efforts contribute value to the total reality, despite the sense in which deity is perfect.

My suggestion, then, is that the mere existence of deity interferes with nothing whatever that is positively conceivable. What follows? Some would say, it follows that the statement, "Deity exists," is meaningless. But then the statement, "Something exists," is also meaningless, for it too interferes with nothing that is positively conceivable! And so far from being meaningless, "Something exists" is obviously true. Accordingly, "There is a reality which is divine," although it excludes nothing particular, is not for that reason without meaning. Its proper status is not that of a fact, but of a claimant to metaphysically necessary truth. The alternative to accepting the claimant is indeed the contention that it is meaningless or contradictory. That this is the issue was Anselm's great discovery.

It is strange how few have remarked that the statement, "There is one who infallibly knows all facts, and who, if other facts had obtained, would have known these instead," cannot itself stand for a fact. It affirms, rather, a *universal correlate* of fact, implying this: to be a fact, and to be known to one who also knows all other facts, are but two aspects of the same thing. The inevitability of the divine knowing means the inevitability of facts being known. To be is to be known to God. (Better: to be is to feel one's value as appreciated by God.[5]) Since God is conceived as having self-knowledge, He also *is*, but not solely in the same factual sense. For whatever the facts, God knows His own existence. Thus His knowledge that He exists is not one of the factual possibilities, but the common feature of them all that, if actual, they are known to Him who inevitably is self-known. Thus the existence of an all-knowing or divine being is affirmed in a statement factually empty, telling us not a single one of the facts which the all-knowing being knows. But although empty the statement is not insignificant. For it provides a correlate to every factual statement which enables us to be conscious of its deeper meaning. Such and such is fact, then, means, such and such is known to one who knows also all other things. If the fact is tragic, then we do not face this tragedy alone. If there is need that this tragedy be taken account of in the ordering of the world, then superior wisdom will respond to this need with some suitable action. We cannot know what this will be, for our notion of what in particular is suitable is not binding in the case, we not being supremely wise concerning the particular situation. But we can take legitimate comfort in the sense that what ought to be done for the world will be done, and that what

[5] See *The Divine Relativity*, p. 141; and my article, "Ideal Knowledge Defines Reality: What was True in Idealism," *Journal of Philosophy*, XLIII (1946), 573–582; also "The Synthesis of Idealism and Realism," *Theoria*, XV (1949), 90–107.

ought to be left to creaturely freedom will be left to it. This comfort is in a sense empty. For it says no more than what every animal, in its fashion, affirms by the very act of living. To live, and to accept that in the universe which is not open to any creature's control, is one and the same action. But man, alone among the animals, is able to confuse himself with ratiocinations, and to imagine that he can quarrel with the essential character of the universe while still living in it. Theistic faith lifts the unity of life with its essential environment to the level of consciousness. On that level this unity has a new value, a new beauty. Yet it is not the beauty of any fact, but of fact as such, neutral to factual alternatives. This is a pure, unsullied, never-failing but empty beauty. It is far indeed from the supreme beauty; for that is the harmony of all things, both necessary and contingent, a harmony which is itself, I hold, contingent — a superior fact which is only vaguely accessible to us in our factual experience. Metaphysics gives us no fact, ordinary or superior, but it gives us the key to fact, on both levels, the clue or ideal by which factual experience is to be interpreted. It gives us a sense of what a German theologian has called the accompanying melody, *Begleitmelodie*, of all existence. The import of the word "God" is no mere special meaning in our language, but the soul of significance in general, for it refers to the Life in and for which all things live.

CHAPTER THIRTEEN

The Unity of Man and the Unity of Nature

"Ethics is the infinitely extended responsibility toward all life."
ALBERT SCHWEITZER, in *Kultur und Ethik* (1923), p. 241.

T HE HUMAN race, alone among the animal species on the planet, possesses the power, and it sometimes seems, the inclination, to destroy large parts or all of itself. The power will be there from now on, unless science and technology sink again to a primitive level, which will hardly happen except through the destruction of the more advanced nations. For centuries at least, the security of much of the world's population will depend almost from day to day upon the will to peace, the energetic, patient seeking of international agreement, in contrast to the will to group-aggrandizement, or in contrast to recklessness, impatience, hysterical fears, among the peoples and rulers of certain nations, including our own. We are one world in danger, if in nothing more. The question is, can the commonness of the peril suffice to produce the requisite sacrifices and restraints?

The history of the formation of nations exhibits two procedures tending to enlarge the scope of action toward common ends: these are conquest and federation against common enemies. If this exhausts the possibilities, then apparently we must conquer or be conquered, or discover a universal enemy of mankind. But we cannot conquer, in the military sense, without a large part, at least, of the very disaster we fear, destruction of a substantial fraction of the world's most civilized peoples. Nor is it probable that we can be conquered without a similar disaster to mankind — unless by our wholehearted adoption of the pacifist role. We should have to destroy our principal weapons, unilaterally disarm. Even then, we ourselves would still be open to danger of violent attack, since our enemies might think it better to finish us off when our voluntary weakness had gone sufficiently far, lest we changed our minds and reversed the process. In any case, we would be accepting some form of slavery for multitudes of peoples for generations or, more probably, centuries. It also seems unlikely in the extreme that we could ever agree to reverse our entire national history in the pacifist direction. We would at best be torn by bitter disagreement and probably in the end fight anyway when the free world had begun to shrink to unbearably narrow limits.

Is there then a universal enemy of mankind, against whom we could unite with all nations in a world federation? Until the men from another planet really do appear, until the "flying saucers" land and permit us all to see their occupants, mankind can have no common foe in the literal sense. "Nature," against whom some say we should war, is not a foe, and we have warred too much against her already. The other animals, or the elements, are not contriving our ruin, or seeking to enslave or exploit us. In many parts of the world, farmers have shot down hawks, including species whose food is almost entirely rodents and insects which do farmers much more harm than hawks. Only biologists have any accurate idea of the total effect of a species on human affairs, and they are slow to classify animals as "harmful," even to man. We cannot learn to love one another by hating nature. (More readily, by acquiring a common love for her!) The plain truth is that man is now by far his own worst enemy, or even his only serious enemy. It is other men, and ourselves in some respects, that we have chiefly to fear. And fear begets hatred. This is our difficulty; for if we give way to hatred, can war be avoided?

Let us survey the motives that might help us here. Men co-operate not only because they have a common enemy to hate, but also because they have common dangers to dread, such as when there is a fire; further, men co-operate because they have common tasks, opportunities for mutual benefits; finally, because they sympathize with or love one another in varying degrees. Now mankind does at present have a very grave common danger. It also has immense common tasks and opportunities, though these, alas, are not so obvious or so well understood as the danger. Moreover, for thousands of years it has been said that "all men are brothers." The question then is, are the foregoing motives to co-operation enough, in the absence of conquest, and of a universal foe outside mankind, to outweigh the divisive and hysterical forces tending to hurl a large part of mankind against most of the rest of mankind? This is where we are, where we come into the play. Will the play have to end with the abrupt disappearance of most of the players?

The uniqueness of our situation is that, for the first time, the same ruin faces both sides. If either side makes the great misstep, multitudes of peoples speaking many languages, many miles apart, are in immediate peril. If we are to hate anyone in this situation, should it not be the irresponsible, wherever they are, whose inner weakness might plunge us into catastrophe?

But surely hatred cannot be our principal resource in this unique danger. Hatred is too blind, and we need to understand the men whose motives will have to be reached if we are to be saved. A safer motivation is fear — not as a vague, ungovernable emotion, but as a rational though keen awareness of danger, and of a danger which is impersonal and universal, the danger of war in which both sides will lose much of what they value. Fear thus understood has no need to be blind. For the danger is there.

We have now defined our problem. Can we achieve human solidarity out of fear, hope, and love? This will be something new. Yet, these factors have always played important roles in the past. When there was a fire, men helped their neighbors. They co-operated in hunting, and in many other ways. If the common danger or the common need is great enough, common enough, obvious enough, why should hate have to be added? And if the probable benefits from common action are very substantial and clearly anticipated, this too has its effect. Release from the burden of armaments would clearly benefit almost everyone, wherever he lives.

There is another consideration. It is becoming apparent that men everywhere have a great stake, only less than they have in the avoidance of war, in a better adjustment between population growth and available food and other materials. For here is a second immense common danger, on the one hand, and common opportunity, on the other. In Asia, Puerto Rico, Egypt, and indeed, for half the human race, at least, the benefits of science have been largely cancelled out by population growth. We lower the death rate which has been natural to man throughout all the past, but we tend to leave the birth rate as it was. Indeed, we North Americans have been raising it.

Science does make it possible to provide for an increasing population, but only with certain qualifications. The population growth must not be too fast and in crowded areas it may be that no growth, or even a decrease, would be the only, or the best, way to avoid misery.

Yet there are very great dangers, not only moral but biological, in the advocacy of birth control. This is one of the extremely difficult questions about which all mankind must learn to confer, pooling its wisdom. We should not simply ignore any sincere and carefully thought-out body of opinions here. For instance, one may reject the absolutistic doctrine of Roman Catholics regarding the unnaturalness of artificial contraceptive measures, including voluntary sterilization as perhaps the most important, and yet see with them that it is a grave matter to make the continuance of the human race independent of nature's primary instinctive provision for this continuance.[1] Alas, it is even difficult to be grateful to those responsible for hygiene, which has confronted us with so strenuous a demand upon intelligent moral insight. But the hygiene is already unnatural enough, and I cannot see any but a relative force in the appeal to the Law of Nature here, even though I agree with Julius Ebbinghaus that this was Kant's position also. He would have held, and I think actually did hold, that the prevention of conception expresses a maxim which could not be universalized without denying the aims for which it was adopted. But it seems to me even clearer that the contrary maxim also will not do as universal. These are deep and rough waters.

Man begins to face the real meaning of being human, a share in power to change the world, not on the tiny scale of savages — yet even they burned great forests to make hunting easier — but on a scale which, though inexpressibly puny viewed cosmically, is vast enough so far as life on this planet is concerned. As baseball players put it, we are "in the big leagues now"; we no longer play for relatively childish stakes, such as what make of car we can afford after paying taxes, or even whether or not we are able to choose the color of skin of people we sit beside. The stakes are, first, to what extent human life (and perhaps other life on the planet) is to go on at all; second, to what extent life is to be free of political interference with the properly private and personal (those who think desegregation is such interference might ask themselves what would happen to segregation and segregationists if there were a puppet government, answerable to Moscow or Pekin, in Washington); third, what genuinely useful help

[1] See the admirably temperate account of the Roman Catholic view by Clement Mertens, S. J., "Population and Ethics," in *Cross Currents*, X (1960), 267–296. For the facts concerning sterilization, see the pamphlet, *Is Voluntary Human Sterilization the Answer*, published by the Hugh Moore Fund.

those of us who are relatively well to do can give the billion and more persons in the world who are extremely poor; fourth, what eugenic practices are to be used (for since we have partly suspended natural selection or thrown it into reverse, we are ethically obligated to use artificial selection)[2]; fifth, how long the peoples of the earth are to go on crowding each other into misery and endless upheaval by the disproportion between birth and death rates.

It is almost impossible to make decent arrangements for our cities and educational systems when every few years practically entire new cities arise and additional millions of children must be cared for. Our plans are forever turning out sadly inadequate; educators will think themselves lucky if their teaching does not fall to lower qualitative levels in the next decades, just when our enemies are improving theirs, simply because of the brutal pressure of numbers upon all resources of equipment and personnel. Yet so long as much of the world increases rapidly in population, there may be dangers in unilateral action to reduce birthrates in the rest of the world. Once again, we must learn to think of and with the whole human brotherhood.

It is reasonable also to suppose that we in the democracies must find ways to employ all our human resources, regardless not only of race, but perhaps quite as important, of sex. Every college class makes it plain to all that women are approximately as educable as men; yet in this country, the percentage of women students relative to men is said to have actually fallen in the past 40 years, both in undergraduate and graduate work! I feel this as a national disgrace. The early marriages, part of our easy-going ways, are doubtless partly to blame. And what do the women do who have been educated? We are far behind some countries in the establishment of nurseries and other devices to help make it

[2] See Hermann J. Muller, "The Guidance of Human Evolution," in *The Evolution of Man* (Chicago: The University of Chicago Press, 1960), edited by Sol Tax, pp. 423–462. Also the remarks by Sir C. G. Darwin on p. 471.

possible for women to do something besides servicing a few children (for a few years) and a husband all their lives. Can we afford this waste of human potential? Our enemies are cleverer than this; it is in some respects they, not we, who are "efficient" in the use of female abilities. Nor will it do to say that children and husbands need all their mothers' and wives' time and energy. Children need love and understanding, rather than constant attention, from parents. (I have seen a child less than two ecstatically happy day after day in nursery school.) And husbands need wives with some content to their lives, as many of them realize, some to their joy, and others, less lucky, to their sorrow.

Our sentimental feeling that while men may be drafted for national service, women must be left to their individual consciences, and their husbands', needs careful scrutiny. We are in a chronic emergency, and half our human resources (less than half, considering the racial restrictions we still have to struggle with and the way we waste the energies of our teen-agers) are not enough. Some forms of skilled work women can probably do even better than men, and they might free men for other work. Somehow we must overcome the shortages of highly-trained people. Africa needs many of these right now. Have we got them, equipped and willing to go? The Chinese are willing; they will go. Russians will go.

If, as seems to be the case, there are not enough men physicists and mathematicians, or doctors, women have amply proved that they can be these things. But are they encouraged to be? Scarcely.

In the cosmic perspective which philosophy ought, but lately has almost ceased, to provide, our provincialisms can more readily appear in their at best limited validity. For instance, we Americans talk too glibly about "abundance" as within the reach of all. In Arabian countries, for example, freedom of the press means little. This is, in part, because there is virtually no press, and there is no press chiefly because there is virtually no paper pulp to be had. No doubt it is conceivable that it could be provided, but the forests of the earth are finite, they are shrinking, and the earth's population is growing with vast strides. True, there are other ways of distributing news. We need not despair, but we must admit a very grave problem in population growth, as it is now proceeding. That this growth produces misery is not a pessimistic prophecy; it is a fact. The misery is at hand. It might seem that the population problem is not our American affair. Yet the Puerto Rican troubles almost cost us the lives of some Congressmen. In the long run, our country also will fill up; indeed, some think it is already too full, and whatever the population situation here, several billions of Asiatics, Africans, and South Americans in misery will scarcely be compatible with any safe prosperity anywhere on earth. And in much of Europe, for example in wretched Sicily, pressure on resources is dangerously great.

Thus in war and population growth we have two great world dangers and hence needs for common action. On the hopeful side, a real relief from the pressure of mounting demands for supplies may eventually make it easier to relax the tensions that threaten us with war and burden us with armaments. So we all have a stake in this matter, especially if our children and our children's children fall within our purview.

It is notable how all our material dangers and opportunities derive from science. Science in irresponsible hands is our mortal foe; but only science in better hands can save us. Unless through vast catastrophes we sink back to a peasant economy, we shall throughout our foreseeable human future face the terrible risks of technological power turned by one group against another, with much or even all of mankind exposed to ruin. The danger can be kept in the background by suitable arrangements, but potentially it will be there. This lane has no turning, except by catastrophic return to the simple, preindustrial method of living and a vastly reduced population.

The moral is that social understanding and good will are our only means of fencing in the abyss that yawns before us. The danger comes, not from nature, but from man. Some express this by saying that social science must catch up with natural science. But this is a puzzling matter. Natural science tells us what men can do with physical instruments, for good and for ill, if they want to. Social science might tell us — even though less precisely — what some men can do to other men, for good or ill, if they want to. But are there enough men who want mankind to be saved from destruction, want it so intensely that they will put their energies and understandings to work to that end? If so, then social science may render their efforts more effective. Science presupposes good motives and keen energies somewhere, if it is to further their development elsewhere. There is at least the semblance of a vicious circle here which Dewey, for instance, never seems quite able to dispel when he talks about intelligence as our hope. Being intelligent about my concrete, unique situation and feelings, in such a way that I devote myself to the highest good in my power to realize for the community — this is a far cry from scientific intelligence in general. The true self-knowledge seems to require an element of repentance for the self-favoring which has ever and anon blinded us to the truth as it concerns ourselves.[3]

The psychologist Skinner, in his effort to show how science may lead to a solution of the problem of the designing and controlling of culture without the abuse of this control, is in similar difficulties, though I confess I find him rather more definite and helpful than Dewey at this point. His hope is that the "control of long-term consequences" over the behavior of the rulers may lead them to renounce any short-term benefits to themselves which abuse might bring in favor of the vigor and ultimate survival of the culture they are designing.[4] A governing agency can take into account those traits in the governed without which

[3] See M. B. Foster, *Mystery and Philosophy* (London: SCM Press, 1957), Ch. 4.

[4] *Science and Human Behavior* (New York: The Macmillan Company, 1953), pp. 443–447.

the agency itself in the end will decline or fail and perhaps the whole group disappear as a cultural identity. Tyranny in the long run undermines itself. This is all probably sound and important, but it leaves the question of motivation finally in vague uncertainty. Does "long run" mean, beyond the individual's own life? Does it mean, forever, and must we assume that humanity is as immortal as any God? The only unrestricted long run I can grasp with any confidence is a superhuman one. Skinner says that science "presumably" cannot deal with "the glory of God" as the inclusive goal; but he can hardly deny that this has proved greatly "re-enforcing" to multitudes of persons.[5] And I submit that it is the only re-enforcement which can survive a merciless stare at the truth of man's situation, when one has divested oneself of flattering illusions.

I must again protest against Skinner's dogmatic assertion, with which his book virtually ends, as well as begins, that a science of behavior must deny human freedom. It is not only not essential to science to dictate to reality in this fashion, to deny in advance any supposedly inconvenient aspects of the world, but sooner or later a scientist who does so will pay the price in missed opportunities to understand existence as it is. Absolute, unlimited freedom would make science an absurd endeavor; but since every animal "knows" in its nerves and muscles that the future is partly open to anticipation, and every careful thinker knows it likewise, this is a red herring and nothing more. Freedom within limits, however, limits which it is exactly the job of science to ascertain, is another matter. Among the means of opposing tyranny which Skinner must renounce, but which there is good reason to retain, is the appeal to every individual to respect in himself and others that subtle fountain of creativity from which in the long run all detailed causation has resulted. I repeat what I said in Chapter Seven, freedom is causality in the making, causality is crystallized freedom, the influence of past acts of self-determination by countless creatures upon this act

[5] *Op. cit.*, p. 358.

now taking place. Causality is the conservative aspect of creation as emergent synthesis, which is always new so far as emergent, but old in so far as its data from the past are so.

The respect for creativity has been employed by a psychiatrist I know with what he takes to be good results. He invites patients to value what little freedom they have and to hope to increase it. He finds this far more helpful to them than telling them that all the future is a tale already told — save for our ignorance.

What does social science include? If it includes the study and guide to the right use of the best religions and philosophies of the past and present, then indeed it is what we need. But if it excludes religion and philosophy, it is not enough. And can it exclude them, and be the adequate study of human social relations? Again, what is the relation of social to natural science? Social science can be wholly independent neither of natural science, especially biology, on the one hand, nor of philosophy and religion, on the other. The first relates us to what is below us, in the scale of existence, the other to what is above us and somehow includes all levels of existence. For science, man is one species of terrestrial animal, among the million or more species; his unity as a species is a special — though uniquely important — case of the unity of animal life and of all life. And the unity of life is only a special case or aspect of the unity of the cosmic system.

There is, however, a serious paradox in modern views of man and his relations to the universe. On the one hand, the old religious views, the primitive animisms, are scolded as anthropomorphic. The poets who feel a sense of kinship with all nature, a sense of life and spirit in all things, are mere dreamers. There are no spirits and no demons, only matter and natural law. But on the other hand, if you say that man alone has intelligence, or social emotions of love, hate, parental solicitude, and so on, you are told that this is quite wrong, that human intelligence, and still more, human emotional reactions and sensations have animal origins and anticipations. But either such things as feeling and sensation are exclusively human, or they are not. You cannot have it both ways. True, you may affirm merely material process at the bottom, and feeling and thinking at and near the top, of the scale of beings. But then somewhere between the extremes, the merely material or physical must meet the material which is also mental. Mere matter meets matter plus mind. Yet science becomes ever clearer that no such dualism can have scientific support. All individuals can be viewed as physical systems, and all, even atoms, can be viewed as responding to stimuli with their own internal feelings. Science does not find it useful to take the latter view, but it can still less accomplish its purposes by denying it. For quantities of energy must then be lost in disputes, impossible to settle, as to where the lower limit of the psychological interpretation should be. Is it the lowest vertebrates, the amoeba, the virus "cell," radioactive molecule, or what? All in some fashion respond to their environment, and the radioactive molecule even initiates activity without having to be stirred up by its environment. The whole gamut of levels from atoms to man is for science basically one system. From this it appears that the poet's notion of his kinship with all nature may in principle be correct.

Admittedly we cannot know what sort of feeling of harmony or discord a deer may enjoy, but we do know that a deer can be in good adjustment or not with its environment, and this would for it constitute the experience of beauty. In principle, all nature can be interpreted esthetically — as correctly, though not so definitely, as all nature can be interpreted in terms of physical structure. Only in details, then, were the animist and the poet in error. Science is eliminating the fanciful details. What it is not doing and cannot do is to establish a dualistic materialism in which the sentient and intelligent arise out of mere bits of dead matter, human evaluations out of a nature devoid of values. *Human* values emerge, sure enough, but are there not simian values, amoebic values — and who dares to assign a first level of values?

If the foregoing is at all correct, then the social point of view is the final point of view. All creatures are fellow creatures. Nothing is wholly alien to us or devoid of inner satisfactions with which, if we could grasp them, we might more or less sympathize. It is merely a question of how accessible to our perception and understanding the inner values may be.

There is an old formula for the universal fellowship of creatures: that all are one family with one supreme parent or creator. It may seem that this is scarcely an aid to human co-operation, since a man and an insect must also, on the assumption, have the same heavenly parent, yet a man cannot be expected to make substantial sacrifices for the welfare of the insect. But the point is that the unity of nature, once granted, admits special aspects. Since even I and an insect are fellows, constituents of one beautiful and valuable whole of life, expressive of one divine wisdom, I will not kill even so trivial a creature, or torture it, merely for fun, and I will hesitate to exterminate any species of creature. On the other hand, should I have reason to kill an insect, I will not suppose that this has the same importance as killing a man. For though each creature contributes to the whole of life, it contributes no more and no less than its nature enables it to. To recognize the ant as fellow contributor is not sentimentally to exaggerate its contribution, but simply to let it count for what it is, so far as we are able to guess this. The same is true of a man; but here the contribution is an incomparably more distinctive one, for individuality is far greater on the higher levels of life.

A familiar objection to the conception of brotherhood under God is that the conflicts and evils in nature are incompatible with this conception. But let us see what these evils are. Animals, other than man, are in general healthy (for the unhealthy or injured cannot long maintain themselves), and they are in general living in accordance with their impulses, without gross frustrations; and what can this be but happiness, so far as they are capable of it? They do eventually die, but is it desirable that they should live forever? Watch any young animal and see how eager and interested it is in all that surrounds it. The longer life lasts, the more has everything (or something like it) been encountered before. The essential charm of novelty gradually diminishes. Death is the solution. Moreover, to die by being swiftly killed by some more powerful animal, as so many do, is to my taste a better way to die than many a human being must endure in our hospitals. The so-called "enemies" of a species are responsible for the fact that, at any time, most of its members are in youth or the prime of life, still full of zest and the enjoyment of novelty. Would it be preferable if they all lived to die of old age, so that, at any one time, a rather large proportion were too old to be more than half-interested in living? I honestly do not believe those who tell us they can think up a much better scheme of nature than the one God has made. I fear they would make a mess of it.

It may seem that I have proved too much. For does it not follow that it would be all right for men to prey on one another? They would only be doing "as nature does." But in the first place, it is somewhat rare in nature for members of the same species to prey on, or seriously damage, one another. In the second place, the possibility of death in the prime of life has a different meaning for man than for the other creatures. Man makes plans which require years or generations to execute; he needs much of his life span merely to learn the basic facts of civilized existence; much of the remainder is needed to bring up his children; he then wants several years to finish his life work, or to follow up some interest which family cares have stood in the way of. Moreover, man knows that he is going to die, and he also knows to what extent men are likely, in his society, to die at the hands of other men. Hence the whole quality and feeling of his life with his neighbors depends upon the extent to which the commandment, thou shalt not commit murder, is respected in that society. After all, it is not merely a man's life that another man ought to respect; we are not to intrude forcibly and needlessly into other persons' affairs in any important respect without their consent.

But animals have no affairs in this sense; nor can a fox discuss with a rabbit whether his appropriate moment to die has come.

A would-be murderer, on the other hand, could discuss with his intended victim the values at stake in his continued existence; that is to say, both men would know what they were talking about, what murder is, and so on. One animal preying on another does not commit murder in this deliberate human sense at all; rabbits, for example, die by an inherited system of instincts bene-fiting both rabbits and their devourers, but this system as a whole is unknown to both parties. Men, on the contrary, are aware of the general scheme of nature but, with their power of conscious choice, are themselves somewhat beyond any fixed system of living and dying. They have to create one, and to re-create it from time to time. As Kant said, man is the one lawless being on earth, unless he makes his own laws and keeps them. He may on the whole be better than the rest of nature, but he does well if he can avoid being, in some respects, far worse. Nothing in the jungle is to my mind so horrible as our gangster youths. The jungle animals are in their appropriate and, as I have argued, useful roles; the youths are not. For one who sees things as they are, it is our cities, not the jungles, that make it hard to believe in a good God. Moreover, the terrifying growth in the human populations of the world is a menace, both to man himself, and to other creatures, like nothing in the rest of nature.

But, you may say, if God is good and allpowerful, why is not the world so smoothly put together, so made and contrived, that every evil is prevented, so controlled that every process reaches a wholly desirable outcome? The reader knows my answer by now: that I believe these are words with no clear meaning. The world is not and could not be a set of mere things, passively put and kept in their places, vessels of clay molded by the divine potter, and arranged each on its appropriate shelf. It will be objected by some that a world of mere non-self-active puppets must be conceivable or we could not even deny that it exists. But there is, I am convinced, a subtle error here. We can conceive, and indeed we experience, entities whose aspect of self-activity is imperceptible from a certain point of view, by certain types of observer, for instance ourselves, and this genuinely significant but relative notion of inactivity is then absolutized to form an alleged concept of a possible world. But absolute negatives require justification in some conceivable observational test, performed by some sort of mind, not necessarily human. The things whose self-activity is imperceptible to us are the things whose individual constituents are so also, and whose causal history and destiny seem to our knowledge entirely extraneous to the events forming a given stage of the history. The only way (according to the argument in Chapters 6, 8) in which we could experience the individual constituents as essentially causal is to experience them as self-actively synthesizing the data furnished them by their pasts. Thus I see no way to distinguish between apparent lack of self-activity and partial ignorance of the thing in question as item in a relatively ordered system called a world, or as object of any possible knowledge.

I conclude that the world is, and any world must be, a community of active individuals. To be such an individual is to make one's own place, in a certain measure, and put oneself in it. No other individual can do this for one, even if the other individual be God. It is not that God is weak, but that my act is mine, and it is senseless to say that God simply makes this act; for if this were so it would be His act and not mine at all. Against this it is often urged that God must determine all our acts; for these must spring from the nature which He gave us. But this "nature" of a man is a neat little verbal package rather than a observed reality. If a person is self-active, currently creating his own role to some extent, then each new act and state of the person is in some degree self-determined. What we call a man's character or nature is a sort of composite photograph of his past acts, not an explanation of them. Each act alters the photo a little, and no new act can ever be exactly inferred from the old photos. Imagine a psychologist predicting a musical composition by applying psychological laws to a composer friend of his. The psychologist then becomes a composer, and since composition expresses individual ways of feeling, there will be two individuals essentially the same in their deepest emotional nature. Moreover, the psychologist would not really be "predicting" the composition, but making it. By these and other lines of reasoning we arrive at the conclusion that, so far at least as any conceivable or usable human knowledge goes, individual acts are really in some measure free, or self-determined.

The tragedy of the world, I conclude, is the price of individuality. The greater the depth of individuality, the greater the possibilities for both good and evil. It is not simply a question of moral evil. The most innocent uses of freedom involve some risk of conflict and suffering. There are many decisions, and thus a composition of decisions, but this composition is itself no decision. It simply happens. It is chance or luck. If each of twenty children decides to shout, has any of them decided that there shall be the confused noise that ensues, preventing any of them from being properly heard? Every individual is fate for other individuals. Divine providence may be a sort of superfate, but its function is to set limits to the free interplay of lesser individuals, which otherwise would be pure chaos. Consider a committee with no chairman and no directives. This would indeed be chaos. Given a chairman and directives, there will still not be perfect order and harmony, and certainly not complete control of every detail according to any plan.

If this view is correct, not even atoms, since they are individuals, are rigidly controlled in their action. Everywhere there is some escape from absolute order. Even physics is apparently beginning to suggest this. The stronger this suggestion becomes, the easier it should be to dismiss the old masochistic notion (almost sufficient by itself to explain the massive failure of Christian missions in Asia, where people have tended to know better) that tragedy is part of a divine plan which wisely decides how much and when each creature ought to suffer. (I shall always appreciate the fact that my father, a minister, never professed this doctrine, nor ever exalted mere "power," in God or anyone else.) The alternative is the view that the creatures themselves decide for themselves and each other, usually unwittingly, when and how they are to suffer.

Scientists and philosophers who have poured scorn upon theologians seeking to extract comfort from the relaxation of determinism in physics have this much justification for their attitude that the system of thought which can best avail itself of this new trend is scarcely the old theology, akin in spirit to Newtonian physics itself, but rather the neoclassical or pancreationist theology, according to which the function of the divine plan is to determine what sorts of limits there are to be for creaturely decisions, what general principles of harmony are to be infused into all beings. The risks of evil which remain are not there because evil is in some mysterious way good, but because without freedom, with its perils, there could be no world at all and neither good nor evil.

At this point I should like to quarrel somewhat with Schweitzer, from whom I quoted at the beginning of this chapter. Schweitzer says, profoundly, that we know reality most intimately as the will to live in all around us. His doctrine is that this will has in the past sought enlightenment in knowledge of nature as a whole, or of a Beyond nature, but that this knowledge has shown itself capable of telling us no more than that the will to live is in all things. No unitary goal of life is manifest, nature appears to us as "wonderfully creative and at the same time senselessly destructive . . . meaningless in the meaningful, meaningful in the meaningless, such is the essence of the universe" as we can know it.[6] The conclusion Schweitzer draws is that we must derive our ethics not from knowledge of nature but from awareness of the will to live in ourselves, from our reverence for the life around us, and our "mystical" sense of the

[6] A. Schweitzer, *Kultur und Ethik* (München: Oskar Beck, 1923), p. 201.

great Will to Live. But why life is set against life, or why there is suffering and death, both of individuals and species, apparently we can never have the faintest idea.

Let us agree that we have a better chance of understanding our own wills than the concrete meaning of nature as a whole. From this it does follow that the former understanding may well be taken as the primary datum for ethics. But that we can have not the slightest grasp, in the abstract, of a possible why of death, conflict, and suffering, seems to me a dogmatic extreme which rests upon errors or confusions in Schweitzer's assumptions. Thus he seems to think about nature as though it were a single individual, or the expression of a single will only, whereas even on his own view, one would think, it is a community of countless wills, whose supreme Will is not a tyrant, however benevolent or otherwise, nor yet the contriver of an all-inclusive machine, but the supreme inspiring genius of the Great Community of partly self-determining creatures. How this could be without risk of incompatibility and hence suffering in the innumerable decisions out of which existence is woven I at least cannot see. But I can see, I think, how sublime beauty and pervasive zest can and do result.

As to death, the notion that it is sheer destruction rests upon the theory, inherent in philosophies of being, that the most concrete unit realities are substances rather than events or experiences. For the latter are as indestructible as truth itself. The life we should reverence consists of actualities, which are past or about to become past and hence cannot be injured in any way, and of potentialities for the future which have a certain claim to actualization, but not an absolute claim, since this would lead to contradiction inasmuch as all of them could not be actualized. Moreover, why should any will other than The Will suppose that it had potentialities of unlimited value?

By overlooking freedom and its implied risk or element of chance, and by misconceiving death, Schweitzer turns his reverence for life into an equivocation, which oscillates between a sentimental rebellion against death (a universal law of life, other than divine) and a blind acceptance of the need to kill, unenlightened by any understanding of what this means.

It is amazing how consistently this great and noble man adheres to his dogma that science can teach us nothing about the meaning of life. The result is that, as a biologist has noted, he reacts to events in Africa much as a European peasant might.[7] He is struck by the brutality of a leopard destroying twenty hens and merely drinking their blood. He poisons, i.e., rather cruelly kills, the leopard. It does not occur to him apparently that in the normal way of nature a leopard would be lucky to get one fowl in a night, and that the cause of the catastrophe was the blunder of a human being who built a coop which failed to keep leopards out but did keep the harassed hens in. Or he compares some army ants with fighting European nations, an extremely crude analogy at best. The wondrous harmony of nature, which biologists suggest by such phrases as "symbiosis" or "the balance of nature" seems to escape Schweitzer.

Only through science has man been able to learn the immense difference between human life, with its unique degree of freedom involved in the capacity to employ elaborate symbols for things and relationships, and all other terrestrial forms. Primitive man, and pre-scientific men in general, had but foggy, or fantastically anthropomorphic, notions of non-human creatures. I almost wonder if part of Schweitzer's popularity, granting his real greatness in remarkably diverse lines, is not due to the fact that to grasp what he is saying you need know no more about nature than any Tom, Dick, or Harry. There are people who have studied natural phenomena; I think we should consult them, when "nature" is in question.

Granted that reverence for life is a good rough description of the ethical attitude, surely it needs to be made concrete and intelligent by understanding of the forms of life around as well as

[7] Paul Shepard, Jr., "Reverence for Life in Lambaréné," *Landscape*, VIII (1958), 26–29.

in us. Of course, we shall never achieve the intimacy with the non-human which we can enjoy with the human. Nevertheless, science can guide our imagination and intuition in many helpful ways. To take one small example which happens to be close to me personally, if we really care about all life, are we not likely to wonder at times what the simple forms of musical beauty in bird songs "mean" to the birds themselves? It is science, and only science (for the poets were at least half wrong), which is finding out to a certain extent "why birds sing," or what song could in a significant sense be said to mean to them, and why it can be that we enjoy their songs, different as we are from birds.[8]

A good test case for the ethics of reverence for life is the gruesome story of the treatment which the African Bushmen received from all other groups in Africa, black or white. The story is movingly told in *The Lost World of the Kalahari*, by Laurens Van der Post. Suppose now that the European settlers in Africa had been inbued with reverence for life: the Bushmen could not have been simply dismissed as "not really human," for even granting this foolish proposition, their claim to reverence would have remained. But would the admission of this have amounted to a great deal in practice? Unless the settlers had been vegetarians, they would have been eating various animals; and in any case it is not feasible to love not only one's human neighbors, but all creatures, "as oneself." One must make a distinction between fellow human beings and mere fellow creatures. So if the Bushmen were to be given any substantial consideration, which it seems they scarcely were by anyone, the first requisite was to have a criterion for "human." What is this criterion? The answer has not been given with much clarity, so far as I know, by any religion, but it has been given with quite adequate clarity by

[8] I venture here to refer to my own work on this subject. See *Born to Sing*, Indiana, 1973; "The Relation of Bird Song to Music," *Ibis*, C (1958), 421–445; also "The Monotony-Threshold in Singing Birds," *The Auk*, LXXIII (1956), 176–192, and "Some Biological Principles Applicable to Song-Behavior," *The Wilson Bulletin*, LXX (1958), 41–56.

science. Apart from the mere test of successful interbreeding, the multiform use of tools, above all, of that kind of tool known as a symbol, is the dividing line between *Homo sapiens* and all surviving animal forms. Any use of tools and of symbols in the best non-human cases is vanishingly small compared to the human. By this criterion, there is no shadow of a doubt, the Bushmen, like the Negroes, were very much human beings. They were masters of the tools of the hunter, trapper, snarer; by shrewd use of these they could secure any animal large or small they wished, from fish to elephant; if they needed poison for their arrows they knew where and how to get it, in diverse kinds for diverse purposes, and they had antidotes in case of accident; if they needed dyes for their paintings (very fine paintings too) this also they could accomplish, and they could store the dyes for long-term use. But above all, their entire life was translated into symbols: they danced their affairs, painted them, put them to music, and stored them up for future generations in words orally transmitted. Even though some of us maintain that bird song is properly termed "music," as such it is next to nothing compared to the Bushmen's artistic-symbolic activities. If the civilized white settler was a Mont Blanc of culture, and the singing bird a mole-hill, then the Bushman was at least among the high hills; to compare him with the mole-hills was either stupidity or a cloak for bad intentions and an excuse for past misdeeds.

But now we can see how our present crisis is different from the past crises of mankind. The affair between the Bushmen and the white settlers was scarcely within the possibilities of human nature to handle ethically. The difference, not so much in degree but in kind of culture, was too great. The Bushman was one of the last of those peoples whose sense of community with all nature was intuitive and poetic, rather than philosophic and scientific, but it was intense and beautiful and highly human for all that. Only a modern biologist or anthropologist can share this sort of attitude, recreated on a more rational plane, and such persons did not furnish Africa's settlers, indeed they did not then exist.

Today we simply have to take our ethical responsibilities toward less powerful peoples seriously, for local affairs now immediately become world affairs. Every people now does what the Bushman could not do, it plays the game of political power on a grand scale. So it is idle to shrug injustice off as unavoidable. The exploitation of the sense of grievance by great powers who make this a career means that we have to seek ways to reach the hearts and hopes of all peoples. Today the peoples have one destiny, or a vacuous destiny — the end.

The history of the Bushman's collective death is a terrible revelation of what man, in all colors and shapes, is capable of. Africa is the perfect exhibition of what Kant called the Radically Evil, and it stalked about in all sorts of skins, and appealed to all sorts of religions. Always it tried to justify itself by telling lies, such as the lie that the Bushman was only another animal. Any time we human beings are tempted to think that our arts and crafts and symbolic achievements are a guarantee of virtue or honesty we might look at the history of Africa as a remedy for our *hubris*.

Man is the most free earthly animal, incomparably so, for by his tool-using and his arts of symbolizing his life, the range of possibilities, among which he creatively actualizes some and not others, is multiplied by an indefinitely great "factor" (in the mathematical sense). Man is therefore the only animal likely to do either good or harm on a large scale. We North Americans tend to see the opportunities for good, but not those for evil; we somewhat lack the "tragic sense of life," expecting our long run of good luck as a nation to go on forever. The news from Africa as I write suggests that this complacency is unwarranted. But if today the perils of human freedom are greater than before, so also are its opportunities. The opportunities can be realized, and the worst perils evaded, only if we decide to make much more use of our human prerogative of conscious participation in the creative process. This prerogative of man does not, contrary to the opinion of some, make him a rival of deity. It is still as true as ever that we all die and that the basic pattern of the universe is out of our power. We do not make the laws of nature at large, and there seems no point in supposing that we ever shall. But we make laws for our own actions, and on this earth only man can consciously do this.

We need in the near future greatly to increase our interest in modes of action calculated to alter the chances of peace and war in favor of peace. This means substantial sacrifices, in part of luxuries for armaments, so that none may think it wise to attack us,[9] and in part it means sacrifices of various kinds to the end of increasing cooperation between nations — not least, sacrifices of prejudice, such as that tragically absurd prejudice which views the color of a man's skin, or of that of one of his ancestors, as the most important fact about him. No longer can such social questions be taken as merely internal or domestic. Every question which the world takes as of world importance for that very reason becomes of world importance, particularly if there is no chance that the world will lose interest in it in the near future, as it certainly will not in the question I have just mentioned.

Biology teaches that aggressiveness, hostility, and self-defence are no more essential to evolutionary success than cooperation, parental tenderness, and sympathy. Suppose for a moment that the great technological powers of the Northern Hemisphere use their resources to fight one another. Unless all mankind is destroyed, will not the less scientific and less aggressive peoples of the Southern Hemisphere, more satisfied with artistic pursuits or with a simple life in nature or, as in Australia, more intent upon games, survive and impart a more pacific tone to what is left of mankind? Our strength might prove our weakness. We are on trial in the world. We are not the human race, but a long

[9] The claim that our military equipment is now adequate to safeguard peace is to my mind decisively refuted by General Medaris in *Look*, September 27, 1960.

way from it. If we can see no constructive alternative to a fighting war, mankind will have to try to step around and, if necessary, over us on its way to survival. Should not our political thinking have as its two basic terms the free world and the human race, rather than the free world and the communists — or white and colored peoples? We are men and we wish to be free; that we wish to be free, and that we are men, should be the two basic grounds of our actions. Neither is a barrier to cooperation with any considerable portion of the human race. For while some men may be so misguided as to see their own destiny in the enslavement of others, there is no large mass of men but has some wish to be free, nor any without potential sympathy for the similar wishes of others.

The notion of human brotherhood does then have a practical meaning. Yet we face this question: when all of us are dead, what will our having lived amount to? What is it that death cannot destroy, to which our lives contribute something of value that abides? Or is there nothing abiding that a man can serve with every moment of his life? And the billions of non-human creatures — what is the importance of their lives? As we have argued in earlier chapters (9, 10) the intelligible answer is that all the values of life, on the various levels, are somehow parts of a cosmic value which abides. It increases, though ever so slightly, with each new creature; an inclusive life, sympathetically sharing in all experience and treasuring it thereafter. We should learn to accept a contributory status in the living whole of reality, and shake off the illusion that each of us (or our group) is the inclusive whole of which other things are constituents, contributing their values to us as the final consumers of all goods, the important ends of creation. Not only at death must we relinquish all contributions to our lives, but at any moment the values of our past experiences are already largely lost to us. Thus all experience is vanity of vanities, unless it contributes to an abiding whole of life that not only transcends us but transcends humanity altogether. This is one way of trying—and of course only trying—to understand that which surpasses human understanding, the old saying that the end of creation is the divine glory.

This glory which we would enhance with our little mite surpasses our understanding; but it need not be the bald contradiction which it seems to become if we define God as in all respects self-sufficient. For then the ultimate end is equally attained whatever we do—the complete is complete, the glorious is glorious. Then, too, there is that other paradox: "Be ye perfect as your Heavenly Father is perfect." This plainly does not mean, be self-sufficient, that is, exist of eternal necessity. For an imperative directed to what cannot be false is absurd. The identification of divine perfection with self-sufficiency thus makes absurdities out of two supreme injunctions of Christianity.

If, however, we define perfection as self-sufficiency, absoluteness, or necessity only in bare essence and existence (here the same), but as infinite relativity or sensitivity in actuality (the concrete *how* of the existence) then, while we cannot reasonably aim at self-sufficiency for ourselves, we can and should aim at appropriate forms of sensitivity. True, our effective responsiveness to other creatures cannot transcend the modest limits of human power. Sensitivity has degrees and levels, necessary existence does not; both are required for theism, the one to mark the absolute difference which distinguishes God from all else, the other to mark the infinite but not absolute difference which makes it significant to speak of the creature imitating the divine archetype, or the servant serving the Master. The absolute is no master, for master and servant are both relative terms. In necessity we are all pure ciphers; in sensitive responsiveness to the experiences of others, we cannot be ciphers and should be as far from such as possible. But still there will be an infinite gap between our little sensitivities and the all-embracing adequacy of divine Love.

Acknowledgments

The author cordially thanks the following publishers and journals for permission to republish, or as the case may be, quote from — in parts of this book as specified in brackets — the following books or articles:

The Open Court Publishing Company — *Experience and Nature*, by John Dewey. [Prologue and Ch. 8] Also *Proslogium; Monologium; An Appendix in Behalf of the Fool By Gaunilon; and Cur Deus Homo*, translated by Sidney Norton Deane. [Chapter 2]

The Macmillan Company — *Religious Realism*, edited by D. C. McIntosh. [Prologue]

Oxford University Press — *The Reconstruction of Religious Thought in Islam*, by Mohammad Iqbal. [Prologue]

The University of Chicago Press — *Philosophers Speak of God*, edited by Charles Hartshorne and William L. Reese. [Prologue: translation of Fechner]; also *Descartes to Kant*, edited by T. V. Smith and Marjorie Grene. [Ch. 2: translation of Descartes]

The Christian Scholar — "The Idea of God — Literal or Analogical?" June, 1956 [Ch. 3]

The Philosophical Library — *The Creative Mind*, by Henri Bergson. [Ch. 1]

T. & T. Clark — *I and Thou*, by Martin Buber, translated by R. G. Smith. [Ch. 4]

The Downside Review — "John Wisdom on 'Gods,'" 1958–59. [Ch. 5]

Longmans, Green & Company — *Some Problems of Philosophy*, by William James. [Ch. 6]

The Journal of Philosophy — "Freedom Requires Indeterminism and Universal Causality," LV (1958). [Ch. 6]

Appleton-Century-Crofts — *The Life and Letters of Charles Darwin*, by Francis Darwin. [Ch. 7]

Journal of Philosophy and Phenomenological Research — "Organic and Inorganic Wholes," III (1942). [Ch. 7]

Scientific Monthly — "Mind, Matter, and Freedom," LXXVIII (1954). [Ch. 8] by permission of the American Association for the Advancement of Science

Journal of Religion — "Science, Insecurity, and the Abiding Treasure," (1958) [Ch. 9]; also *"Time, Death, and Eternal Life,"* XXXII (1952). [Ch. 10]

Geoffrey Bles Ltd. and Harper & Brothers — *The Destiny of Man*, by Nicolas Berdyaev. [Ch. 11]

Review of Metaphysics — "Total-Unity in Russian Philosophy," VII (1954) [Ch. 11]; also "Some Empty Though Important Truths," VIII (1955). [Ch. 12]

The Emory Quarterly — "The Unity of Man and the Unity of Nature," XI (1955). [Ch. 13]

Index

creation, neoclassical view of, 273f.;
ex nihilo, 123, 273f.
creative synthesis, 199f.
creativity, xi, xv, 14, 18–23, 78, 89f.,
98, 106, 123f., 143f., 147, 164, 166,
180, 185, 207, 209, 307f; and
chance, 169; and psychology,
172f.; as positive side of contingency, 75; philosophy of, 27
creator, 39, 89, 137, 208; of myself,
183

Darwin, C., 191, 205ff.
Darwin, C. G., 12
death, 11, 145f., 234f., 240ff., 245,
249ff., 266, 310, 316f., 322; ends,
does not destroy, book of life, 253
democracy, 204
dependence, feeling of, 133; for existence, 74f., 80, 136; for qualities,
74, 76, 80
Descartes, R., 24ff., 28ff, 33, 48f.,
57, 60, 63, 68, 96, 124, 183, 201,
277
design, argument from, 156
determinism, xiii, 18–24, 44, 126,
161–90, 207, 210; and discontinuity, 186; and ethics, 169; as absolute, 165; as relative, 163fn., 164;
implicitly atheistic, 143; in psychology, 180; relaxation of in physics,
315
devoted imagination, 257, 262
Dewey, J., vii, xii, 92, 216, 279, 306
dialectic, Marxian, 145
dichotomies, thinking in, 182
discontinuity in nature, 220ff.
dispositional properties, 188
Dogen, 118
Dostoyevsky, F., 265
Driesch, H., 212f.
dualism, xiii, 126, 128, 191, 309
Du Bois-Reymond, E., 229
duration, 79

Ebbinghaus, J., 103fn., 302
Eccles, J. C., 166fn.
Ehrenfels, C., 9
Einstein, A., 167, 188, 190, 206fn.
electron, 183, 186, 195f., 220f.; feelings of, 225
emergency of mind, 124f., 210f.
emergent synthesis, 232
Emerson, R. W., viii
empirical criterion, 34, 198ff.
empirical atheism, 116
empiricism, x, 14, 104, 116
encounter with God, 4
ens necessarium, 149
Epistemic proof, 70ff.
essence, 4; of God, 4; *see also* God
as abstract, *and* God, definition of
events, as primary units of reality, v, 10, 17f., 121f., 218ff., 231,
273; as unpredictable, 163, 184
everlasting, the, 132, 143
evil, and providence, 12, 44, 143f.,
157, 189, 203f., 214fn., 295, 310–
15; moral, 44
evils, always contingent, 287f.
exclusive concepts, 70
exclusiveness of actualization, 285
existence, eminent, 58, 113; necessary, 25f., 28, 33, 65f., 89, 91fn.,
93f., 103 f., 149f., 208, 277, 280;
of God, meaning of, 110; two
kinds of, 32, 63f.
existentialism, 7
experience, data of, 227; how influenced, 227; unity of must be
created, 232
extension no criterion of mere matter, 124

facts, defined, 150, 285; never wholly negative, 69; two levels of,
290f.
faith, 47, 114f.
Fall, the, 14, 265